Dr Elisabeth Croll is Reader in Chinese Anthropology and Chair of the Centre of Chinese Studies at the School of Oriental and African Studies, University of London. For more than twenty years she has conducted frequent field studies in China and has written widely on women, women's movements, marriage, the family, family planning, domestic food supply and rural development in both historical and contemporary China. Her research has often been undertaken in association with various NGOs and international organizations. Among her numerous books are *The Family Rice Bowl* (Zed Books, 1983), *Chinese Women Since Mao* (Zed Books, 1984), *Wise Daughters from Foreign Lands* (Pandora Press; Allen & Unwin, 1989) and *From Heaven to Earth: Images and Experiences of Development in China* (Routledge, 1994).

Changing Identities of Chinese Women

Rhetoric, Experience and Self-perception in Twentieth-century China

ELISABETH CROLL

Hong Kong University Press

Zed Books
LONDON AND NEW JERSEY

Changing Identities of Chinese Women was first published in 1995 by:

Hong Kong, China, Taiwan and South-East Asia
Hong Kong University Press, 139 Pokfulam Road, Hong Kong

Rest of the World
Zed Books Ltd, 7 Cynthia Street, London N1 9JF, UK, and 165 First Avenue, Atlantic Highlands, New Jersey 07716, USA

Cover designed by Andrew Corbett
Cover photograph by Gong Guorong/Women of China
Typeset in Monotype Baskerville by Ewan Smith, London
Printed and bound in the United Kingdom
by Biddles Ltd, Guildford and King's Lynn

The author has asserted her moral rights.

A catalogue record for this book is available from the British Library.

US CIP data is available from the Library of Congress

Hong Kong, China, Taiwan and South-East Asia
ISBN 962 209 limp

Rest of the World
ISBN 1 85649 341 5 cased
ISBN 1 85649 342 3 limp

'A girl changes eighteen times before she becomes a woman' (Old Chinese saying)

Contents

PART III   Not the Moon

Gendered Difference and Reflection: Women of Reform   109

Acknowledgements

I am indebted to the reflections of others, be they in text, interview or conversation. Indeed this book owes much to the writings of Chinese women, both those few who have left a record of their own experiences during the earlier decades of this century and the many who have written and are writing either of their own lives or of women's studies during the present period of Reform. Without their works this book could not have been written. I also would like to thank the many Chinese women with whom I have had such interesting talks during my numerous field visits to China over the past twenty years. In particular I would like to thank Dr Mary Ann Burriss and Zhang Ye of the Ford Foundation for sharing an important field experience in 1991 and helping to arrange some interviews with some of their Chinese colleagues in the summer of 1994. I am grateful to Professor Dai Kejing of the Academy of Social Sciences in Beijing for jointly undertaking some recent research exercises in Chinese schools.

Additionally I owe much to the writings of women in my own culture on women, China and autobiography which have stimulated my own thoughts over the years. I am especially indebted to Emily Honig and Gail Hershatter's very fine *Personal Voices: Chinese Women in the 1980s* (University of Stanford Press 1988) and Virginia Woolf's reflections in *Moments of Being* (Triad Grafton 1978). Finally I would like to express my thanks to many colleagues at the School of Oriental and African Studies of the University of London and to friends who have given much personal and professional support during recent months made uncertain and arduous following an accident in China. For reasons that will become clear in the course of these essays, this book is generally dedicated to daughters who, though wounded in cultures the world over, more often than not become strong women; in particular it is dedicated to my own daughter, Katherine, whose young confidence is a source of pleasure.

Elizabeth Croll
London, July 1994

ix

Introduction: Living with Rhetoric

Much has been written about Chinese women, thus it is with some trepidation that I offer yet another study that attempts to combine historical, contemporary, scholarly and popular approaches.[1] This book incorporates many discrete moments of reflection: those of Chinese women over the past few decades, those of outside observers and scholars, and my own, born of more than twenty years of documentation, observation and interview. It might be said that this study marks what has been a substantial shift in my own interests from the Chinese revolution and the gendered revolution within the revolution to the revolution within women themselves. For many years as an anthropologist of China, I have been interested in experiences of rebellion, revolution and reform, as opposed to their images, and in lives beyond the rhetoric, the slogans and the statistics. Simultaneously, I have long been interested in the deployment of rhetoric, slogans and statistics by those seeking to direct and introduce social change in a society where rhetoric and politically correct language have been employed to underwrite image, capture consciousness and define or even deny experience. From previous studies of women in historic and contemporary China, we know more about the rhetoric prescribing female subordination or equality and the gap between rhetoric and experience than we do about how it feels for women to live with that rhetoric and with that gap. In this respect, one remark made by a Chinese woman sociologist and family counsellor was instrumental in giving impetus and shape to the three sections of this book: 'Many Chinese women feel alienated by the rift between the government's official policy of equality of the sexes and the day-to-day reality.'[2]

This comment, almost an aside in a recent interview, raised anew a number of questions: during the thirty years or so of revolution what did it feel like to be female workers and comrades surrounded by talk and images of equality and yet daily experience inequality? Did a feeling of alienation significantly affect women's attitudes to, participation in and support for the revolution? Was there a female-specific experience of revolution which was rendered invisible or denied by the rhetoric of equality and which gave rise to gender-specific images of revolution? To what degree did the discrepancy between rhetoric and experience lead to the rejection or erosion of that rhetoric and the diversification and plurality of female images and new emphasis on female experience during the recent years of reform? Might it be said that during reform the living of rhetoric has given way to living in the absence of rhetoric or alongside rhetoric or even with the search for new rhetoric? Moreover, it is not just during the past decades of revolution that Chinese women have lived with an all-pervasive rhetoric daily prescribing correct thought and behaviour; in the preceding centuries they lived with a state-supported Confucian rhetoric that emphasized their subordinate position as daughters, wives and mothers. Again, we know more about this rhetoric defining and directing female behaviour and the texts from which it was derived than we do about the experience of young daughters. How did they become acquainted with this rhetoric and come of age amidst daily talk and images of inequality? How did daughters and granddaughters respond to messages of secondariness from their mothers and grandmothers who, though individually strong, might themselves live ambiguously, confounding the rhetoric of inequality? Does the experience of preceding generations of daughters help us to understand how more recent generations have experienced, lived and managed such a rapid and sharp substitution of rhetorics? Could it be said that Chinese women, perhaps more than any other social category, have lived with a hegemonic rhetoric closely defining female qualities first in opposition to and then in emulation of their male counterparts? The questions are many, and of course living with rhetoric is not just confined to the female half of the population. Although this book focuses on the female-specific experiences of rhetoric, it does so with constant reference to the other gender. What becomes clear throughout this book is the importance of definitions of male qualities and categories of masculine behaviour in the defining and redefining of female qualities and appropriate categories of behaviour. The importance of the male other is such that the process of becoming a woman might just as easily denote a process of 'othering': differentiating oneself from or imitating the masculine or male other.

In China the rhetorics of both inequality and equality were derived from a set of well-known texts, which were reiterated time and again in an official attempt to define and direct female behaviour. Before the revolution, text was translated into the oral via folk adage, homily and story, with the accumulated rhetorical heritage providing many a colourful, succinct and memorable metaphor communicating messages of female subordination, inequality and inferiority. During the revolution, slogan replaced folk adage and homily to punctuate both oral and written texts. But whether rhetoric takes the popular form of maxim, homily, folk adage or slogan, it primarily reaffirms socially correct thought and behaviour. To live with rhetoric is to live with constant cross-referencing of formalized and familiar quotation designed to be effective and persuasive in intent.[3] In a rhetorical encounter, the delivery of homily imposes the authority of the speaker seeking to shape or subordinate the will of another; for the other, the listener, the import of the generalized abstract, apparently irrefutable, places language beyond reach of the particular or the individual, thus denying or at least discouraging the possibility of appeal or protest. Although the deployment of rhetoric may be instrumental, its presence does not necessarily imply a single message, for slogan and everyday saying may also juxtapose messages of some incongruence, and just as these may show some variation in content so may also their utilization. Even a hegemonic rhetoric does not exclusively serve those in authority; it can also constitute an important weapon of the weak: that is to say, women may be both agents and victims.

To elicit female perceptions and experience of rhetoric both historically and in contemporary China is a daunting task, largely because of the presence of a well-developed and all-encompassing rhetoric explicitly defining female characteristics and a virtual absence of recorded female experience. For documentation of female living it has been necessary to turn to the few available written accounts of women's experiences and, given that these are largely omitted from official historical records, the accounts are largely confined to a small genre of twentieth-century autobiographical or personal narratives. For those whose gender and class have excluded them from the formal historical accounts, it is the distinctive contribution of this genre that these narratives record one person's individual and often intimate perceptions of their self, of other significant persons and of their times and thus add greatly to our knowledge and understanding of people, relationships and events of the past. Gender differences in definitions of the self are often premised on the unique importance of relationships and connections for the female self or, in Nancy Chodorow's words, 'the more complex relational constellation of women's emotional lives'. Thus, women's autobiographies tend to create the female self by exploring her relations with others, thereby also illuminating both interpersonal relations within domestic, family and local communities and the visible and invisible 'presences' that keep her in her place.[4] In China, some of the most explicit of these 'presences' fashioning the female self were rhetorical constructions – Confucian or Communist – defining female qualities and behaviour. However, if personal narratives are to provide an opportunity to explore how women interpret, negotiate and experience gender rhetoric, their interpretation also has to take into account the contexts of their production and the use of the personal by the narrator.

It is now well recognized that the process of writing personal narratives or autobiography entails the creation or construction of selves that represent rather than exactly reproduce lives.[5] Much as a self-portrait can only be a created likeness reflecting what the painter perceives, so the writing of an autobiography is a self-constructed and thus a conscious attempt to link moments of being and fragments of the past into a coherent life story. In constructing retrospectively, they are entirely reliant on memory which is itself a reflective recapture or retrieval of past events and experiences inevitably imbued in their recall with a retrospective significance often dictated by present imperatives.[6] Reflexivity bearing on relationships between past, present and future is thus an important factor in both the production and the reading of autobiography.[7] This is especially so in periods of great socio-economic and political change when what is new, marginal and rebellious or normal, appropriate and approved may be rapidly defined and redefined. Autobiographies may provide the only evidence of the ways in which women respond to a changing and frequently fragmented rhetorical environment, of the instances of female rebellion against the old and of the individual circumstances surrounding the acquisition of the new. In China, autobiography or any form of personal narrative was a form seldom adopted by either male or female writers in the centuries before the late nineteenth-century Western presence.[8] In almost all cases in the twentieth century, the production of substantial female personal narratives has been encouraged or facilitated by European or North American mentors who either prompted, recorded or even jointly authored them, leaving the reader uncertain of the degree to which foreign writers or imagined foreign readers mediated the recording of lives. However, although no single voice can be said to be the 'authentic' or 'representative' voice of female experience in any one period or location, there is an interesting congruence in the gendered moments recalled by these female narrators although their accounts may be separated by time and space. Where few personal narratives coexist to document female life experiences, these have been set alongside other research sources.

To explore and understand the female experience of rhetoric in China, as elsewhere, is to generalize on the basis of an analytic category, Chinese women, who are nevertheless divided in interest and identity by age, generation, class and ethnicity. As both Henrietta Moore and Rosalind Delmar have noted, the category 'woman' has to be investigated rather than assumed given the amount of research by feminists demonstrating the tremendous diversity of the meaning of womanhood across cultures and over time.[9] This study recognizes these sub-divisions but cannot always take as much account of them as would be desirable with more varied sources. However, there is one sub-category which this book does emphasize and it is that of daughters. All women begin life as daughters, and young girls, perhaps more than any other social category, are concentratedly socialized into and subjected to rhetorical imperatives in order that they become 'women'. As Simone de Beauvoir so succinctly and memorably stated in the opening lines of her international best-selling text, *The Second Sex*, 'one is not born, but rather becomes a woman'.[10] In writing and talking of their lives before the revolution, many women still referred to themselves as daughters – daughter of China, daughter of Confucius, daughter of Han, as well as first, second or third daughter of a particular family. Subsequently women became 'daughters of the Revolution' to be promised 'half of heaven'. More recently still, during the years of Reform, it is the fate of daughters that has attracted national and international attention as they have been discriminated against and even denied existence in increasing numbers, first through female infanticide and then through sex-selective abortion. Yet the familial and social experience of daughters, their images of themselves and their routes to womanhood have been much neglected in studies of Chinese women undertaken both inside and outside China and in policy by those redefining women's roles and status in China. In an attempt to make good this omission, this book focuses on the relevance and the reticence of rhetoric in relation to the process of becoming a woman during three major eras of the twentieth century.

This book is made of three complementary but interrelated essays on the upbringing of daughters during the first half of the twentieth century before the Revolution or of the Republic (1911–1949), during the Revolution (1949–1978) and following on from Revolution in the present era of Reform (1978–). I make no apology for taking a broad temporal view or engaging in yet another look at Republican and revolutionary pasts and even images of projected futures before focusing on the present. Although it is the present process of reform or the contemporary, the cosmopolitan and the new in China today that engages our immediate attention, the experience of the present can only be appreciated and understood in a broad context of meanings that embraces both past and future. Throughout this study it is the living in and of time and its apprehension that takes centre stage. Many previous studies of women in China have focused on the relation of women and space and particularly the implications of movement in virilocal marriage between households, villages or regions for investment in daughters and the status of daughters-in-law and wives. Certainly, as becomes evident in this study, anticipated spatial movement in marriage affects daughters' concepts of their selves and their families, but less researched are the implications of this movement for their apprehensions of time. In our own culture feminist research and writing that sets out to illuminate temporal perceptions of women throughout their life cycles have highlighted women's uneasy relations to exterior or dominant and imposed linear time which Julia Kristeva has called the time of project or of history.[11] She sees this as a male construct that not only estranges women but fails to acknowledge female concepts of their interior time based on bodily rhythms or cycles of repetitive, circular or cyclical time, which are largely based on fertility cycles and place birth rather than death at their centre. In these studies interior female time is also conceived of as existing primarily in the mind or in fantasy or mental constructs that put women outside of measured time so that they have an imagined time alongside measured time, distancing them from it.[12] This study argues that in China it is the discontinuity, rupture and uncertainty of daughters' anticipation of and experience of becoming a woman through marriage that underlies female-specific concepts of both measured and fantasy time and it is their uneasy relationship with time's linearity that has differentiated male and female attitudes towards rebellion, revolution and reform in China.

Part I, Not the Sun, is based primarily on book-length life stories written or told by women who have left unique twentieth-century records of girlhoods lived in widely disparate places and times. Given explicit rhetorical definitions of appropriate female behaviour, it is not surprising to find that female narrators have quite independently recalled so many of the same gendered moments and commonly identify them as pivotal to their experience of girlhood. These gender-specific experiences of text, time and space inscribed upon female memories can be categorized into three main clusters. Influenced by a well-developed rhetoric defining female qualities and daughter behaviour, there was a number of uniquely female moments that were still compulsory *en route* to womanhood in pre-revolutionary China. These included concealment, confinement and crippling of the female body. There was also a category of moments that, though common to both male and female childhoods, were gender-specific in terms of participation and therefore served to separate female from male experiences of childhood, family and society. Such moments included naming, kinship rituals, the birth of siblings and marriage, all of which had the effect of estranging girls from their own families of birth. Finally, there were the events that were memorable precisely because they involved daughters in the crossing of gender boundaries to become 'boys of girls'. They entered male spaces normally or hitherto denied them and a few were even dressed and addressed as boys in their childhood. The accumulated effects of these categories of moments signified female difference, secondariness and defiance of conventional routes to womanhood.

There was one theme that predominated in these personal narratives and that was the idea of rebellion. The rejection of prescriptive norms was both the theme common to the published narratives of female lives during the first decades of the twentieth century and the predominant thread running through each life story as individual authors pursued one of the new opportunities for school education, employment or freedom in marriage and thus rejected confinement, a betrothal or an arranged marriage. Whether or not a young girl rebel succeeded in resisting convention very much depended on her source of support within the family, the strength of her own resolve and outside peer and public support. Even those with the strongest resolution and personal support found themselves, in defining the new, having to cross cultural and gender boundaries in the search for new cues or patterns of behaviour based on either Chinese male or Western female role models. Few daughters, even those who escaped their families, rejected past conventions and embraced new forms with comfort and confidence. Frequently they found themselves still strongly bound by inherited rhetorical ropes and straddling both old and new, male and female and Chinese and Western behavioural patterns in their endeavours to break free from Confucian rhetoric, the family and the past.

For Part II, The Sun and the Moon, there are very few source materials beyond official reportage of the role models or women who spoke with the tongues of rhetoric, albeit of a new revolutionary rhetoric expounding gender equality. For longer personal narratives voicing the experience beyond the rhetoric this account has had to rely on records mostly retrospectively produced either in China during the recent years of Reform or outside China by those who have left. A new and pervasive revolutionary rhetoric of gender was generated not only to erode Confucian rhetoric but also to exclude the language of experience, despite the obvious discrepancies between rhetoric and lived experience. The new rhetoric not only prescribed male and female equality but also either denied gender difference altogether or reduced it by collapsing male and female categories. What this meant in both rhetorical and practical terms was that women were invited to assume male qualities and enter male spaces, whether temporal or spatial, including work, the public sphere, the revolution or heaven as the male landscape of the future. They were invited to enter on terms that were the same as or equal to men's, with very few concessions to female-specific qualities. It was as if the female body did not exist; reproduction was ignored and the continuing female-specific inheritance of the Confucian-bound family and society was negated. Revolutionary daughters crossed gender but not cultural categories so that becoming a Chinese woman was likened to becoming a Chinese man or a Chinese 'man of a woman' with few references to outside, foreign or cross-cultural influence or experience. However, this section argues that the rhetorical feat of associating female with 'half of heaven' was undermined by the rhetoric's flawed disregard of gender-differentiated concepts of time, so that women remained strangers to heaven and thus to the revolution. Therefore, despite enormous efforts by the revolutionary government of China to introduce a new rhetoric of female equality and the establishment of new androgynous categories reducing gender difference and hierarchy between comrades and workers (perhaps unmatched by any other government at any time), women's living of their own mode of time before and after marriage continued to estrange them from the heaven of revolution and reduce the efficacy of the new hegemonic rhetoric to reach its desired ends. However, whatever the discrepancy between rhetoric and lived female experience and the flaws inherent within the revolutionary rhetoric focusing on the future, it was only during the more recent reform period that unexpected events were to detonate the rhetoric of the future in favour of living the present.

Part III, Not the Moon, focuses on the contemporary and new aspects of the Reform period, which is characterized by a plurality of state-sponsored female images inclusive of consumer and cherished infant daughter. The billboard presence of these females (in the absence of their male peers) advertising both material and family completion is important, intentional and of rhetorical significance. One of the most marked characteristics of the Reform period is the open recognition of the discrepancy between the rhetoric of equality and the female experience of inequality. The first years of Reform were marked by an increasingly open acknowledgement of all forms of female discrimination, whether in education, employment, politics, or the family, and particularly in the single-child family, which has alone been responsible for a rapid and radical increase in daughter discrimination and death. The rhetoric of equality did not survive the open acknowledgement of inequality and discrimination, and this separation of rhetoric from experience drew attention to experience as a legitimate area for investigation. In the open presence of discrimination, the rights of women were increasingly separated out from those of the general population, culminating in 1992 with a separate law promulgating women's rights for the first time in Chinese history. In the absence of an all-pervasive rhetoric of equality masking discrimination, women's studies too have become a separate field of investigation and discussion. Much of the new debate has centred around what 'being a woman' or 'a modern woman' mean; definitions of female as opposed to male and what are the female images and sources of self-esteem appropriate to the new woman in China today. In the absence of a well-defined rhetoric and of role models, there is also some confusion of cue and norm, and a plurality of images and patterns of female living has emerged.

Perhaps the most significant change has been the separation out of the female image from the previous generalized definition of comrade or man and the rejection of the revolutionary 'masculinization of the female', 'female man' or 'superwomen's masculinization'. In the new pursuit of a modern image and life, daughters and women no longer have to cross gender boundaries in their search for female as opposed to male qualities. Much discussion however has centred on the degree to which women should cross cultural boundaries in their attempt to be modern and on the appropriate influence of both Western feminism and Western femininity in the construction of China's female images and lives. While there is an official attempt to construct what might be described as a new 'feminism with Chinese characteristics' and new 'femininity with Chinese characteristics', many Chinese women have found themselves still strongly bound by inherited rhetorical shackles and by their straddling of old and new, male and female and Chinese and Western definitions of womanhood. In contrast, China's younger generations of daughters have increasingly begun to assume characteristics that are cosmopolitan and global. If gender-specific images and experiences have been quite distinctive in Republican, revolutionary and post-revolutionary eras this century in China, the study of each era demands not only an understanding of the rhetoric of the living, but also of the living of the rhetoric.

PART I

Not the Sun

Gendered Moments and Memories: Daughters of Rebellion

'Are women not also human beings?' *Canton Girls' Daily*, 1919[1]

In China before the twentieth century, there were few recorded experiences of childhood, much less of girlhood, until the publication throughout the twentieth century of a number of female life stories dating girlhoods from the early decades of this century. Narrated by unusual women, albeit mostly literate and advantaged, they placed women's experience at the centre of textual attention during times of rapid and radical social change. For daughters who have left a record of their girlhood memories, there is evidence of a dawning recognition that there were both general and gender-differentiated norms and expectations with which they were expected to become familiar. Indeed some literate daughters could 'recite whole books of Confucian Classics by heart'. One young woman chose to entitle her memoirs *Daughter of Confucius* because of the influence of his precepts and 'the strict Confucian discipline' with which the household was ordered.[2] Another noted that her parents, 'undoubtedly kind but strict' wanted to bring her up 'properly' according to their precepts, that is the precepts of Confucius'.[3] Yet these same daughters also saw themselves as rebels, and indeed it was the opportunity for the citation of their own history of rebellion which commonly underlay the autobiographical impulse.

At the time of writing or relating their life narratives, the women writers saw themselves or were seen to be unusual women who had followed novel and independent personal and/or professional paths culminating in new occupations, sojourns abroad or unusually modern marriages. It was the novelty of their life stories that had invited comment and generated an invitation and/or the will to relate how they had arrived at this 'unusual place'. This impetus was clearly stated in many of the prefaces to their life stories. Perhaps one woman writer,

Bu Wei-chao can be permitted to speak for the others as she introduced herself in the preface to her *Autobiography of a Chinese Woman*:

> I am a woman with an unusual experience. I had four parents. I broke my engagement at a time when engagements were never broken. I was principal of a school before I went to college. I joined revolutions and took refuge from wars. I healed grown ups and brought a few hundred children into the world. When I was married, I was married without a wedding. I have travelled in twelve provinces and three continents. I have lived six years in Japan and thirteen years in the United States ... People often pay me the doubtful compliment of saying that I am not like a woman. Maybe there is something in that statement.[4]

Most wanted to remind their readers that, in becoming new women, theirs had not been an easy journey and had involved struggle, defiance and rebellion. Thus in the preface to another, *The Lotus Pool of Memory*, the author Chow Chung-cheng had stated:

> This is the story of my childhood and my youth in China ... I had to wage a bitter war against my parents; it was a battle between the old traditions and the new in China ... perhaps my story will remind all women that there were times in China which obliged mother and daughter to inflict pain on each other.[5]

In adopting rebellion as the central theme, these life stories in China can be read as counter-narratives identified as such in other cultures because they revealed that their subjects did not necessarily think, feel or act as they were 'supposed to'. Without exception, these female narrators of the personal focused on the dissonance between their lives as new women in early twentieth-century China and Confucian prescriptive codes or expectations.

Filial daughters

Much has been written about the Confucian rhetoric underlining gender difference and hierarchy and inclusive of female secondariness and seclusion. From the earliest of times girls had been taught via the Confucian Classics that they were not the sun, the heaven or the lightness of day. These Classics had cosmologically enshrined those most basic of equations – of yin and yang, of earth and heaven, of moon and sun and of night and day – with female and male. Originally conceived as complementary, such oppositions were early arranged in a series of hierarchical relationships juxtaposing superiority with secondariness, authority with obeisance and activity with passivity. It was their cosmological foundations which removed these prescriptions beyond debate to apparently universal, natural and immutable status, so that gendered difference became integral to cosmic order with the preservation of harmony dependent on the maintenance of such complementarity and hierarchy. As one scholar of classical China wrote: 'Woman's place in the classical canon was not determined by the fiat of any supernatural force or piety, but rather by the Confucian certainty that order and harmony were supreme values and that only in hierarchy were they preserved'.[6]

The *Book of Changes*, arguably the most ancient and influential of the Confucian Classics, before suggesting a correlation between unrestrained woman and destruction or disorder, stated that 'great righteousness is shown when man and woman occupy their correct places: the relative positions of Heaven and Earth'.[7] According to the *Book of Rites*, compiled in the second century AD and later to become one of the venerated Confucian Classics containing rules of correct conduct: 'to be a woman meant to submit' and in the sexual division of labour 'a woman was to take no part in public affairs'.[8] From these principles were derived gender-specific norms and expectations detailing correct behaviour for women, be they daughters, wives or mothers, which were subsequently elaborated in sets of classics expressly written for a female readership.

Among the several texts bequeathed to succeeding generations of girls for their instruction were the *Nu Jie* (Precepts for Women) and the *Nu er Jing* (the Classic for Girls). The *Nu Jie* was written by the famed woman scholar Pan Chao in the first century AD who was unusually well-educated and became a court historian following the deaths of her scholarly father and brother. In the *Nu Jie* she elaborated on the qualitative difference between male and female resting on the very different but complementary virtues of firmness and flexibility. The texts went on to exhort women to be obedient, unassuming, yielding, timid, respectful, reticent and selfless on the basis of 'first others then herself'. A woman should endure reproach, treasure reproof and revere her husband for 'a husband, he is Heaven', 'Heaven is unalterable it cannot be set aside' and 'if the wife does not serve her husband, the rule of propriety will be destroyed'.[9] The *Nu er Jing* similarly catalogued the ideal qualities of women. It outlined in more detail the rhetoric that was to be lived for subsequent generations in what became known as 'The Three Obediences' and 'The Four Virtues' which were familiar in their abbreviated form to women who, throughout their life cycles, were subject to the three authorities of father and elder brothers when young, of husband when married and of sons when widowed. The four virtues comprised first a 'general virtue' meaning that a woman should know her place in the universe and behave in total compliance with the time-honoured ethical codes; second, she should be reticent in words taking care not to chatter too much and bore others; third, she must be clean of person and habits and adorn herself with a view to pleasing the opposite sex; and fourth, she should not shirk her household duties.[10]

The more popular *Lie Nu Zhuan* or series of women's biographies from which stories of filial women were drawn was compiled in the first century AD with a general preface that read: 'The wife leans on the man. Gentle, yielding, she early listens to the words of others. She has the nature and emotions of those who serve others and controls her person in the way of chastity.' The biographies included featured filial daughters, chaste maidens who would sooner meet death than dishonour and sisters-in-law, wives, mothers and widows whose chastity and devotion to duty was above reproach and worthy of emulation.[11] One commentary on the *Lie Nu Zhuan* categorized nineteen of the women as far-sighted and benevolent in service; nineteen whose chastity was above reproach and eighteen widows who refused to remarry; eighteen whose downfall should serve as a warning for girls; sixteen who were great mothers; and sixteen who were primarily celebrated for their docility and constancy.[12] From the first centuries AD onwards, an endless succession of Confucian writers took these codes as the basis of new prescriptive texts defining female behaviour. In particular, the Neo-Confucian philosophers of the Sung dynasty (960–1279) further elaborated on codes of feminine ethics by emphasizing spatial prohibitions via the practices of segregation and seclusion and by introducing the practice of bound feet. Confucian precepts were also frequently reduced to one-line quotations, proverbs and folk sayings for oral repetition among both literate and illiterate such as: 'The woman has her correct place within and the man his correct place without' or 'To be a woman means to submit.' Many phrases beginning with the negative injunction that 'a woman does not ...' were invariably and relentlessly inscribed upon the young female consciousness in both gentry and peasant households. However, daughters in gentry and peasant households also inherited an oral tradition different from the homily and adage of Confucian rhetoric, for the upbringing of small daughters was marked also by stories of heroines and of swordswomen who were both filial and roamed in wide open spaces combining male and female roles. Story-telling was both domestic and public with familiar stories passed from grandmother or mother to daughter and old tales too were spun and embellished by servants and itinerant storytellers. Both foreign observers and women themselves have frequently noted how female residents of household, village and town loved to hear stories. In one village in Guangdong, an anthropologist resident there in the 1920s commented on the 'powerful control' that popular ballads exercised over the imaginations of women and girls who often identified themselves with the heroines of the simple stories which were told in rhythmic and popular language.[13]

In their autobiographies, grown women remembered with fondness the patriotic and romantic heroines and narratives of intricate myth, legend, fairy tale and popular story recounted to them by mother, nurse/servant or sibling. Tsai Chin remembers:

> We were usually told a bedtime story, not by our parents but by the servants, but they were never read from a book for the oral storytelling tradition is strong in China. We preferred ghost stories, and the servants being country folk well acquainted with nature and the supernatural, had them in abundance. Sisters and brothers would huddle together wide-eyed with terror and rapture, listening to talks of fantastic apparitions. When my elder sisters began to read, Cecilia in particular became a fund of stories herself. And always any story that could be interpreted as remotely sad would have the tears streaming down my face.[14]

One of the most popular and favourite stories commonly recalled in memoir was that of the courageous warrior woman Mulan, which was set in the sixth century AD. She was the daughter of an old and ailing general who was suddenly called upon to lead the Imperial troops into battle. To save her father she donned the dress of a boy, left home and for twelve years fought 'as a man' in the army. She was a leader of men, performed great feats of courage and was rewarded for her heroic service to the Emperor. None suspected her female sex, her chastity was preserved and it was not until she returned home and exchanged her linked-iron tunic for a skirt that her true identity was discovered. One woman described how when she was a young girl she sat on her mother's knee 'round-eyed and still, and listened enchanted to the old legends of the past'. Of all of them, the story of Mulan was her favourite and she never grew tired of hearing about her and begged for the story over and over again. She later described what she thought the story of Mulan had meant to her mother who was herself the daughter of a general and had led an unhappy life. As a young girl her mother herself had dreamed of freedom and happiness, all dreams which had been frustrated as, physically timid and without education, she had suffered as a junior member of a large stifling household. The girl thought that since her mother was a victim of this and other facets of the system, 'the story of Mulan was actually a projection of the dreams she held originally for herself and later gave to me.'[15] Another girl learned of the story from her brother, for whom she waited impatiently each day to begin another story:

> As I was a girl, my brother would tell me of many heroines who sacrificed themselves for their fathers, brothers, or husbands, always practising the virtues of humility, modesty and servitude.

My favourite heroine was one Mu-lan or 'Wild Orchid' ... These daily stories, exemplifying basic Chinese obligations and principles, made an enormous impression on me, and would affect my attitude and personal philosophy throughout my life.[16]

Another young daughter recalled a memorable occasion when her father took her to the theatre to see a play entitled *The White Snake*, the story of which she already knew well. In it a beautiful white snake spirit took on human form and married a youth who died of fright when his bride reverted to her serpentine form. After taking a draught of regular wine, the heroine travelled to the Enchanted Mountain to fight the celestial deer and storks who were the guardians of the magic herb that could restore her husband to life. Simultaneously and with a male energy she repelled the barrages of spears hurled at her

now fending them off with the springy shaft of her own weapon; now knocking them back, one or two at a time, with her ankles or hands; now ducking one aimed at her head and kicking it with the back of her calf, so that it rebounded to the enemy who had thrown it ... until she vanquished her foes, wrested the herb from its niche in the mountainside, and performed her wild dance of triumph.

What the little girl was to remember above all was the quality of the heroine's love and fearless determination. In male spaces and with male energy 'she was a thrilling model of female power: strong or tender, gentle or menacing, and straightforward or clever, depending upon which trait was needed at the time. She could wound or heal.'[17] Chow Chung also recalled her nurses recounting folk-tales they knew by heart although they didn't dare tell her too much for fear of being overheard 'filling young minds with nonsense'.[18] For another small girl the ghost stories of the slave girls also remained 'some of the most vivid memories of these early years'. She particularly remembered that of one young vengeful woman ghost who compensated for previous wrongs by aiding and abetting an unhappy young man to hang himself.[19]

The power of story and folk-tale is also reflected in an autobiography from another country, another age but not another culture. Maxine Hong Kingston colourfully recalled the influence of her mother who 'told stories that followed swordswomen through woods and palaces for years. Night after night, my mother would talk-story until we fell asleep.'[20]

Later her daughter reflected that she:

had been in the presence of great power, my mother talking story. After I grew up, I heard the chant of Fa Mu Lan, the girl who took her father's place in battle. Instantly I remembered that as

a child I had followed my mother about the house, the two of us
singing about how Fa Mu Lan fought gloriously and returned
alive from war to settle in the village. I had forgotten this chant
that was once mine, given me by my mother, who may not have
known its power to remind. She said I would grow up a wife and
slave, but she taught me the song of the warrior woman.[21]

However, if stories like that of Mulan juxtaposed messages of the filiality
of 'good' daughters and wives with the exercise and agency of the
'warrior' woman free of body and roaming in male guise in wide-open
spaces, the split between fantasy of fable and reality of rhetoric broadened as daughters grew up. These stories had provided neither an
alternative rhetoric nor a practicable role model enabling daughters to
become a woman different from that defined by Confucian rhetoric.
Thus Confucian Classics and allied gender-specific texts were adopted
as authorities or prescriptive codes for right and proper feminine
conduct becoming to a Chinese woman for succeeding generations
right up to the twentieth century. How daughters were socialized into
and experienced this rhetoric is an important theme of many a female
narrative written or related by women whose girlhoods dated from the
early years of this century.

Daughters' life stories also document the dawning recognition that
not only were there gender-differentiated norms and behavioural
expectations, but that female lives were to be substantially and increasingly different from those of brothers and other males of family or
neighbourhood. That becoming a woman was not the same as becoming
a man was apparent even to the very young. Reflecting this burgeoning
consciousness, these women writers reconstructed narratives around a
number of remembered moments which commonly gendered their
experiences and memories of childhood and documented the unique
journey from girlhood to womanhood. Indeed the terms 'daughter',
'journey' and 'memory' frequently appear in the titles and subtitles of
their life stories. Given explicit rhetorical definitions of the female, it is
not surprising to find that, quite independently, female narrators from
disparate times and places have recalled so many of the same moments
commonly identifying them as pivotal to their experience of girlhood.
The gendered moments inscribed upon their memories can be categorized into three clusters. There are those moments uniquely female *en
route* and still compulsory to 'becoming a woman' in pre-revolutionary
twentieth-century China; moments common to both male and female
childhood but gender-specific in their participation and consequences
separating female from male experiences of childhood; and moments
that were memorable for girls precisely because, in crossing gender
categories, they were dubbed 'boys of girls'. In the beginning though,

combining all categories of remembered moments for daughters, was play.

Girlhood play

If in the beginning for all children there was play, play with siblings, cousins and sometimes neighbouring children of both sexes and in- and out-of-doors, childhood play was all the more significant in female memory because it constituted a unique phase in the female life course. Whether it was in the secluded gentry home, peasant village or small-town street, girls were permitted a freedom of movement when they would get muddy, roam the fields as they played the games of their brothers. Grown women remembered 'acting just like the boys'. Hsieh Ping-ying remembered that, when spring came to her village:

> lovely grass was all over the fields. Red and white flowers bloomed everywhere. Gentle ripples whispered in the streams. The birds began to sing their spring song incessantly. This was just the time for the farmers to plant their rice and for the children to start catching their fish and river prawns.

Going out in the rain with a bamboo-leaf waterproof hat on her head, she would act 'just like the boys', taking off her socks and shoes. Her playmates were all very naughty boys and 'quite like a boy' she joined them in wading in the dirty shallow water, trying to catch prawns and fish and arriving home wet through and covered in mud.[22] In a town, another young girl played with her brother and sister and neighbouring children on the streets and in the garden next door. Like the others, she enjoyed climbing trees and was very fond of swinging. One of their favourite games was to hang by the rope from the windlass letting themselves down into the well![23] In gentry households little girls' play might be confined to the innumerable apartments and courtyards surrounded by high walls, but they too recalled playing with an unusual spatial freedom alongside their brothers. One little girl born in Canton in 1896 lived her first years entirely within a clan compound in which

> there were apartments for the men and young boys; for the women and small children; and, of course for the servants – the whole connected by innumerable little courtyards, east gardens, south gardens, west gardens, with the main banquet halls and reception rooms at the core.[24]

Here throughout the compound, she liked to play with her brothers and play their games inclusive of mud pies and death matches in which live crickets contested to their untimely ends!

From early days, however, play for girls was increasingly punctuated

by spatial and physical prohibitions emphasizing constraint and confinement concealing of the female body. Each grown woman could
remember well the steady erosion of play and the recurring number of
prohibitions curtailing their liveliness and freedom which did not apply
to their male playmates. Girls were perpetually reminded that they
were 'female' and therefore increasingly subject to gender-specific expectations: 'you know you are a girl', 'girls must stay at home' and not
'play too much'. Wei Tao-ming was reprimanded time and again and
reminded that 'play had become an unseemly pastime for a properly
brought-up little Chinese girls'.[25] Hsieh Ping-ying also remembers how
she, the lone female of her playmates, was upbraided very severely by
her mother. According to her own account she put up a valiant defence:

> 'You know you are a girl, why do you mix with those naughty
> little brats?'
> 'Why cannot a girl go out and play in the fields?'
> 'She just can't. She must stay at home!' Then I would have a
> good thrashing, and my mother's angry voice and my howls would
> fill the house.[26]

Soon her 'loose' behaviour attracted disapproving talk in the village so
that her mother began to hear things against her from outside:

> It was said that as I was growing up and my feet were still
> unbound it was most probable a future mother-in-law would refuse
> to accept me. Moreover, it was scandalous to see a girl mixing
> with boys and playing at making mud pies, throwing stones and
> playing at commanders and soldiers. They maintained that, ac-
> cording to the proprieties of ancient times, children after four
> years of age must be separated, and boys and girls should not
> occupy the same table, and that my mother, being a well-educated
> woman, should realize the importance of these rules.[27]

In gentry households a sense of physical restraint and decorum
began to be instilled from an early age. Little girls were taught to be
ashamed of a dirty face and dress: 'A girl must always keep clean and
neat no matter what she is doing.'[28] Chow Chung recalled how her
liveliness as a child was frequently subject to parental restraint. She
remembered the sense of wanting to be able to say whatever occurred
to her and to laugh and cry whenever she felt like it but of always
being reprimanded for talking too much, laughing too loudly and
walking too quickly. Play too was curtailed:

> In the garden was a swing, but Mother did not allow us to use
> it. Once I did, with Ch'ang, and Mother saw us through her
> window and was angry with me. 'Fancy a girl swinging!' she

exclaimed angrily. So afterwards I could only gaze at the swing from afar.[29]

Liang Yen also remembered how from childhood she was continuously admonished that 'a lady must never run, never shout' and that 'she may smile but not grin, titter but not guffaw, weep but not wail.' She was continually warned not to let any of her body except hands and head be seen by others, even by parents and brothers.[30] Wong Su-ling, also taught not to laugh too loudly, not to talk too much and above all to walk with short steps, remembers her mother constantly repeating: 'Smile not move lips, walk not move skirt.'[31] In a working household the mother of another young daughter, who was accustomed to street life, wanted to beat her for liking 'to play too much' – so much so that she would be forced to run and jump over the wall so as not to be caught.[32]

Daughters' feet

It was not only the steady erosion of play, which did not apply to their male peers, that was inscribed in the memories of each woman narrator, but the gradual confinement and silencing of the female body, which was sharply advanced by the binding of feet. For most young girls, the 'biggest upset' came at the moment their feet were to be bound. More than any other event the binding of feet, paining and physically restricting young girls, marked the end of liveliness and freedom of movement ending the non-segregated spaces of childhood. Commonly girls anywhere up to seven or eight years of age had their feet wrapped tighter by the day for over a year until the arch was broken and the toes bent permanently under so that they could no longer run, even walk freely and frequently could only hobble or be carried. Thus was their physical mobility devastatingly crippled. Little girls might be told that the practice dated from the fashion of small bowed feet current among the court dancing girls in the tenth century. First practised among the upper classes, small feet became associated with wealth and status so that eventually they constituted an essential prerequisite for an advantageous marriage. The degree of binding might vary by social class with matchmakers sometimes asked not 'Is she beautiful?', but 'How small are her feet?' A plain face was said to be given by heaven, but poorly bound feet were thought to be a sign of laziness and poor breeding. Many an aspiring mother thus subjected her daughter to this painful process and soon girls of all but the poorest families and of certain ethnic groups had lost their original agility and freedom. The agonies of their first moments of footbinding remained forever etched in women's memories as they moved instantaneously and with such pain from active liveliness to passive lifelessness.

It is noticeable in the personal narratives that, while most mothers recognized that feet had to be bound, many did delay binding the feet of their daughters as long as possible. In one gentry household a mother had decided to put off the binding of her second daughter's feet so that she could have a different experience from herself and the girl's elder sister, who could walk no more than two steps without having to support herself by holding on to the wall and was thus 'no better than an invalid'. However, she dared not delay it for too long, for if her daughters' bones became sufficiently hardened there would be little likelihood that she would ever be able to have small feet and therefore 'be welcomed by those looking for daughters-in-law': 'Would not anybody who saw such a girl exclaim: "her mother must have died when the girl was young!" With a pair of feet as big as palm-leaf fans it is really ugly'. On the chosen day, her mother asked her daughter to kneel down before the Goddess of Mercy to be blessed to ensure a pair of small feet'.

The daughter remembers remonstrating with her mother and re-called her feelings and thoughts on that eventful day:

'I don't want to bind my feet,' I said and dared not go near her … 'Mother, it will be very painful. I won't be able to walk. Please do not do it to me.' I pleaded in tears and full of fear.

'I must bind your feet because I love you. If I do not bind your feet I shall not be doing the right thing by you. You must realise that a girl with huge feet will never be accepted by a husband.' Then she … started to bind them. Of course I began to howl and struggle.

'Oh Mother I am dying of pain! I had rather never marry all my life than have my feet bound!'

'You little wretch, what is the use of howling and struggling? I will bind your feet the tighter for that.' While she was binding my feet, I kicked as hard as I could, and with my hands I tried to snatch away the cloths and to throw the shoes away. My mother was very angry and called out to my sister-in-law to take hold of my hands. Putting my right foot under her seat, so that I could not kick with it, my mother held my left foot very tightly and made a very good job of it. I, like a condemned prisoner who was going to be beheaded, shouted and howled, hoping to get people in the neighbourhood to come to my rescue. My sixth grand-aunt came … all grown-ups were hard-hearted for not one of them had any sympathy for me, and my heartrending cries were of no avail. Alas, they were all like my mother, no better than executioners.

When I put my new vermilion shoes on, not only my feet but my body felt rigid and numb. My mother planted me on the ground to try whether I could walk. I felt as if the bones of my feet were broken and I cried and fell down on the ground.

From henceforth I spent most of my days sitting by the fire spinning. Sometimes I could manage to walk very slowly in the hall. It seemed as though my feet were fettered, and to walk was very difficult. The days of enjoying beautiful flowers and of catching fish and prawns would never come to me again.[33]

In village and working households women were as likely to have experienced footbinding as girls in gentry households, and mothers here too were also influenced by their own memories and delayed the moment for their daughters. As one working woman remembers:

They did not begin to bind my feet until I was seven because I loved so much to run and play. Then I became very ill and they had to take the bindings off my feet again ... When I was nine they started to bind my feet again and they had to draw the bindings tighter than usual. My feet hurt so much that for two years I had to crawl on my hands and knees. Sometimes at night they hurt so much I could not sleep. I stuck my feet under my mother and she lay on them so they hurt less and I could sleep. But by the time I was eleven my feet did not hurt and by the time I was thirteen they were finished. The toes were turned under so that I could see them on the inner and under side of the foot. They had come up around. Two fingers could be inserted in the cleft between the front of the foot and the heel. My feet were very small indeed.[34]

Most young daughters pleaded in vain against their mothers' and others' remonstrances that bound feet were an essential female attribute enhancing a girl's marriage prospects and family status. For a fortunate few born into gentry households in the early decades of the twentieth century and influenced by Chinese reform and Western example, the violent response of daughters to the pain and sudden loss of mobility was so great that they unusually succeeded in winning in their entreaties against footbinding. Even for the successful few however, the very attempt to bind their feet left an indelible scar. One young girl, who could bear the pain no longer, 'suddenly started screaming without tears but in great volume' with the aim of ending 'the torture'. She remembers hearing that her feet were to be bound, broken and thus prevented from growing to normal size because of an ancient version of the Cinderella story:

The legend was that, a prince, travelling through the countryside, came upon the footprint of a woman, so small and beautifully shaped that he cried out immediately that he must find her. He gave orders that the footprint should be preserved, and stated that the woman whose foot it would fit should become his consort.

From that time on no daughter could expect to escape the fate of small feet. She remembered how on the appointed day the bandages were first put on her feet:

> I submitted not only because it was being done to all the little girls of the house, but because I knew if I rebelled it would bring fresh humiliation on my mother. But I simply could not stand it, and the first night when I was alone, I took off the bandages. Next day they were put back on, and I was reprimanded. After that, I stood it for three more days, and then I knew I could not bear it any longer ... so on the morning of the third day, while we were all sitting miserably listening to our tutor, I suddenly started screaming, without tears, but in great volume, I lay on my back, kicking, and yelling. I kept up this bedlam for the greater part of the morning, disturbing the entire household, horrifying everyone, and generally creating such a turmoil that my grand-mother – whose final word was necessary to make any decision – came to pass judgement. She looked down at me with great distaste and said: 'Very well, then. Take the bandages off. Her feet will grow the size of an elephant's. No one will ever marry her, but so be it. I wash my hands of the whole business.'[35]

Thus, barring a few bruises, a hoarse throat and some lost sleep, Wei Tao-ming recalled that she came out of the whole episode with normal feet and she was fortunate in that no girl could have rebelled in such a successful manner before the twentieth century. This was because by this time the practice was no longer regarded with such approbation by the educated and travelled men of gentry and official households. They frequently took the unprecedented step of persuading the women of their households to abandon the process and spare their daughters. One grandmother was even taken to Hong Kong by one of her sons to persuade her of the utility of natural feet,[36] and for a family of Bu-wei Chao's standing, it took a revolutionary like her grandfather to success-fully oversee its demise. Her father, feeling that he was adopting a 'son' was also willing to let her feet 'go where they wanted', although this irked her Aunt Ch'eng, her prospective mother-in-law, who remonstrated:

> What kind of a looking bride will that girl turn out to be, with a pair of webby feet thumping along in front of the red skirt! When she arrives at our house, how will the servants be able to tell whether it's the bride or a newly bought slave girl?[37]

For all but the most privileged however, bound feet in the early years of the century remained the hallmark of the well-bred, restricting daughters' mobility, preventing them from running freely and for some, running at all. An oft-quoted verse in *Nu er Jing* asks of women:

Have you ever learned the reason
For the binding of your feet?
Tis from fear twill be easy to go out upon the street.
It is not that they are handsome when thus like a crooked bow,
That ten thousand wraps and bindings are enswathed around
    them so.[38]

A similar rationale underlies a Yuan dynasty rhyme: 'Why must the foot be bound? To prevent barbarous running around'[39] and a folk ditty from Hebei province: 'Bound feet, bound feet, past the gate can't retreat.'[40]

Walled daughters

Subsequent to footbinding and during the approach to adolescence and the early age of marriage, young girls were increasingly confined to domestic spaces. Virtually secluded within their own households and increasingly segregated from all but the women of their family, older girls lived within designated or demarcated spatial boundaries. It was common for such girls to be almost entirely confined to their households whether they be the large gentry-style courtyarded compound or the humbler three-roomed peasant dwelling. In their personal narratives women meticulously recalled the minute details of spatial configurations perhaps because for much of their girlhood they had been confined to domestic spaces which in turn had been subdivided and bounded into men's and women's spaces in the interests of segregation and seclusion. Thus even within households, the girls' experience was clearly bound up with gendered definitions and allocations of space. It is not surprising therefore to find that women's earliest memories frequently reflected the importance of permitted and prohibited spatial divisions and subdivisions. One young girl described in great detail the three court-yards within which she came to live her life. Each courtyard had rooms on all four sides with the main ones facing south with wide upcurving eaves to shut out the sun. All the rooms only had interior windows opening on the courtyards, which added to their bounded seclusion, protecting them from 'prying' from within or 'depredation' from without. In one of the rooms her mother passed her days, leaving it only to go to the women's dining rooms, to pay her respects to her grandmother or to visit the rooms of the other ladies, all of which opened off her courtyard or the one just behind it. She observed that beyond these spaces her mother only infrequently went on visits to relatives in the city and had no curiosity about the world outside. Perhaps, her daughter surmised, this was because her mother, like her grandmother, her two aunts and her first sister-in-law had bound feet. Her mother's were the smallest, of which she was very vain, and it was no accident that she was the one who moved about least. Her daughter later described this women's world as the 'world of her childhood' and as a 'world within a world' in which women lived limited and enclosed but safe lives within a framework fixed by female generation and seniority.[41]

Near the end of her childhood Wong Su-ling remembered a conversation quite clearly which brought home to her the rigidity of separation and segregation that lay ahead:

> I had never fully realised the rigidity of this sex separation until one day as I was nearing the end of childhood I heard First Aunt and my mother talking about my grandfather, who had been dead for several years. Aunt told how she had built up a picture of him based upon his voice, which she heard almost daily, although she never saw him. 'His voice was so bright and strong that I always thought of him as big and fat and powerful,' she said. 'Then when it came my turn to make my bow and knock my head in front of him before he was put into the coffin, I thought that it would not be impolite, seeing that he was dead, for me to take a good look at him.' First Aunt paused as if the picture were fresh before her eyes. 'There he was, sitting in an armchair in his official robe embroidered with golden dragons, just like life. It gave me a shock. And he was not at all as I had imagined him. He was a tall thin man with a white beard on his pointed chin.' My mother nodded understandingly. 'It was just the same with me,' she said. 'I expected to see a dead man, but he looked alive, sitting there that way, and not at all what I had thought he would be like.'

It seemed almost incredible to the young girl that her mother and aunt had lived in the same house with her grandfather for years and in daily sound of his voice, yet had gone as brides into their own rooms and had never appeared outside them when he was present. She remembered, however, that:

> once when we were in one of the workrooms off the back court-yard, mother had heard First Uncle coming that way, which he very seldom did, and had run for the door, and whisked from one back room to another until she had regained her own apartment, quite out of breath. I had not known that she could move so fast on her tiny bound feet. 'But did you not see him at the time of your wedding when you and First Uncle bowed to him?' I asked First Aunt. My mother laughed. 'We were both too shy and flustered to look at anybody. Besides, it is the proper thing for the bride to keep her eyes fixed on the floor and not look at any of the people at her wedding ceremony, and then when she puts on

the Dragon Crown headdress, the red silk gauze veil which hangs down to her waist makes it impossible to see things very clearly anyway. I never saw him either.' 'But,' I persisted, 'every morning and night you went to grandmother's room to pay your respects. Grandfather shared the same room. How could you miss seeing him?' 'He always left when he heard us coming,' said First Aunt. Perhaps he knew our voices or our footsteps.' 'Perhaps', said my mother, 'grandmother told him that a daughter-in-law was coming.'

I thought about the other possibilities of contact. Both attended various weddings and funerals where it would seem that they would inevitably catch a glimpse of each other. But not so. Women usually went earlier and made a stay of several days. Even if they came when men were present, their closed sedan chairs would be set down at the door to the inner apartments into which they immediately vanished. Nor was it considered good form for the men to look at them. They politely turned their heads the other way.

I looked at mother and aunt with new eyes of admiration. Here was the modern counterpart of the celebrated women of old that I had heard of, Po Chi, wife of Duke Jung of Sung, who perished in her burning house rather than violate the rule of not leaving at night unless the matron and governess were there, or the very proper Meng Chi of Chi who preferred to die rather than ride home in a cart without curtains when her own cart broke down.[42]

She was to later marvel how this was not a seclusion maintained by guards and locked doors, but a voluntary one based on Confucian ethics which had given her and others a safe, secure though confining 'world of childhood'.

In other gentry households the rules of segregation also led to the increasing isolation of girls from all save the women of their family. Few were the occasions in any household when girls and boys or men and women were permitted to observe each other, be in close proximity or touch. Indeed in one household the rules of segregation were so strict that clothing belonging to the opposite sex could not be hung in the same closet or on the same bamboo pole to dry; girls were not allowed to sit on a seat that had recently been vacated by a man; and fingers were not permitted to touch when objects were passed. In almost all households men ate first and separately from the women. Thus a predominant theme of the early years of privileged female life stories was the narrowing of permitted public, domestic and interior spaces or the heightened experience of boundaries as they gradually enclosed the experiences of growing gentry daughters. Although in working house-holds women customarily had more freedom of movement, daughters of marriageable age also were frequently confined. However, their living quarters afforded them less seclusion than the rambling courtyards characteristic of gentry dwellings. The very size of the peasant dwelling made impossible the degree of seclusion that was maintained in gentry households and where the light inside was poor, peasant women fre-quently sat and worked on their doorsteps. In the village, peasant women sometimes gathered water from the well and did their washing at the river, and had no servants to shop for them. They had some contact with local shopkeepers and pedlars, but even so the movements of most young village women were still restricted. They were often not permitted to leave their courtyards before or during the first three years of marriage. One traveller in nineteenth-century China found that tens of thousands of women had never been more than two miles from their villages and this was often only on the occasion of their marriage. They were generally said to live the existence of a 'frog in a well' and one lady told the traveller that in her next life she hoped to be born a dog, for then she might come and go where she chose.[43] The common sayings 'A man travels everywhere while a woman is confined to the kitchen' and 'an incompetent man can get about in nine counties but a competent woman can only get around her cooking stove' arose because appearances of women outside their household yards were rare. In a small city working household too, a woman remembered the importance of spatial prohibitions:

> When there was a knock at the street door, no matter what we were talking about we had to stop. If a stranger came into the court we had to disappear into the inner room. When my father came home, even if we had been laughing and talking, we were silent the moment we heard the latch fall in the socket as the front gate was opened.[44]

Even the appearances of adolescent working and servant girls outside their household yards was rare. As one working woman recalled in her memoirs, she and her sister were not allowed on the street after they were thirteen. She also recalled that when a family wanting to know more about a girl, who had been suggested as a prospective daughter-in-law, asked neighbours for an opinion, the highest praise and compli-ment in response was: 'We do not know, we have never seen her.'[45]

If memories of these spatial prohibitions remained vivid, women also remembered their curiosity about the world outside. One even recalled 'asking a bird' for knowledge of places and events beyond the family walls.[46] Standing on thresholds and observing from doorways apparently hidden and unnoticed was a favourite childhood occupation.

In most households it was a taboo to openly observe a member of the opposite sex in and between courtyards, although all the accounts of childhood suggest that there was much closeted peeping from behind doors and screens even though punishment for so doing was swift and direct. If younger girls had any doubts as to the segregation and seclusion that lay in store for them as they approached the age of marriage, they had only to watch the fate of their elder sisters, female cousins or neighbours. Several younger daughters remembered observing the increasing seclusion of their elder sisters as they were confined to their rooms sometimes doing very little but embroidering their trousseaus. Wei Tao-ming sometimes wondered if her older sister was really a sister given that 'her whole being and approach to life were incomprehensible'. She did not seem to regret her tightly bound feet, had little interest in the outside world and spent all her days in painting, embroidery and domestic detail.[47] Chow Ching-li's older sister was also 'so quiet, so slow, and so delicate'.[48] Hsieh Ping-ying's elder sister had started to embroider when she was only eight and until aged eighteen, when she was married, she seldom left her room:

> In her tiny room, from six o'clock in the morning until six o'clock in the evening, she did nothing but embroider. In the evenings she had to spin. My poor elder sister, even when she was weary and panting, would not dare say anything about it to her mother. All she did was to sigh in secret. Of course my mother wished that I would be like my sister, doing a lot of embroidery work, so that by the time I married my trousseau would be very attractive.[49]

Hsieh Ping-ying, for her part, could not understand why a girl was bound to be nothing but a wife, to give birth to children for her husband and to be badly treated by her parents-in-law just as was happening to her elder sister.

It was the increasing confinement that distinguished girlhood and the contrast with the boys of the family could not have been greater. Many girls compared their cloistered experience with that of their brothers and male cousins; almost without exception the boys attended schools, travelled far and had access to outside knowledge as they trained for familial and non-familial occupations. The contrast with the lives of their brothers had been anticipated by the poet Fu Xuan from ancient times:

> Boys standing leaning at the door
> Like gods fallen out of Heaven,
> Their hearts have the Four Oceans,
> The wind and dust of a thousand miles ...
> When she grows up she hides in her room,
> Afraid to look men in the face.[50]

Nevertheless, the contrast with the lives of brothers was experienced by each sister anew. One sister recalled very movingly the dislocation between boyhood and girlhood experiences and the parting of the ways between brothers and sisters:

> They were young men with their lives ahead of them, the world at their feet, their hopes high. I was a mere girl, and a girl was not even half a man. A girl belonged to a man, her only future was to marry, to be true to a husband and give him children … My dear brother, my brother of the little green door showed no interest in me now. He was leaving me, step by step, and I was retreating, step by step. We were growing away from each other and would soon be strangers.[51]

Stranger daughters

While girlhood was marked by a number of female-specific events that spatially confined and concealed the female body, there were also a number of events and experiences common to both male and female childhood that, although shared, drew attention to differences in male and female experience of family and to girls' estrangement and separation from their families from birth. Most such moments were occasioned by family and kinship rituals emphasizing the contrast between the transience, secondariness and exclusion of daughters from their natal families and the experience of their brothers who as sons were both permanent and preferred members of households. Adult daughters still remembered the growing sense of exclusion and injustice they felt as young girls when they became aware of their secondary place in the familial hierarchy – a place that seemed to be based solely on their gender. A common such moment and first memory of exclusion had to do with gendered naming practices. There were no cases in the autobiographies where girls had been given names meaning 'better luck next time' or 'wish you were a boy', but even those with conventional girls' names felt discriminated against. It was customary for boys to have a clan name, a generation name and an individual name which clearly defined their place and position in their family. Girls were usually given a number and an informal child name, perhaps of a flower, a fragrance or a precious stone. In every case women remembered how as small girls they noticed and commented on the naming differences, given the array of names of their brothers and male cousins. This difference was forcefully brought home to 7-year-old Wong Su-ling in a way that she 'never forgot'. She was known as 'Miss Seven' to senior relatives and servants and 'Ling', meaning bell, to immediate relatives. One New Year on the occasion of the birth of the first grandson of the household when she was looking at the book of ancestral records, she

found not her own name but just 'a number seven female'. She remonstrated with her father:

> But I am Ling Ling and that is only a number,' I told him.
> 'Where is my name?' 'You are a girl,' he said, unconsciously
> dashing my enthusiasm and merely stating a fact. 'Boys have a
> name and a serial number, girls have a number only. When you
> grow up and marry, the words will be added "married to so and
> so", and your name will also be entered on the record book of
> your husband's clan.' I was hurt, and could not understand why
> I could not share the name of my generation. It was the small
> beginning of a sense of injustice that was to continue and grow
> more and more sharp.[52]

Interestingly, one of the first and symbolic actions that adult women
later took on leaving home was to acquire an additional or new name
to symbolize their equality with their brothers or to stress their new
status as persons separate from their families.

If practices of incomplete naming made an early impression on
small daughters, so also did familial ceremonies and ritual occasions
such as the worshipping of ancestors or making of offerings at family
graves at which they were either marginalized to spectator status or
excluded altogether. One small girl who made as if to pay her respects
after the smallest boy of the family had completed his bows to the
ancestors was pulled back and told to keep quiet. She described how
'suddenly she felt orphaned.' On this occasion all the men and boys of
the branch of the clan had gathered before the ancestral shrine in the
great reception hall in the late afternoon of the last day of the year, but
the females of the family were not present. Wong Su-ling remembered
how she and her sisters were permitted to stand at the far end of the
hall under the supervision of the steward, Kiu Kung, to watch the men
of the household light candles, kowtow and make presentations to the
ancestral tablets in a ceremony in which every move was dignified and
formal:

> This gave me a deep impression of the presence of the unseen
> spirits. These were good spirits, and my feeling was quite different
> from my chronic fear of ghosts. It was my first real intimation of
> the spiritual. It was partly the ritual ... the portentous solemnity
> ... It was even more the consciousness, shared by all of us, of
> being in the presence of a mystery greater than ourselves. I looked
> at the ancestral tablets and, in my imagination, saw an old, gray-
> bearded man sitting in his set inside the cabinet. Perhaps he was
> my honourable grandfather come back home to pay a visit to his
> family.

I watched until the smallest boy had completed his bows with the help of his father, and then turned to Kiu Kung. "Shall I also bow to our ancestors, Kiu Kung?' I asked. He shook his head, 'Keep quiet', he said in a low voice of finality, 'Say nothing'. I suddenly felt orphaned. This was my family and my home and yet I did not really belong. I felt unaccountably and unjustifiably shut out. I wanted to ask him why my brothers could worship our ancestors and I could not. But I didn't dare.[53]

As the servants began setting the tables for the feast the males of the clan would then enjoy in the reception hall, sharing it with the spirits of the ancestors, 'the mysterious realm of the spirit ... was suddenly clouded over' for this daughter who had the overwhelming feeling that 'she did not belong'.

Likewise Chow Chung-cheng remembers her feelings of exclusion on ritual occasions such as New Year when sacrifices made to the Kitchen God were for boys only and the annual journey made by her grandfather to make offerings at the graves of her great-grandparents and great-great-grandparents, which was also the occasion on which grandsons were shown the graves of their ancestors. When her brother was taken how Chow Chung-cheng envied him! 'But, of course, Grandfather would never take a girl with him.' In the increasingly extravagant celebrations of her elderly grandfather's birthdays much enjoyed by the men of the family, 'the daughters of the Chow family, whether married or unmarried also had nothing to do.'[54] Tsai Chin did not witness her grandfather's burial, for he was almost certainly taken to his ancestral plot in Ningpo to be buried with his forefathers as every Chinese dreams of doing. But in a procession following the coffin from one part of the temple to another she was told that her younger brothers took precedence in the procession, while the girls were obliged to walk deferentially in their wake. They protested in surprise, but even her mother had to bow to conformity and their protests were in vain. 'At that moment,' she said, 'I discovered that I belonged to the lesser part of mankind.' After the funeral she persisted in finding out the reason for the discrimination. An old-fashioned aunt, Father's cousin, finally lost her patience:

'A girl should know her place,' she said firmly. 'What place?' I echoed, in genuine ignorance. 'Don't you know that women are inferior?' 'No, but why?' I asked, even more surprised. 'Because we are unclean.' I did not understand what she meant. It was before my puberty. But the message seeped through somehow. I wrote an essay in school entitled: 'To Fight for the Greatness of Womanhood.' I got nil for the assignment, since the content was no longer than the grandiose title. I hadn't the faintest notion how to go about it. I was eight years old.[55]

Daughter order

Women recalled that as small daughters they felt a growing sense of injustice in the face of son privilege and son preference. Sisters with brothers all directly experienced son privilege as they were passed over in the distribution of favours, but more important in sharply giving shape to this awareness was the difference in ceremony and felicitation greeting male and female births. The secondary status of daughters was frequently and incisively confirmed on the birth of younger brothers and sisters. The eyes and ears of small girls were quickly alerted to the differences in sentiment and ceremony greeting male and female births within their families. Even those daughters who were cherished frequently realized at this moment that they could never be the equal of or substitute for sons. It was not always true that in the ancient words of the poet Fu Xuan 'No one was glad when a girl was born and by her the family sets no store.'[56] Although many daughters felt particularly cherished and wanted by one or both parents if they were the first or last born in a family of sons, a girl was generally welcomed into the family with fewer expectations and less ceremony than a boy. The *Book of Poetry*, one of the richest and most authentic source materials depicting social life in ancient China, recorded the unequal perceptions of sons and daughters from birth:

> When a son is born
> Let him sleep on the bed,
> Clothe him with fine clothes.
> And give him jade to play with.
> How lordly his cry is!
> May he grow up to wear crimson
> And be the lord of the clan and the tribe.

> When a daughter is born,
> Let her sleep on the ground,
> Wrap her in common wrappings,
> And give her broken tiles for playthings.
> May she have no faults, no merits of her own
> May she well attend to food and wine,
> And bring no discredit to her parents.[57]

None of the women writers witnessed female infanticide within their own families, which is not surprising given the socio-economic status of most of them. However, one daughter was very much affected by the sight of the orphanage established by her grandfather for abandoned baby girls. She walked home much sobered by the thought that there were daughters who, unwanted, had been abandoned by their families.[58]

All daughters however could not help but notice that the births of girls and boys were treated differently. Usually girls were made to feel less welcome than boys although the autobiographies reveal a range of birth circumstances. They either remembered being told of the circumstances and the degree to which they themselves had or had not been welcomed into the family or, more importantly, they observed the circumstances surrounding the births of their siblings. Chow Ching-li learned that she had been daily prayed for by her Buddhist mother as compensation for living within a miserable marriage. She owed the fact not only that she was born but that she was permitted to live to her mother's conversion to Buddhism. In the final months of confinement her mother, who had already borne a son and two daughters who had both died, prayed daily for a daughter.

> If the baby were a boy, he would belong to his father and father's family; a daughter, on the other hand, would belong to her; no one would want to lay claim to a girl. Such a child could be a source of joy and consolation for the miserable life she spent under the domination of her implacable mother-in-law with a husband who was too weak to protest or to demonstrate any tenderness toward his wife, or who perhaps didn't care.

However, there was not the slightest doubt that grandmother expected the baby would be a boy and she ran speechless and unforgiving from the room at the time of birth. Her mother's wish for a daughter was, according to her daughter, all the more remarkable for her grandmother had early been widowed and her life had been made miserable without either husband or son. She had harshly lashed out at her mother when she was small: 'Why weren't you born a boy!' she used to shout at her, striking her.[59] Another daughter, born after a difficult labour, was subsequently told that her 'little eyes were like two brilliant lamps' and that she could roll them very rapidly. She had shaken her little fists and kicked so incessantly that her sixth great-aunt had sighed and said, 'what a pity this is a girl. Had it been a boy I am sure he would have become a great official. Look at the quick-moving eyes.' Her mother, not approving of her words, objected: 'what difference does it make whether it is a boy or a girl: they are the same to me.' So she was told by her grandmother that she should know that her mother, although having suffered so much for her sake, loved her the instant she had been born.[60]

Many daughters, however, did not remember being made to feel welcome and for some, born after a succession of sisters, childhood memories as 'unwanted daughters' were all the more traumatic. The extent of secondariness and discrimination felt by girls seems to very much have depended on their birth order in the family. Many second and third daughters felt that they had not been born in the right sequence and were a 'disappointment from the start'. Chow Chung recalled that although she was born at the right hour, she certainly was not born in the right order:

> My eldest brother died when he was five; two years after the birth of my second brother, my sister was born, and then, two years later, myself. So we were two girls and a boy. Why did I have to follow my sister? A year later my third brother arrived and four years afterwards my fourth brother; nine years later came my fifth brother, and five years later a sixth, but he was still-born. I did not choose the right order, and, moreover, my mother liked boys but did not care for girls. When I was born, she was hoping for a son, so I was a disappointment from the start.[61]

On the birth of one of her baby brothers, she recalled the events of that 'lucky' day:

> One morning my nurse said to me: 'There has been a happy event. Last night your mother brought you a little brother. Now you will be more highly esteemed, for your mother has four sons and only two daughters. So you should be pleased.'

This daughter knew immediately what the birth of this child meant to her parents. But she doubted if as a consequence she should be more highly esteemed:

> Would my mother ever esteem a daughter? ... where had my little brother come from? It was a mystery to me. When we were with our parents that evening I asked: 'Mother, where did our new brother come from? Where?' She smiled. 'Far away, on a mountain peak, there are children, boys and girls,' she answered. 'People who want children go there to fetch them. I brought all of you from that mountain, including your littlest brother.' We must have been cold and hungry, I reflected. How good of Mother, how kind of her, to have brought us home! 'When did you go to fetch him?' I asked. 'One night,' she answered. 'You have to go at night and search'. I would have liked to ask why she brought back girls when she could have had only boys, but I didn't dare.

This was the daughter whose own childhood memories were to be such that, when she later began to write poetry, she ended one poem with the plea: 'Father and Mother! A daughter is as good as a son!'[62]

Another second daughter remembers not only the feeling that she herself was unwanted, but witnessing a particularly unforgettable and disturbing event when her younger sister was born. She had watched her own mother revelling in her difference from other women around her and known that she enjoyed being regarded as a spirited modern woman free of the conventions that others unthinkingly accepted. Still from time to time her mother's carefully controlled modern façade would crack. When that happened it became painfully clear, even to a child, that she was not entirely free of the bonds of tradition and particularly of the ancient injunction of bearing sons. This daughter later came to understand that despite her Western ways, her mother's failure to give birth to a son – the first requirement of a Chinese wife – came as a blow she 'could not parry'. This second daughter described her personal ordeal, which 'began at the time of her own birth'.

> when I was six I learned that Mother felt a wrenching personal shame at having failed to bear my father a male heir ... No one had paid more dearly than I for what she saw as her one failure. In the Chinese culture, it is no tragedy if the first-born is a female. There is time yet for a son to come. As the proverb states it, 'first the blossom, then the fruit' ... it was I, the Second Daughter, who bore the stigma.[63]

But if she was very aware of the cumulative effects of her own order of birth, she also never quite got over one particular event occurring immediately after the birth of her younger sister. On the occasion of the birth of yet another daughter, her mother 'luckless' and 'distraught' attempted to pretend that she had given birth not to a daughter but to a son. When she screamed at the hospital nurses for mistakenly swapping a boy for a girl, her young second daughter attempted to correct her mother. She thus found herself at the receiving end of an angry gesture the effect of which she was never to forget for the rest of her life![64]

Maxine Hong Kingston, again in another country and another age but not another culture, was to capture memorably the sense of difference and injustice felt by daughters without brothers. She minded that the emigrant villagers shook their heads at her sister and herself saying 'One girl and another girl', thereby making her parents ashamed of taking them out together.

> The good part about my brothers being born was that people stopped saying, 'All girls', but I learned new grievances. 'Did you roll an egg on *my* face like that when I was born?' 'Did you have a full-month party for *me*?' 'Did you turn on all the lights?' 'Did you send *my* picture to grandmother? Why not? Because I'm a girl? Is that why not?

She early surmised that the reason the girls were left at home was the street approbation which would greet the line of boys:

'Come children, hurry. Hurry. Who wants to go out with Great Uncle?' On Saturday mornings my great uncle, the ex-river pirate, did the shopping. 'Get your coats, whoever's coming.' 'I'm coming. I'm coming, Wait for me.' When he heard girls' voices, he turned on us and roared 'No girls!' and left my sisters and me hanging our coats back up, not looking at one another. The boys came back with candy and new toys. When they walked through China-town, the people must have said 'A boy ... and another boy ... and another boy!'[65]

If their own birth order was a common theme distinguishing their experiences as daughters, their increasing awareness of injustice in the face of son preference contributed to their growing sense of exclusion from their families of birth.

It is very noticeable that even as young girls and long before marriage, daughters reported perceiving themselves to be somewhat estranged from their families, frequently regarding themselves as detached or 'outside of their families' in comparison to their brothers. They observed that there were times when women were excluded from the family and they early formed images of themselves as outsiders, as observers and as less than full family members or had feelings of being 'less than a person'. Even in relation to the family of their birth they had a status like that of a stranger; they both were regarded as and perceived themselves as detached, transient outsiders. Katherine Wei noted that the predominant theme in relation to the family was one of roundness and wholeness, with descent lines maintained by sons who feed the dead and the old, who in turn look after the family; that is, of a wholeness from which women were excluded even if necessary. Her image of herself was of 'an observer who witnessed every nuance of an unchanging regime' of the family.[66] Chow Chung wrote that in the events and discussions of her household: 'They ignored what I had said. I was only a daughter to marry ... only sons were people.'[67] As another daughter duly surmised, she was in the family but not of the family for was her presence not temporary?

In our household the women who had come in as wives from other clans, and the girl children who had been born to them and would be married out into other clans, constituted our woman's world and had a psychology of their own. We were in the family but not of it.[68]

Marriage too was an event common to both males and females ending childhood, but the event had a very different significance in the lives of sons and daughters. Within the secluded quarters of gentry women or in peasant and working households, girls were reared and trained in anticipation of one single future – marriage.

One single future

If at 10 years old a girl was considered 'almost a young woman' and embarked on her apprenticeship as a wife, marriage marked her passage to womanhood. Mothers frequently ended their instructions about obedience and service to their daughters on the eve of their marriage with the words: 'Tomorrow, your life as a woman will begin.'[69] From her earliest years a daughter was reminded not just that marriage was a pivotal moment in 'becoming a woman', but that she was destined to become a daughter-in-law and wife in another family. She was reminded that a girl's happiness, well-being and welfare depended on marriage and a successful marriage at that; this was her future and her only future. For girls it was thus a moment of discontinuity, dislocation and rupture like no other. Indeed most young girls first associated marriage with movement: 'All I thought it meant was leaving home and going to live somewhere else, where I would eat and sleep for the rest of my life, and never again see the outside world.'[70]

On the eve of the girl's marriage it was her weeping mother's words bewailing the imminent departure of her daughter that finally brought home to Chow Ching-li the significance of the events of next day: 'Her words shocked me into finally realizing grim reality. Tomorrow, I would be gone. I would have to leave my house, my beloved parents, and go to live with strangers. Tomorrow! I broke down again and began to sob.'[71]

Another young girl, Alice Lin, watching wedding processions with their sad and tearful scenes, later thought that it 'was no small wonder' that she 'did not remember any stories of happy brides'. Above all she remembered the tears shed as brides were about to become separated from all that they knew in order to enter a future unknown. She remembers how as a child she once joined other children to watch a wedding procession in the neighbourhood in which the bride, under a heavy veil of scarlet brocade covering her entire head and face, was led to a waiting carriage by her family, with her mother sobbing incessantly. Face unseen, the bride also seemed visibly shaken. Puzzled by the sad and tearful scene, Alice followed the carriage to the house of the bridegroom's family. Watching brides arrive at their new residence was apparently a favourite pastime for neighbourhood children! Struggling to reach the bedroom window, she saw the new bride 'sitting on the bed wiping tears from under her veil' and heard an older child mutter 'wait until she sees the bridegroom. He's as ugly as a toad!' Brides in Alice Lin's memory were inevitably 'linked to separation, tears, fear, and uncertainty about the future'.[72] Separation was a uniquely female experience of marriage in contrast with the confirmation of the certainty and permanence of their place in the family that marriage gave their brothers. Girls commonly remembered their envy of boys, especially of their inclusion and permanence in the family, and many at one time expressed a wish that they had been born boys. Indeed most girls associated any unconventionality in their childhoods with being 'honorary boys' – both at the time and in retrospect.

Boys of girls

There was thus a third category of moments inscribed in girls' memories, delineated precisely because they had stepped outside of conventionally defined female expectations and crossed gender categories by temporarily assuming male dress or male forms of behaviour. Unusually, some small girls had won a temporary reprieve from girlhood constraints because they had for some reason been addressed and dressed as boys. This practice sometimes occurred when a couple had given up hope of a son and adopted a girl or when the youngest of several daughters had just been born. Bu Wei-chao, adopted at birth in lieu of a son by her childless aunt and uncle, was addressed as 'Little Master three', dressed as a boy and treated as male by both family and strangers. She recalled being privileged to do things that none of her sisters or female cousins 'would dream of doing'. She described her childhood as one marked by an 'unlimited range of activities' and one in which 'I never bothered much as to whether I was a boy or a girl until much later.'[73] The outraged parents of Chow Ching-li were particularly incensed by her 'going about in pants, since, under the rules of propriety and elegance in the French concession, little girls wore dresses, not trousers.' Her mother was always shaking her head and predicting: 'You'll never get married, you'll wind up a hoodlum!'[74] On the other hand, the father of Wei Tao-ming was so greatly taken with her unusual curiosity, exuberance and insatiable mind that 'she became a sort of mascot to him.' He began to take her everywhere with him, explaining everything to her as he went about and generally treating her much as he would a favourite son. She recalled:

> it soon became necessary for me to wear boy's clothes because the appearance of a little girl in a public place or in an open carriage would have aroused untoward comment. It just was not done. So, to get around this problem, Father had me dressed in little short trousers and a loose blouse. As my hair was cut short at that age, I passed easily for a little boy.[75]

Another young girl who also passed easily as a boy could not help but wish she had herself been born a boy. When Chow Chung heard someone ask her nurse if her charge was a boy, she feared that the questioner could even read her thoughts: 'Why should he ask that? Did

I look like a boy? Could he read my thoughts? Oh, I wished I were a boy!'[76]

Young girls evading the practice of footbinding were also seen to be crossing gender categories. Bu Wei chao thought that her unbound feet were a 'vitally important part of her male attire'. Her elder brother made up a jingle about her feet: 'Boy of a girl, with great big feet'.[77] Many small girls had not such a direct experience of male attire or attributes, but they had memories of stepping into exclusively male or female-prohibited spaces that were all the more sharply inscribed because of their exceptional qualities. One of the earliest childhood pictures recalled by one woman was of her 'grandmother in our front courtyard. It is especially vivid because we were seldom able to go out there, since it was territory ordinarily reserved for men, and women could only use it when they were away ... '[78] One of her most precious memories was of happily and triumphantly looking down upon the face of her smiling father as she sat astride the branch of a tree in the family orchard. Had she not entreated her reluctant father to let her climb that tree? Had he not initially looked as if he found it impossible to imagine a girl in his family doing such a thing but had he not also found it impossible to resist her entreaties? She remembered how when she was again back on the ground 'we looked soberly at each other. We were partners in crime. We both knew that grandmother would scold him far worse than she would me if she ever heard of it.'[79]

In less strict city households or later into the century, daughters remembered outings, perhaps a walk in the park or a shopping expedition, the excitement of which was derived from their rarity. Although such visits and journeys were usually made in a closed, curtained sedan chair, walks in parks and shopping expeditions were certainly not taken for granted as a normal part of girls' lives. Katherine Wei remembered 'glorious carefree outing days', the most memorable of which were visits with some of the servants to the market-place, the sights and sounds of which long remained in her memory.[80] Chow Chung-cheng remembered the elaborate negotiations with her parents to get them to take their children for a walk in a park, to the cinema or to a restaurant and how 'these rare outings were the more deeply engraven on my memory because our negotiations with Mother were so often unsuccessful.'[81] Older girls, too, were less likely to have such 'treats'. The longest and most important journeys that unmarried girls made might be pilgrimages to far temples, usually undertaken because their mothers wanted to worship or placate the gods and fulfil some promise made to the gods on behalf of daughters in past times of adversity. For instance, Hsieh Ping-ying's mother, on noticing that her daughter's feet were unwell, concluded that this was because the promise of such a pilgrimage at the time of her birth had still not been kept.

She and her daughter thus set out on a strenuous ten-day sedan chair journey to a mountain site to make their obeisances, with the daughter closely guarded all along the way.[82]

Several Western visitors to China remarked on the absence of women on city streets and described Chinese cities as 'cities of men'. In most of the households depicted in the personal narratives, if one of the women wanted to visit a relative or friend or leave the compound, she had first to get permission from her grandmother or mother and was required to go in a closed sedan chair. Just how rare visits were outside of some of the stricter households is beautifully portrayed in the early twentieth-century novel, *The Family*, in which the author describes a New Year custom that persisted into the twentieth century of allowing women on to the streets: 'The women of the family ... walked smilingly through their main gate and out on to the street. This was the women's annual comedy of going 'abroad'. It was only during this brief interval each year that they were permitted to travel freely in public other than in the closed sedan chair. 'The women feasted their curious eyes on the sleepy little street. Then fearful of meeting any strange men, they hurried back into the compound.'[83] In one Christian household, women and girls went to extraordinary lengths to avoid being seen in the streets. When they wanted to take the short journey to the nearby church, for which sedan chairs posed an unaffordable luxury each week, the women who had never walked on the streets before found it to be an unacceptable ordeal:

> We always met people we knew, and all of them looked at us in the greatest astonishment and stared unmercifully. We would lower our eyes and hurry past, blushing down to our necks. This at length became unbearable, so we got up at cockcrow, walked to church in the early dawn and thus avoided meeting any of our relatives. There was a shed on the high-school grounds, next door, and in this we hid until the church doors were open and we could enter.[84]

However there was one space hitherto only inhabited by males that young girls increasingly could enter and that was the local village or city school.

Schooling for daughters

As the twentieth century progressed, girls previously secluded were more successful in negotiating their entry to schools hitherto open only to the males of the family, village or city. The twentieth century was unique in that it was marked by increasing popularity among certain classes for the public education of daughters. Mission schools for girls first founded from the mid-nineteenth century began to expand and to multiply in number. After a long struggle to establish their schools, the missionaries no longer had to entice and bribe pupils to attend as, increasingly for a certain group of Western-orientated Chinese, the mission schools, with their high teaching standards and foreign equipment, seemed to provide the most advanced courses for their daughters. Others of the gentry class, unwilling that the education of their daughters be left entirely in foreign hands, began themselves to sponsor the establishment of girls' schools. The first Chinese schools for girls were established with the patronage of wealthy merchants and officials from the turn of the century, although for many decades they were predominantly, but not exclusively, confined to the main cities such as Peking, Shanghai, Tientsin and Nanking. The majority of those leaving records of girlhood had entered one of a variety of new schools.

Young girls like Chow Ching-li and Tang Sheng attended these mission, government and privately-sponsored new schools for girls from a very early age because their parents wanted them to acquire literacy, a knowledge of the classics and foreign languages. Girls such as Liang Yen and Hsieh Ping-ying first attended primary schools in villages and towns that girls were now sometimes permitted to attend. However, most girls had to struggle against considerable family and village opposition in order to attend school, primarily because they were seen as entering spaces hitherto denied them or as entering a boys' world and thus once again becoming boys of girls. One young girl, taught in the family school usually only for boys, was told that it was 'not fitting to have older girls associate with all those big boys'.[85] Another girl, Hsieh Ping-ying, entered her village school at 10 years of age although, in her native village, they had never seen a girl going to school:

I never thought that a girl's ambition to study would meet with so many obstacles. Not only was the teacher reluctant to accept me as his pupil, but also those people who had nothing to do with us or the teacher protested against it. My greatest enemy was a woman with a snub nose who had the nickname of 'Sharp-mouthed Grandma'. She was well known in the village as a cattish woman. Her only son was studying in that private school, and so when she heard that I was going to it she went out everywhere spreading tales about me. She said that if girls were allowed to go to the same schools as boys, then the wisdom of the boys would be stolen by the girls, and the boys would become stupid dolts. Then she condemned my mother as being ignorant of the proprieties. She said that girls and boys should be separated was well known by everybody; how could it be allowed for me, a nearly grown-up girl, to go to the boys school? Although people were sympathetic to her, all they could do was to talk behind my mother's back. They were so afraid of my mother that none of them dared to approach her to stop me from going to the school. The 'Sharp-mouthed Grandma' was the bravest of all. She said she was afraid of nobody, so she came to see my mother and asked her not to send me to the school. This was all to the good because my mother was of a very perverse nature. At first she had not been quite keen on sending me to school, but after this interview, she was more determined than anyone to send me there immediately.[86]

While so many of the women narrators remember the girlish excitement of entering new spaces hitherto denied them on account of their sex, they also remembered how as girls they were often reminded that not only was their education of less consequence to the family, but also that their attendance at school did not mean that they had 'become as boys'. Bu Wei-chao knew that she was allowed to go unpunished at school when she was a mischievous pupil because 'it was not so important for a girl to study anyway.'[87] Liang Yen, who was sent to a local public school which was much cheaper than the normal private school that other members of her family attended, overheard her father say 'Besides, she is only a girl.' Later, when she wanted to go on with her studies her father's tolerance turned into opposition: 'What's the use of Daughter learning a lot of drivel?' Not only could his daughter 'not earn a copper' but 'To pay for marriage, yes – the sooner the better – but' – his hand rocked the desk – 'for this imbecility nothing'.[88] Chow Ching-li's family fearing for her chastity and reputation prevented her from entering the Shanghai music conservatory. 'A fine thing!' her mother exclaimed. 'A pretty girl like you in the middle of all those disreputable, shifty boys. The first thing that will happen is that someone will try to seduce you.'[89] Hsieh Ping-ying's mother, at the same time as assisting in her education, grumbled:

> Oh, a girl wanting to study? Really, the heavens will fall and the earth crumble! To study is the work of your elder brothers. You were born to be confined to your boudoir. Just think, what is the use of a woman who has studied?

Later when Hsieh Ping-ying had been to the village school, her mother again remonstrated 'What is the use of your studying any more? A girl who has read as many books as you already has done quite enough. You are not a man.'[90]

The nearer they came to marriageable age, the greater was the difference in treatment or discrimination they experienced even at the hands of the most liberal of families. In the early decades of the century

almost all daughters who were fortunate enough to have an early
education experienced some subsequent attempt to end or narrow their
education. Once brothers left home for school family tuition was
discontinued or girls were brought home from school to prepare for
marriage. As increasing seclusion and preparation in domestic arts
replaced public or family school, literate girls, having experienced an
alternative, increasingly chafed at the confinement. Many was the ex-
school pupil who took drastic action to advance her educational cause.
Liang Yen, faced with complete family opposition, secretly took a
tutoring job, turned to Buddhism and escaped from the family. Hsieh
Ping-ying felt her quest for further education against the implacable
opposition of her mother was so hopeless that she considered all forms
of suicide. 'At last I determined to starve myself, and I stayed in my bed
determined to die of hunger.'[91] Some days later she only 'won a reprieve
from death' and the promise of school if she consented to be a 'good
girl' at home for two more years. In order that Chow Chung was able
to attend higher school she had to wage a bitter war against the
combined opposition of her parents and family in a 'battle between the
old traditions and the new China'. Fearing no resolution she ran away
from home:

> I had packed a little bundle which I could carry unobstrusively
> under my arm. It contained a well-lined jacket, underwear, the
> three hundred dollars and Sse-shan's letters. It measured only
> about eighteen inches by ten, but it was very heavy. It was my
> first and only luggage for my journey into the world.[92]

Her entreaties to a progressive girls' newspaper for support in negotiating with her parents became a celebrated cause, and as a result of the
publicity she received in its pages she was able to persuade her parents
to permit both her and her sister to immediately re-enter school, then
go on to university and if possible thereafter go abroad to study. In the
light of such opposition to education, a common theme in all the life
stories was rebellion – rebellion against past restraints imposed by
rhetorical definitions and behavioural conventions surrounding Chinese
girlhood.

Daughter rebels

It is above all the notion of rebellion or rejection of prescriptive norms
that is both the theme common to the published narratives of female
lives during the first decades of the twentieth century and the predominant thread running through each individual life story. Each of
the narrators not only primarily perceived herself as a rebel, but also
denied having had a conventional Chinese girlhood. From the stand-

point of grown women they recognized that from an early age they had 'a lively curiosity', a 'strong will' or an 'independent spirit', all characteristics more likely to apply to sons than daughters. In categorizing themselves as girls of an unusual physical liveliness or curiosity of mind, they frequently thought of themselves as boys of girls. Almost without exception they dated their rebellions back to their earliest years speaking of themselves as 'infant rebels' or as engaged in 'nursery rebellions'. In retrospect, for example, Hsieh Ping-ying said she was ashamed to confess that from an early age 'I was just a rebel.'[93] If each daughter, whose parental attitudes and actions occasioned rebellion against conventional daughterhood, saw herself as an 'original rebel', she was encouraged in this rebellion by her schooling, a unique experience for some daughters of the twentieth century. Education in new girls' schools began to constitute an accepted practice for gentry daughters and the literate, and although its ends or goals might still be defined as additional correct preparation for good wifehood and good motherhood in the interests of rearing good sons, the main beneficiaries were the daughters themselves, for schooling increasingly took them outside the confines of the family and into the company of female peers and teachers. The new institutional environment not only served to insulate daughters from the exclusive influence of their families and tradition, but also brought them into contact with a new rhetoric, frequently Western or mission-sponsored, emphasizing female equality. As Wei Tao-ming recalled, the new school curriculum 'was a radical departure from the kind of education which Chinese girls received at home throughout the centuries.'[94] At school girls glimpsed an alternative future to the prescribed patterns of the past.

It was the freedom of movement, the example of the teachers and the relaxed talk with peers and with and between teachers of both sexes that made for indelible first impressions. For Wei Tao-ming 'the sight of Western women walking arm in arm with the men, on their big feet, talking and laughing with an equal lack of shyness', was stupifying.[95] When Hsieh Ping-ying first crossed the threshold of the advanced Datung school for girls and saw many lively girls playing with india-rubber balls, jumping, or playing at other games, she thought she had 'entered into Heaven'; 'I was almost crazy with delight, and my heart was full of unutterable happiness.' Suffering a severe drawback physically with her tightly bound feet, she took off the bindings:

> my feet began to enjoy freedom. After I had done this I went out into the courtyard with bare feet one day when it was raining very hard. It was a very exciting sensation to let one's natural feet get into touch with the good earth – a pleasure that I had not known for many years.[96]

Katherine Wei was particularly taken with the woman principals of the various schools she attended although she wondered if it was 'common in America for women to occupy positions of authority over men'.[97] Similarly, Chow Chung dubbed the university she attended 'that little world where men and women were equal.'[98] Liang Yen observed that the freedom between Western men and women extended to the point where 'women were sometimes heard talking back to men.'[99] Wong Su-ling, a new pupil, wrote at length on the influence of school on her as a new pupil:

> The school was a new world to me. There were new relationships I had not previously experienced, and new freedoms I did not know how to use. The girls were less formal than in my home, and more free in talking and discussing together than in our old family school. The relationships between students and teachers were friendly and democratic. Soon I found myself joining with the girls in their games and getting acquainted with my teachers ... Until this time I had never seen any but men teachers. Indeed it had never occurred to me that a teacher could be anything but a man ... but here most of my teachers were young women. And they were Chinese and not foreign. I looked upon them with amazement and admiration and followed their every move. How well they seemed to know their subjects. How self-assured they were. What dignity and authority they possessed. Just as much as my old teacher. And then the light dawned. Their status was just the same as if they had been men. Here was real equality. This was what I had been feeling the lack of, without quite being able to put it into words for myself. This was the meaning of my growing feeling of injustice over the disabilities imposed by family and clan because I was a girl. I decided then and there that I would be like them ... This was a feminine world. So was the women's part of our home in which I had grown up. But this Christian school was different. Women had a status here in their own right and not by virtue of being the mother or wife of some man, and in danger of losing it in case of the death of the man on whom it depended. Here women stood on their own feet.[100]

As one sociologist travelling in China noted, even in the most conservative mission school, which primarily taught girls the qualities of restraint and obedience, every lady principal and teacher was at heart a sworn enemy of bound feet, forced betrothal and the subjection of women in China. Although they might protest and be reluctant to admit to this role, he argued that this was the case:

> It is not her role of course – she will fence with you at first, but

finally if you seem trustworthy, she will own up. She does not egg the girls on to assert this or that right, but strives to build up in them a personality which will not accept the old status.[101]

The new opportunities for education in girls' schools not only took girls out of the confines of their homes and introduced them to new role models, but also introduced them to Western ideas, literature and institutions based on the ideals of 'freedom', 'individualism', 'self-fulfilment' and 'equality of the sexes', which came to have popular appeal among students in the first decades of the twentieth century. It was the new schools too which produced and published the first newspapers specifically aimed at a female audience. By the end of the second decade, hardly a periodical appeared that did not raise 'the woman's problem' or 'the woman question' as the issues surrounding female roles and status were collectively termed. The woman's problem was usually viewed in terms of the emancipation or independence of the individual from traditional familial and societal restraints and in particular took up the cause of free-choice marriage and romantic love. Indeed the most compelling contemporary concern of the privileged and educated younger generation was with the institution of marriage, in which their bid to free themselves from the authority and control of the older generation came to centre on their right to choose a marriage partner free from parental interference. Daughters who had glimpsed a different future refused to bow to the hitherto inevitable or a fate predestined by Confucian code and to be married out by the families of their birth.

The avoidance of fate

Nearly all the daughters who narrated their life stories had been promised to another family either at birth or at a young age. Early marriage was well-nigh universal and the negotiations regarding the choice of marriage partner, the financial transactions and ceremonies were arranged and conducted on behalf of their families by a go-between or broker, with the younger generation playing no part. After the quest for an education, a second major area of rebellion for daughters as related in many of the autobiographies was the avoidance or cancellation of a betrothal arrangement promising them to a husband unseen and to another unknown family. In rejecting an arranged match Wong Su-ling showed considerable and memorable imagination. In the negotiation of a match it was customary to place the divination cards of potential bride and groom showing the year, month and hour of their birth on the bride's family altar, a ceremony which, if followed by a period of harmony, order and peace in the household symbolized the 'rightness' of the arranged match. Wong Su-ling, despite calling herself 'Daughter of Confucius' had her younger sister and cat bring such disorder into the ancestral hall that the match was instantly called off![102] Bu Wei-chao, who had been betrothed before she was born, first began to rebel on hearing that her prospective mother-in-law opposed the non-binding of her feet. 'This made me hate her and started my thoughts of getting out of the whole arrangement.' She was fortunate in that her father opposed her being wed at fifteen years of age and managed to delay the marriage so that both prospective son-in-law and daughter could first get an education and thus be more independent. This delay was not sufficient a guarantee for Bu Wei-chao, but her mother refused to discuss it and her father advocated delay:

> Let's not talk about it any more. The sky may hold unpredictable winds and clouds. You just keep quiet for a few years. Even girls in foreign countries cannot decide their own affairs until they are of age ... You should also settle down to your studies ... become a teacher ... I think our country is due for some revolutionary changes.

In the meantime she had to attend her own engagement party at which she:

> talked loudly and joined fights over fruits and nuts. I meant to tell them by my behaviour that I regarded the whole thing as somebody else's affair with which I had nothing to do. Apparently they did not or would not understand me. They just remarked that I was too much used to being a boy.

Once she was about eighteen years old she felt she had no choice but to deal with the problem of betrothal for 'her freedom was at stake.' Although her grandfather had said that he would help her with all his authority, there remained:

> the question who should bring up the question to whom. There was no precedent to follow, because the thing was unprecedented. I thought at first that, since the families had made the engagement, they should be responsible for breaking it. On the other hand, since it was on the ground of freedom of the individual that I based my move, I should write to my cousin myself.

She wrote him what she hoped was a tactful letter with the most important aim of winning her freedom, which brought forth threats of forcing the marriage and even of putting her to death. Fortunately her grandfather overrode all saying:

> I have no illusions about happy marriages always resulting from

free choice, but you can be sure that no good can come of
compelling a girl to marry someone against her wish. I have seen
too many abuses in the old system. If a family like ours cannot
make a start in reform, who else's can? You are always talking
about your mother's orders. All right, I am your father. I now
countermand her orders. That is final.

Thus ended successfully Bu Wei-chao's nineteen-year fight for un-
conditional freedom: 'For the first time in my life,' she noted, 'my self
was my own.'[103]

Katharine Wei's husband was chosen for her so that her family
might have the chance to emigrate to America. For the previous five
years her mother, having no sons, had groomed her to fulfil the first-
born son's responsibility to ensure the family's security in his parents'
waning years.

I was to have played the role of the male heir Mother had never
borne my father. At least that was now understood ... It would
have served no purpose to accuse her of wanting for herself the
best of the new and old social orders – the privilege of selecting
not only her own husband, but those of her daughters as well.
She would not have listened.

Her mother had chosen a husband for her and encouraged his suit
without even informing her own daughter. In return Katharine Wei

wanted to punish her mother terribly for the five years she had
made me think I was earning her respect and affection, but all
that time she had been dealing in a different currency. Now I
would put her arranged marriage out of my mind and risk the
lawless violence of the city streets. I felt free of the need to win
mother's love, yet enslaved in a different way. Now I was driven
to make her hate me. I was angry at Father too. He must have
known something of what Mother was up to, but he had been too
weak to stop her. By his silence, I felt, he had collaborated in her
exploitation of me; in her long-term strategy to barter her way to
America.[104]

Feeling the weight of tradition and lacking support, the daughter
eventually bowed 'to the inevitable' and entered the arranged marriage
– to her mother's satisfaction.

Wei Tao-ming remembered that at thirteen years of age there was
a party to celebrate her engagement to a young man she had never
met. 'Marriage had always seemed a remote and unreal idea but ... I
acquiesced with the vague idea in my mind that this would keep peace
in the family.' She was not involved in the party and she ignored the

whole situation as best she could, but once the marriage date was set, she too became panic-stricken at the idea of marrying a total stranger. Moreover, reports of the young man himself were not promising for he had the reputation of a spoilt playboy from a conservative family who did not approve of telephones, which she thought was 'an indication of my betrothed's family's attitude towards everything'. Furthermore, she found that her father-in-law did not approve of 'modern education for women'. He was also reported to have said that 'She knows too much already. She spends too much of her time outside her parents' house, and a woman of our society should not run after learning.' In response to Wei Tao-ming's pleadings, her sympathetic father did begin to try to find some way in which the engagement could be broken off without either family's losing face. He spent weeks trying to locate an inter-mediary who would handle these difficult negotiations. In the meantime, Wei Tao-ming, very impatient, persuaded her sympathetic brother to write to her fiancé and tell him 'in tactful phrases' exactly how she felt:

> Finally, I took the bull by the horns. As a matter of fact, I did not realize what an extraordinary thing it was that I did. I not only thought of myself as quite grown up, but in my determination to be emancipated, my plan seemed a very minor detail … the hubbub which ensued was unbelievable. To the best of my know-ledge no Chinese girl of good family had ever done such a thing before. Both families, especially mine, lost an enormous amount of face. My father was shocked beyond words, and, needless to say, my grandmother took to her bed and gave every appearance of dying of shock. My only support was Mother, who, though miserable at the disgrace which had been brought on the family, was still secretly happy that I had not been forced into the marriage. She cried a great deal, but she cried more from affection for me and general emotion than because of the end of the engagement. I had won the battle at a terrific emotional cost to the whole family.[105]

Thirteen-year-old Chow Ching-li suddenly found that she was being groomed for marriage and introduced to the son of a family far from modern but of great wealth. She could not believe it:

> Was *he* the one they wanted me to marry? Surely Mama couldn't seriously be considering marrying me off to *him*! No, it was too ridiculous. It was a joke, it was some kind of a game cooked up to frighten me.

She opposed the match so vehemently that her father hesitated to give his consent, while her brother and sister supported her against the arrangement, with her brother making a hysterical declaration of family war to the effect that 'you can't sell our sister – you have no right.' The resulting tension and conflict within the household became so violent that Chow Ching-li could not hold out:

> I finally came to the conclusion that the only thing left was for me to submit to my destiny. I had no right to prolong my family's anguish – particularly my father's. I would have to do what was expected of me. I would have to agree to the marriage.

Her brother and sister were furious with her for giving in, but she went ahead with the engagement party. All the while she:

> felt numb, nothing at all, defenceless to argue ... the certainty of my fate filled me with fear and despair. And even though it had been my own mother who had pushed me into this trap, I still clung to her. I couldn't believe that she wouldn't take pity on me and relent.

She pleaded with her mother against 'disappearing into that family', she lost sleep, didn't eat and even lost much of her hair. After living through several days of tears and lamentation in the final throes of defiance, Chow Ching-li wrote that she 'bowed before my destiny, this time without hope, praying only that my path would not be too difficult'. She concluded that as a 13-year-old schoolgirl with alternative hopes of her own she had in effect been sold to a wealthy family, albeit under the guise of marriage and condemned to live with a stranger she didn't love. She had resisted, but 'the child I was could not hold out against either my own family's greed or, more important, the ancient and rigid tradition of strict obedience to your parents, regardless of their wishes.'[106]

Hsieh Ping-ying had been betrothed when she was 3 years old to the son of one of father's friends. After fleeing home and entering one of the revolutionary girls' armies she returned home to break her betrothal even though home felt like a 'family fortress'. She thought she had enough will-power to be strong enough to break away. In the meantime though her mother had been preparing her dowry and thus began a long exchange of views between mother, father and daughter which is interesting for the range of the arguments marshalled on each side:

> I had thousands of things to say to my mother, but I knew not how to begin. However I decided that until my father came back I would say nothing about the breaking-off of my engagement. I knew my mother was a very obstinate woman, and to raise the subject with her would be just like pouring water on the back of a duck. It would be sheer waste of energy.

She recorded her memories of the exchanges between mother, father and daughter following her announcement that she would not marry her betrothed:

'What! Not marry him? You want to break off the engagement?' My father looked very angry. 'Yes, certainly, father,' I replied calmly and firmly. My mother could not keep silent any longer and began to scold me by saying: 'Beast, beast! ... Marry you must, and I will see it to myself ...' I knew it would be no good to continue the discussion with my mother, and I retired to my bedroom to write a long letter, about five thousand words, giving my father all the reasons for my proposal to break off the marriage. I handed the letter to my father the next morning, and I was surprised to see that after he had read it he was not moved in the least, but began to upbraid me even more severely than before:

'As you say in your letter, the reasons for breaking off this engagement are chiefly these two: first there is no love between you, and second, your ideas are different. Let me answer you very frankly. First, love can only be created between husband and wife after their marriage. To have love before they are married is ridiculous. As you have not yet married Kwang, how can you expect to have love for him? The second point is his ideas. Now that term can only be applied to revolutionary people, and has nothing to do with man and wife. Your marriage into the Shiao family is not a revolutionary affair, but is to fulfil your duty as a woman. The best you can do is to follow our ancient teaching, so that you can have a family in which "when the husband sings, the wife shall join in," to present descendants to the family and look after the cooking and all other domestic affairs of the house, and then you will become a good wife and a kind mother. Since this is not a revolutionary affair, what do you care about ideas? ... Ideas? Why should women have such dangerous things?'

'Please stop arguing with her,' my mother shouted to my father. 'This beast cannot be considered as a human being! Don't you realise that "father and mother are greater than heaven"? How dare she oppose our wishes? I sent you to school hoping you would learn propriety, righteousness, temperance and purity, but who would have thought that education would turn you into a beast without respect for your father and mother! Your marriage had been arranged by your father and mother when you were still at my breast. If you dare to oppose your marriage arrangements, it is as good as daring to oppose your father and mother. That would be a very shameful act indeed, and it would ruin our reputation and bring your ancestors into disgrace. I would rather die than allow you to do this ... Do you know that "a marriage may be arranged thousands of miles apart by a single piece of immortals' red thread?" Man and wife were arranged actually before their present existence. How dare you oppose the will of the immortals?'

When Hsieh Ping-ying heard these ridiculous quotations, she laughed hysterically and preferred not to waste her breath. Her father conceded that although he did not wish in these modern times to force her in the spirit of the proverb that says 'When you are married to a rooster you have to follow the rooster, and when you are married to a pig you follow the pig,' he went on to argue his case on the particular merits of the young man and his family. Hsieh Ping-ying did not agree but she did recognize that her father was a little more moderate than her mother, who was implacable in her opposition and vowed that she would be the last of the family to attend school:

'Schools are not much better than hell! Anybody who has been to school can act just like a devil. When they come home, no matter what happens they must break their matrimonial engagement carefully arranged by their parents.'

'Of course! What can parents know of the kind of husband or wife their children should have? Marriage is one of the most important things in one's life and should be left to the persons who are directly concerned. He or she would make a better choice than the parents.'

I knew these words would not meet with approval, and that on the contrary I should be scolded for them, but my mind was going to burst if I did not air some of my views.

'Aren't you ashamed of yourself, you, an unmarried girl, to talk about selecting a husband! The Shiao family is a very respectable one … they know the rules of propriety … Now in return you want to commit this outrageous act against them. What face shall I have to see them again? You should remember the old proverb: "A good horse will not turn back to eat the grass behind him, and a good girl will never marry a second husband."'

Before my mother had finished my father put in:

'She would never read anything like that now. What girls of her type read nowadays are love stories in which girls commit suicide simply because they are not allowed to marry a young man of their own choice. Also stories in newspapers about girls breaking away from their homes because of their differences with their parents. Since they are influenced by these novels and newspaper stories, it is quite natural that we should have a girl who is dead set against her parents and the rules of propriety!'

'This is ridiculous! How can one set oneself against the rules of propriety?' my mother shouted in anger. 'They were established by our Sage, and for many thousands of years they have been governing our lives. How dare a mere girl like our daughter act against them? How can it be possible that with all pagodas and monuments erected in honour of chaste women of all ages, they cannot be a reminder to the girls of our generation? When we learn that a girl of twelve could determine to remain a widow when her future husband died, can it be possible that the modern girl would think of marrying twenty-four husbands in a year and still be without a husband when New Year's Day comes?'

I said nothing because I had now decided that to argue any further would be entirely useless. The only way was that I should be resolute in my struggle and never stop until the engagement was broken off.[107]

For daughters like Hsieh Ping-ying there was no alternative but to either give in to their parents' demands or run away; Hsieh Ping-ying chose to run away and escape from 'the fortress' that was her family.

Family fortresses

Daughters opting to pursue new forms of behaviour either negotiated with their parents and established a new path of behaviour for themselves, gave in to the old conventions and submitted to an arranged marriage or ran away to escape conventions. Several of the daughters, who later wrote their autobiographies, had taken a highly unusual step and placed themselves at risk in a society outside their families and therefore beyond its support. For them, seclusion had became imprisonment and the home a fortress from which they had to escape if they were to break free from custom either to further their education or to choose their own marriage partner. Chow Chung, impatient to attend school, grew more and more unhappy behind 'the great unscalable wall of the family fortress'. She knew it would not be easy outside of the family but still she was convinced that it could not be as bad as sitting in a corner of the family fortress, despised and abandoned and waiting for marriage. After she had taken what seemed to her to be the only alternative course of action and escaped from the family household:

I rocked to the rhythm of the train. But I couldn't relax. I was tormented by too many confused thoughts. Two hours ago I had been at home, behind the walls of the family fortress, condemned from birth to absolute obedience. Now I was free. I could feel my chignon behind my head. Only married women wore chignons. So, from today I was married, married to my campaign. The days of pigtails, of young ladies, of embroidery and sitting and waiting, of disappointment – these days were over. A chignon had replaced my pigtail, and this symbolized my struggle against the conventions and my hope of winning. I would not sit and wait any longer, I was going to stand firm and go forward. I would only think of the future ... the future which had begun today. The train jolted and rattled, but my resolution was like a rock.

Her resolution was to be sorely tested as she passed from pillar to post trying to find a way to support herself:

I had always been restless, always wanted to talk and to do what was not allowed. My father said I was like a monkey. Why couldn't I stay quietly at home like my sister? But I even wanted to drag Hsing [her sister] to school as well. I wanted us both to go out into the world and mix with other people, and do something for our country, for humanity ... To live for just my own family was not enough for me. I had tried to explain to my parents, but they would not understand. Now I no longer even hoped to be understood. I had deliberately run away from home because there had been no other way. Now I was sitting alone in a little dark room, more alone than I had ever been before: without family, without parents, sister or brothers. But it was my own choice ... I was a combatant, fighting against my family and my parents ... free to dream of my future, free to laugh and cry, as I wished!

When she finally escaped home by leaving China, Chow Chung pondered the moment of freedom and happiness as she sailed away from her family and the fate of her siblings:

At last I could no longer see my brother or the harbour. There was only a line on the horizon, and I was sailing over the sea, to freedom, hope and happiness, away from my family, away from the conflicts which lay behind the horizon: away from Ho [her older brother], fighting to take his wife and children to Peking; from Ch'ang [her second older brother], fighting for the girl he loved and for his education; from Hsing [her sister], fighting to marry the man she loved; away from the battles which little Ch'un [her younger brother] would certainly have to fight as he grew older. We all had to fight my parents. I had crossed the line of the horizon. I was the luckiest. But I was alone, I had left them all behind.[108]

When Liang Yen left home to escape the threat of marriage and the threat of 'an empty life', she remembered too how she closed the gate behind her to face an unknown that lay ahead: 'I knew I could teach; I was sure I could learn other jobs. I would make my own way to my dreams.' In retrospect however she was amazed that she had had the temerity to set out with her aunt at the age of seventeen and without even a change of clothing: 'Looking back, I'm amazed at my audacity in this venture, unheard of for a girl in China.' She supported herself by tutoring and writing articles and remembers how she lay in her bed after leaving home:

> It was the same moon, the same sky, but I was a different girl now. Not only was I a grown-up eighteen but my life had become something that, in my girlhood days, I could not have foreseen – could never have dreamed: a life of adventurous independence away from the compound, free from the slavery that is a wife's lot in China.[109]

With no family resources many lone daughters like Hsieh Ping-ying found it difficult to support themselves and often became ill, sick and homeless. In circumstances such as these, Hsieh Ping-ying referred to herself as 'a fallen leaf in the autumn wind'.[110]

The scale and the success of daughters' rebellion against conventional codes defining the transition to womanhood very much seems to have depended on the degree of support they received from within the household and the source of that support. Fortunate daughters like Wei Tao-ming or Bu Wei-chao received encouragement from their fathers and grandfathers or another male relative who gave them some form of support. Such daughters were encouraged in their quest for further education even as they reached marriageable age. Wong Su-ling was to be forever grateful to her third uncle who having already supported the unbinding of feet in his household argued that many families:

> nowadays have girls who are exceptional and allow them to take special training as teachers, nurses, or for other careers. It is a good thing. Ah Chih is such a girl. She qualifies on two counts, her scholarship is good and she is ambitious. My proposal is that she be not betrothed but allowed to continue her education.

Wong Su-ling was 'wildly elated':

> I was really on the way to achieve my ambitions to become a teacher, which had been steadily growing stronger. My mother sold a larger consignment of her jewels than usual to provide for the heavier expense at the famous school in the capital to which they decided to send me.[111]

Several fathers and grandfathers played a role in the cancellation of a child betrothal thus supporting their daughters' bid to free herself from an arranged marriage. Both Wei Tao-ming and Bu Wei-chao had cause to be grateful to them. A sister also might be fortunate in having a brother who took her under his educational wing. Chow Ching-li's brother, six years older, told her stories, supervised her schooling and generally took it upon himself to be her teacher. Hsieh Ping-ying's older brother encouraged his younger sister in her schooling and frequently sent her packages of books to read as well as interesting letters. Wong Su-ling's brother suggested that his sisters be given generational names when they went to school and Chow Chung's brother, who was a passionate reader and poet shared his stories and poems with her. Encouragement from a 'modern' and educated brother might be influential in deciding his sister to embark on a struggle with her parents, but because they were less authoritative and often involved in their own struggles, brotherly support was less likely to help their sisters in any serious way to win over other members of the household.

Mothers and daughters

Support from mothers tended to be less overt, secretive, indirect and felt by daughters rather than openly articulated within the family. Many daughters were later to remember their mothers' eyes or facial expressions gesturing their unspoken or indirect support. Wei Tao-ming remembered her mother's stories, her frustrated dreams of freedom and happiness and her unspoken determination that her daughter should not share her fate. She felt she had her mother's support 'in breaking away from the stifling tradition which surrounded Chinese women',[112] but whenever she was rebellious she also watched helplessly as her mother took the blame for her misdemeanours. When daughters asserted themselves within the family, their mothers merely tended to shake their heads and say 'she wants to do what she wants to do'. When Tang Sheng's father reminded her gravely that a girl's happiness and whole life depended on a successful marriage and that nothing in the whole world is better than marriage and a family, her mother, however, 'said nothing and bundled her into bed'. In the family row that ensued when she attempted to set out on travels away from home, it was her mother who came to her support:

> Finally my mother, from whom I had inherited both a physical resemblance and a stubborn character, came to the rescue. She, being a woman who in her maiden days had followed the call of revolution and had played her part in the establishment of our present republic thirty years ago by smuggling revolvers and performing secret errands under the very eyes of her father, an official in the old Manchu government, could – and did – understand my desire to be independent and my wish to get away from the sheltering roof of 'the family'. Being a mother, and a very

affectionate one, she was fearful of all the dangers that well-protected and innocent girls might meet once out of the friendly family circle, as well as the perilous fate that might befall girls who took the risk of crossing over the borderline. But she was also a mother who once, several years earlier, had decided to send my sister and myself to an American grade school, provided specially for the few American children in China, for no other reason than that she wanted us ... to be stronger and more self-reliant than other girls of our acquaintance, and naturally she sympathised with my desire to be independent. We had always known she was an exceptional Chinese mother, and as soon as she realised that I was really keen on going to free China, she banished all her fears and anxiety over the dangers and quietly backed me up. With such a mother behind me, the battle was won without too much effort.[113]

Daughters whose battles were not won after a struggle and who submitted to the ways of the family, thus abandoning plans for further education or for acquiring a husband of their choice, felt particularly sore at their mothers: 'Like all girls, I blamed my mother, as everyone knows that men didn't understand things the way women did.'[114] They recorded in their autobiographies their sadness, frustration and anger not just at the lack of personal support and affection from their mothers, but at the collusion of their mothers in lending support for 'the old ways so detrimental to women'. So many tried time and again to earn their mother's affection and were so grateful for small signs of favour. Many astutely sensed, at the time and retrospectively, that it was the pain of their mother's own experience and unacknowledged identification with the woman in their daughters that led to an apparent absence of affection for them. At best, the messages that daughters received from their mothers were ambiguous: they observed the discrepancy as mothers either spoke the Confucian rhetoric and lived differently or spoke new norms and succumbed to custom. Chow Chung watched a mother who 'only came to life' when she was back staying in her childhood home and who apparently did not like herself or her daughter:

When she was staying with her mother she was like a fish suddenly back in water. Married life must have been a burden to her. She had been married at seventeen to my father, who was the same age; ten years later she was the mother of six children, the eldest of whom had died. When she was staying with her mother, she was a completely different person from the one we knew. I began to think that married life must be horrible. It was the end of a girl's life. She must forget her own life to adapt herself to that of her husband's family. Was that perhaps why mother did not like girls? She didn't like herself, she felt it was shameful to be a girl, she saw a woman's life as unmitigated suffering. I did not want to be a girl either. I wanted to be a boy, to win my mother's love. Gradually I began to understand and sympathise with her. And I too, wanted to stay with Grandmother for ever ... mother did not like girls of any age, and she thought it shameful to be a woman, for women could only suffer. Probably she thought it shameful also to have brought a girl into the world.[115]

This daughter always felt that her mother wished that she had brought a son, a 'brave and enterprising son', into the world. Was not her mother overheard to say 'to have a daughter is a misfortune but to have a daughter beyond control was a double misfortune'?

Hsieh Ping-ying observed how her mother of 'very strong personality' simultaneously spoke the Confucian rhetoric but 'was not afraid of anything in heaven or on earth'. In her family of birth, she had had no brothers and two sisters and since she was the eldest she had been allowed to run the whole household at 16 years and after. After she had married, she became the most prominent woman in the village. According to her daughter:

She was extremely clever, and seemed especially endowed for managing affairs. In her mind she followed the old teachings of the 'three obeys' and the 'four virtues' of the model woman ... She also had the fixed idea that the man is higher than the woman. She held the old-fashioned moral code dearer than her own life. In her own family and in her dealings with other people, she was always the one to give orders, which had to be obeyed. In fact, she was nicknamed the Mussolini of Hsieh-To-San. All the people in the village obeyed and respected her. She also undertook to look after the public property of the village. She was a trustworthy person, absolutely honest and full of public spirit. In the management of the affairs of the village she was simply indispensable ... She was born with a resolute, or rather an obstinate, character. The people feared her and therefore would do her bidding. As she was the dictator of the village, naturally she was an absolute tyrant to her family; all her children were her slaves, and had to act exactly according to her instructions.[116]

Katherine Wei, on the other hand, watched her strong-willed mother, who had joined the ranks of the first generation of emancipated women in 1920s China, still submit to time-honoured demeaning ceremonies in her husband's home, reject her daughters on the grounds of their sex and calculatedly manipulate her daughter into an arranged marriage to the son of a very rich and conservative family 'within which she would be lost'. Whatever the experience of daughters of their mothers, few daughters in the early twentieth century thought their mothers provided practicable role models appropriate to becoming new women.

Past and future

Daughters, who did rebel against the Confucian rhetoric in their bid to move from a past to a future, took their role models from western women and/or male behaviour in their own society. In rejecting the past and moving towards the future, their yardstick in adapting to the new was so often the too apparent contrast between the confining conventions of their mothers and grandmothers and their own lives, which contributed to their own 'sense of escape' or 'sense of liberation'. Wong Su-ling remembering how not so long ago her aunt and her first sister were kept inside their rooms like birds in a cage instead of going to school like herself, describes herself as of 'thankful heart'.[117] A 'thankful heart', relief and exhilaration were common sentiments expressed by the younger generation of women, whether they had been encouraged, negotiated with a struggle or fled the confines of the domestic. Tang Sheng, writing in 1949, summed up the changes within three successive generations of Chinese women in her family:

> Sixty years ago when my grandmother was a young girl, her greatest pride was in her pair of tiny-lily feet; she had no other ambition in life but to marry; on the merit of her Lilies, a nice man and be a good wife. Women of her time were obedient and docile; they sat in embroidered gables and read *The Virtuous Women's Books*; they believed, as the book taught them, that women should be quiet and submissive, obey traditional teachings, stay in the family and be real ladies. But thirty years later, when my mother was a young girl, the mode of the time had switched away from Lily Feet. People of her generation were intoxicated with revolution and drunk with the desire for change. The old system of ancient China was crumbling and traditions were being doubted; Western ideas wafted across the oceans and stirred the imagination of the young. Women started to loosen the binding tapes around their tortured feet, and virtuous books were tossed out of the window in scorn of old restrictions. Liberalism and freedom became the popular words, and men and women alike demanded equality of the sexes and emancipation of the mass. With great zeal they shouted 'Down with the old, up with the new!' They were rebels against the oppressive ties of ancient traditions and proud to proclaim themselves as such.

However, when Tang Sheng went on to talk of her own generation, she was less sanguine about the effects of change on their lives:

Unfortunately, we, the sons and daughters of the Republic, children born in a period of change and turmoil, were neither ladies and gentlemen nor wild rebels, we were just hybrids with a queer mixture of western influence on Oriental culture. In schools, we were taught in the modern way: we still recited our classic books and memorized our historical dynasties, but we learnt English and natural sciences as well.

At home, under the direction of the 'Family' – that mysterious body composed of grandparents, aunts and uncles and numerous cousins and in-laws – we were not allowed to escape from developing a traditionally Chinese philosophy of life; we learnt to observe the proper code of behaviour handed down by the sages, and our contact with relatives formed our concepts of society.

But Westernized ideas and new thoughts were constantly permeating through the shells of the surrounding family circle; they came to us through novels, magazines and movies, all of which influenced our beliefs and coloured our viewpoints.

In the thirty years after the [1911] Revolution, China was struggling and swimming in a rapid, whirling tide where the influx of the West met the traditions of the East, where the two streams combined but were, as yet, not thoroughly mixed. Into this great whirlpool we, the hybrids, generated and were engulfed. We became in a sense neither a foreigner nor a real Chinese, and yet, we were the new generation ... [118]

The category that Tang Sheng uses twice in this passage and that could be said to sum up the confused feelings of her generation is the label 'hybrid'. In her case, she was referring to the uneasy combination of Chinese and Western ways or characteristics suggesting that they were neither one nor the other. Thus the definitions of modern woman to which the young aspired were vague.

In rejecting the past as their measure of the future, most daughters set out to realize 'a future', 'a dream' or a life of 'adventurous independence' by which they usually meant a new life different from the female conventions of the past rather than any clearly defined or refined definitions of the new womanhood of the future separate from the family. Chow Chung in her struggle against her family could only think of the future: 'I was going to stand firm and go forward. I was only going to think of the future.'[119] Liang Yen 'closed the gate' behind her so that only the future lay ahead when, as she said, she would make 'her own way' to 'her dreams'.[120] Tang Sheng too saw how the 'die' was cast as she abandoned the past, so that within hours of leaving home, she was writing:

It seemed incredible that less than twenty-four hours ago, I was in Shanghai protected by my parents and under the wings of 'the family'. I found it hard to realise that the seeming eternity that I went through was in fact only one short day. Already the home atmosphere, college activities, friends, books, dances and movies, that had so filled my past life had faded into the dim background as if all of them were things in a dream, I could no longer think of them as part of my life' ... I knew the die was cast, I had stepped out of the dream land and could never go back again to my old sheltered life. I myself had chosen this new life and it must be better or for worse; whatever might lie ahead I must face the future as well as I could.[121]

When daughters stepped out of the past and into the future they had little idea what form the future would take for their female selves. It is clear that there was a confusion of expectations surrounding the becoming of new women – both the process of becoming and of new womanhood itself. There were numerous popular periodicals and magazines that offered advice to the young and solicited their letters so that their problems might be shared and solved. Indeed in many instances the magazine itself assumed a mediating role between conflicting members of the older and younger generations. Ai Li S. Chin, a sociologist who studied a number of letters published in a popular periodical in 1947, concluded that so many personal problems of the young were caused not by conflict or even by the existence of alternative or competing patterns of behaviour but by the sheer lack of patterns and cues, making for confusion of expectations both inter- and intra-generational.[122] Most of those who wrote to the advice columns were involved in some form of parental conflict to do with education or marriage in which those who were trying to reject old and adopt new forms of behaviour found themselves faced with new unfamiliar situations for which there were no established patterns and no agreed cues with which to judge or interpret other persons' behaviour. Moreover, this uncertainty as to how to behave had to be seen against a background of the general anxiety and guilt aroused by conflict with the older generation. Not only did the young incur much criticism and hostility from their parents and the tradition-bound majority of the population in breaking away from old patterns, but also, because parents had been negated as models and labelled backward and old-fashioned, young people were left without any clear-cut models for adulthood or family support with which to fight against tradition. It is not without significance that the name of the periodical studied by Chin Ai-li S. was *West Wind*, symbolizing the influence of western ideas and practices. The old rhetoric had been questioned and found wanting in the face of new ideas from abroad, but it had not yet disappeared or even been weakened except within a small minority of mostly Western-influenced and urban-educated gentry families. For them and their daughters there were few cues or established patterns of behaviour to support rebellion or rejection of past conventions that did not derive from crossing gender or cultural boundaries.

If the new generation of daughters thought themselves to be boys of girls they also thought themselves to be neither Chinese or European, largely because they had taken as their model the example of Western women. It was the freedom to move on the streets, to mix with men and talk with peers and teachers of both sexes that made an impression. Wei Tao-ming, for whom the sight of Western women 'walking arm in arm with the men, on their big feet, talking and laughing with an equal lack of shyness', had been stupefying or incredibly odd, still thought 'that something about their bodily freedom alone stirred responsive chords in me. Watching them, I decided that somehow I rather liked the way they moved and acted – so unrestrainedly.'[123] In Wong Su-ling's household, it was the grandmother who first had been impressed with the sight of western women on the streets following her travels in Hong Kong. The rest of the household had listened open-mouthed as she said that the thing that impressed her most was the way women went freely about the streets whereas in her own city only servants and working women did so, or women of little reputation. But in Hong Kong she had observed many beautiful and refined women of evident good breeding. She repeated over and over again that men and women there were 'just the same'.[124] In several households women said they had been attracted to Christianity because of the example it had set of women's equality with and independence from men. Symbolic of much was the adoption of the hat as an item of outside attire worn as it was by Western women in public spaces. Wei Tao-ming did her hair in the Western style of the day and was so taken with her hat that she could not be persuaded to take it off indoors.

> I did my hair now in the Occidental style of the day; in retrospect it seems to have been rather an unattractive cross between a pompadour and a bun at the nape of the neck. I dressed in what I thought was the latest and smartest style … I wore a hat – I think it was one of those high, flaring plates loaded with assorted trimmings. Since it was the first one I had ever had on my head, I was so fascinated with it that I could hardly be persuaded to take it off indoors.[125]

If Western women had provided cues and clues for new behaviour outside of the home, so also did brothers or other males of the family. So many of the writers either at the time and or retrospectively referred to themselves as boys of girls or men of women and so many report that at the time they were so accused by others. Brothers and male cousins too might provide an alternative pattern of behaviour in domestic spaces, but it seems to have been much more difficult for daughters to evolve new patterns of behaviour inside the home. Perhaps this is not surprising given that the focus of Confucian rhetoric was on domestic roles of daughter, wife and mother. Moreover, alternative gender or cultural forms or models of behaviour did not add up to or give rise to a new rhetoric sufficient in strength to challenge the old. As Hsieh Ping-ying was reminded by her brother, it was much more difficult to introduce change within the domestic compared to outside the home:

> Our mother is a more terrible person than any famous tyrant in the histories, ancient or modern, Chinese or foreign. Do not you know that already? Because I took your sister-in-law to Yi Yang without getting her consent, I was condemned by her as one who would oblige his wife by disobeying his parents, and was made to kneel down for more than two hours with a big basin of water balanced on my head. That is a thing which no one should forget. Besides, the marriages of your second and third elder brothers and your elder were arranged by her, and they are all suffering and miserable, but none of them dares to breathe a word about divorce. Although you are braver than any of us, I think your bravery would be much better applied on the battlefield than at home. We cannot possibly have a Revolution in our own house![126]

Daughter separation

What does become apparent on reading the personal narratives of this new generation of Chinese daughters was the difficulty experienced even by the most rebellious in separating from their families perceptually and practically. To separate out their own lives from the family either of their birth or of marriage and shape their own futures was a new and difficult undertaking for most daughters. As their autobiographies illustrate time and again, much of this rebellion against the old and tug of war between old and new became that between the 'I' of the individual and the 'we' of the family. Despite the fact that daughters felt less included and identified with the family than sons, they still had great difficulty in separating their lives from those of their families. Bu Wei-chao remembered the:

> stirring crises there had been, both emotional and physical, … but they had all seemed to be part of the events of the family, rather than inside myself. Even after I began to think that I was thinking about myself, my thoughts about me continued to consist largely of echoes of words of Mother, Father, Grandfather, Big

Uncle, Auntie, sisters and brothers, etc ... When I thought about myself, there was little of 'I' or 'me' about it.[127]

It was only after she broke her betrothal that she felt 'for the first time in my life, my self was my own.' For Liang Yen too, there was little of the 'my' of the individual as opposed to 'our' of the family remembered from her childhood: '*My* courtyard, I say. *My* bedroom, *my* study, *my* clothing. In China, it should be said, nothing really belongs to '*me*'; everything, it was impressed on me from early years, belongs to the family. Everything, that is, except one's spirit ... '[128] Wong Su-ling too felt that in Chinese households the 'I' is different because it is circumscribed by the family order: 'not me but us'.[129] 'Without the family, the individual is nothing' reverberated in Wei Tao-ming's mind.[130] In building up her resolve to leave the family home Chow Chung recounted in some detail her thoughts on her departure:

Suddenly I felt certain that I was going to lose my parents and my brothers and sisters; that I was going to follow a road which was not theirs. I had to be different from them all. I had to find this road, and when I had found it I would be alone ... I did not want to learn embroidery, but embroidery helped me to make my rebellious plans. I had to get away from home, and go to school and eventually to university. I must become a person, as a man was a person. I must be able to be proud of being a girl, not ashamed. I wanted to shape my own destiny, to see the world to serve humanity. I must leave home, or I would have no life at all. I must fight, it was a matter of life or death. Yes I must fight, I said to myself as my needle went under. Our tutor corrected my stitches, my flowers, my leaves, my birds; but she could not correct my thoughts. I wanted to live, to live in the world, not to die in the family ... I was alone in a fortress and I wanted to get out. I did not believe in fate or bad luck or superstition. I wanted to be reborn, under a star of my own choosing. Where and how? Soon I would find out. First, though I must leave home and leave for good, not just for a day or a month or a year. I must be reborn and by my efforts. I must make my own life. These were the thoughts which preoccupied me. But nevertheless, Mother praised my embroidery and my handicrafts whenever I showed them to her ... I sang not for joy, but for sorrow. I seemed to be always unhappy. Whatever song I sang, the words in my heart were the same: 'Soon I must leave home, parents, brothers and sister. I belong to the world, not here. The world is big. I must find a place in it. Don't love me, for I must go.'[131]

When Tang Sheng, finally setting out on her travels, saw the houses of her home town retreating into the distance one by one, and realized that she was going further and further from home and family, the very idea brought 'pain, dread and confusion. The idea of venturing into the world on my own, and leaving all the protection and shelter of the family behind, assumed a frightening aspect.'[132]

In the absence of an alternative rhetoric upon which to pattern new behaviour becoming to new Chinese womanhood, many were tempted to avoid the domestic altogether by remaining single. For some, rejection of the past or fate meant the rejection of these institutions or relationships themselves as they avoided marriage, families or even adopted celibacy as a cause. For example, some daughters who had not had a good experience of family life or had insufficient confidence in imported models for new forms rejected marriage and the family altogether. Wei Tao-ming, a very successful lawyer, not only rejected an arranged marriage but for many years rejected the very idea of marriage. Only years later did she begin to look at marriage more favourably, even if only slightly, as the foundation for the continuity of family life: 'I began to see that no one is complete alone' and 'without the family, the individual is nothing.'[133] Another young woman employed as a schoolteacher also refused to contemplate marriage. Her grandmother, though proud of her granddaughter's occupation, strongly disapproved of her rejection of marriage and family life:

> My granddaughter, Su Teh, is a successful woman. But she has not married. I tell my granddaughter she should marry. She says that marriage is not necessary to working for the country. That is new talk. We all know that the family is more important than anything else. Every woman must have a husband and children. How can there be a country if there are no families and children?

As her granddaughter was 35 and she had not married, she went on to muse:

> Life must go on. The generations stretch back thousands of years to the great ancestor parents. They stretch for thousands of years into the future, generation upon generation. Seen in proportion to this great array, the individual is but a small thing. But on the other hand no individual can drop out. Each is a link in the great chain. No one can drop out without breaking the chain. A woman stands with one hand grasping the generations that have gone before and with the other the generations to come. It is her common destiny with all women.[134]

New destinies?

Other errant daughters who had stepped outside of women's common destiny in the public sphere and for whom there was little in the way of rhetoric to sustain and support their adoption of new patterns of family behaviour found themselves living two lives, that is defying convention and living the future outside the home but still being influenced by the past when returning to their homes. Although many of the women of this rebellious and newly educated generation adopted new public roles, it is interesting to observe how, on their own admission, they very much reverted to traditional ways once back in their own family homes. What distinguishes their lives, especially those who had dramatically escaped, was the contrast between their public lives and their behaviour on their periodic returns home – frequently to a home where custom and rhetoric lay largely unchanged or much as they had left it.

When daughter Chow Chung, who lived her own life at university, returned to her home 'everything was exactly as it had been when we were children.' Indeed, her parents could not understand the university or that 'little world where men and women were equal'. They asked 'why should women want to be the same as men?' Nature had made them different, they were intended to walk different and separate roads, working to attain harmony but from opposite sides. Surely it was wrong for women to want to be like men? At home as in society, women followed time-honoured codes so that for these parents it was their daughter who alone was thought to be 'out of her mind': 'for they knew that without me my sister would certainly have stayed contentedly at home. What did I really want? Why couldn't I study at home?'[135]

Many an errant daughter found herself, and almost despite herself, compromising and embracing the old customs once they returned home. When Wei Tao-ming returned home she was 'always struck by the peaceful contrast between home and the outside world of my Party activities':

> Home was such a different world that the life I had led outside seemed only to be a dream vaguely remembered. Everything in the house went on as if there had never been a revolution – nothing was changed. The daily routine consisted of a hundred little domestic details and the general pattern of life was leisurely and calm. Grandmother insisted on the strict observance of the traditional rigorous etiquette: we kowtowed, kneeling and bumping our heads smartly on the floor, when we entered her presence; we observed all the correct ceremonious forms when we sat down to meals. This return to the ways of the old, strangely enough exerted a soothing effect on my frayed nerves. I always came out of it refreshed and strengthened. Revolutionary though I was, the thought impressed itself on my mind that, in some imperceptible but definite manner, the stability and the permanence of the age-

old Chinese family system imparted to one a sense of well-being and comforting security.[136]

Similarly, Bu Wei-chao behaved differently within and outside of her home. On the occasion of her father's funeral, she found herself behaving 'as good as an eldest son' and stepping out of an all-black foreign-style dress into traditional coarse hemp: 'what difference did it make to wear coarse clothes for a few days – it would make a good impression.' As for her family, they were surprised that having been abroad for six years she had returned and ceased to agitate for revolutions. For her family, she had came back 'knowing propriety', which suggested that it might be good to let other children go out to study. This sentiment pleased her greatly and as she felt that she had won her revolution in advocating education for women, she did the kowtowing of the eldest son 'no longer insisting that the Republic had abolished the kowtow'.[137] When Wei Tao-ming's grandmother died, her death was blamed on her granddaughter's revolutionary independence and violence, which had finally been more than the now frail old lady could stand. Although her modern grandaughter did not think this to be true, she recalls how she 'fell prey to a flood of atavistic emotion':

> Remorse and grief engulfed me ... For many nights I took part in the ceremonies, watching the monks circling the body, wailing and chanting, until towards dawn I would fall into an exhausted sleep. It is extraordinary to me today to see how quickly I reverted to the old customs at that time. The years in which I had been engaged in various forms of revolutionary activity, completely absorbed in seeking Western knowledge, and had thought and talked in foreign languages, all slipped away from me; however it must be remembered that I was only about twenty-one at the time and my modernity was still largely skin deep. But there must have been considerable conflict within me; a part of me must have rebelled against this orgy of useless emotion, because at the end of the official period of mourning, I fell violently ill with fever, overwhelmed, no doubt, by the tug-of-war between two different worlds which was going on inside me.[138]

The different worlds involved in the tug-of-war inside daughters might refer to those either Chinese and foreign, family and individual or male and female. As their autobiographies illustrate time and again, daughters had few role models or accepted cues that they could follow in embracing new patterns of behaviour; nevertheless, the daughters of the personal narratives were proud of their own examples of rebellion and many deliberately constituted themselves as 'new women'. However, it would not be surprising to find that these daughters, in understanding

their own lives as of the future rather than of the past, had retrospectively exaggerated both the degree of their rebellion against their fate
and their abilities wholly to live the new. There being no daily journals
or diaries, the life stories available for study are all reconstructions
relying on memory. It is significant that many of the narrators think
that they had an unusual ability to recall because their memories had
been trained 'like cameras' due to many early years of retaining and
reciting Chinese characters and classics. But these life stories, like others,
are unlikely to have escaped problems inherent within reconstructions
based on memory. As one of the women narrators very astutely anticipated when she wrote in her preface, 'a true description of me cannot
of course be a coherent, consistent, description … all this is only what
I think I am – no, not even that, it is only what I *now* think I am.'[139]

Above all, these life stories offer reflections of the moment on past
lives. Even with this caveat however, the published life stories do reveal
a remarkable female congruence in choice of moments pivotal to
'making a woman' in pre-revolutionary China. Their perceptions of
themselves as unconventional daughters in mostly conventional families
embarking on difficult struggles perhaps testify above all to the continuing strength of past Confucian female-specific prescriptions and
prohibitions that still had to be countered in establishing difference
from mothers and grandmothers and in the establishment of new codes
becoming to the new woman. Rebellion against the Confucian female-
specific codes and the adoption of new patterns of behaviour still
required the prior rejection of female-specific events pivotal to being a
woman in another family and the crossing of cultural and gender
boundaries. For women who had stepped outside of women's 'common
destiny' as defined by Confucian rhetoric, there was little in the way of
a new rhetoric to sustain and support their adoption of new patterns
of behaviour.

If during the first decades of the twentieth century these autobiographies are testimony to the difficulty of shaping new lives after the
example of women from another culture and the men of their own
culture, by mid-century there was a new government in China committed to providing women with a new rhetoric which supported far-
reaching and radical changes in public and domestic female lives. In
challenging the Confucian rhetoric, the new rhetoric, while reducing
the relevance of cross-cultural examples, highlighted the crossing of
gender boundaries in an attempt to produce a new Chinese Communist
comrade or 'man of a woman'.

PART II

The Sun and the Moon

Gendered Sameness and Strangers:
Comrades of Revolution

'How Should the Problem of Women be Viewed?' *Hongqi*
(*Red Flag*), 1964[1]

In 1949, when Mao Zedong stood on the rostrum in Tiananmen Square, the ruling centre of China, and pronounced in his now familiar words that 'the Chinese people, one quarter of humankind have now stood up', he was prescribing agency to China's women as well as its men. Indeed, that Chinese women should be given the opportunity to 'stand up' was symbolically apt given the bound feet of recent female history. Women, like men, were henceforth not only to formulate rather than follow 'fate' but also to participate in the holistic redefinition of that fate. The female half of the population was said to be the equal of men and for the first time to be entitled to 'half of a heaven' encompassing both the sun and the moon. In this, one of the most popular revolutionary slogans of the next thirty years, women were variously said to support, hold or shoulder, be entitled to or even constitute 'half of heaven' or 'half the sky'. Indeed, the term 'half of heaven' became a popular synonym for a new female fate in that the very juxtaposition of the female half of the population with heaven constituted a rhetorical feat, challenging as it did the age-old binary oppositions underlying the now outmoded divisions separating female from male, earth from heaven and sun from moon. While imaging a heaven to which women had an equal entitlement and in which women had an equal place constituted a revolutionary claim and a rhetorical feat, it also, perhaps surprisingly, generated rhetorical defeat. Feat was to become defeat largely because 'heaven' had hitherto been synonymous with a male space and in inviting women to enter this male space they were invited to become men of women. Instead of the anticipated creation of a new androgynous category, combining women with men denied both the unique qualities of the female body and female-specific experiences of daughterhood and marriage.

A new rhetoric

If Confucian precepts recognized and reaffirmed gender difference and hierarchy, the Communist Party set out to reduce gender difference and hierarchy in the interests of equality and sameness. In anticipation of a gendered as well as a general revolution, a new language incorporating new names and titles aimed at establishing new androgynous categories inclusive of both female and male. First, women like men were to be addressed by an individual name, thus ending the practice whereby, without a personal name, they had been addressed as daughter, wife or mother of ... During land reform in the early 1950s, it was often reported that women heard their own names spoken in public for the first time in their lives. Once given names, women like men were to be addressed by new terms delineating new androgynous categories combining males and females in new unisex modes of address. For example, one all-inclusive new title, comrade, was used uniformly and nation-wide, from village to urban street and from national leader to peasant, to address both men and women. The import of this new term eliminated with one stroke the use of an array of multiple titles which were gender- and generation- specific, distinguishing not only men from women, but married from unmarried, old from young and close from distant kin. Similarly, the terms peasant, worker and proletariat became common forms of identification of men and women. Within the family and more intimately, the term *airen*, 'loved person', was used interchangeably for both husband and wife replacing *neiren*, or 'inside person', with its domestic or secluded connotations and previously used exclusively for 'wife'. In addition to the introduction of new androgynous categories, many existing terms were redefined in accordance with new constructions of the family, the workplace and society in general, incorporating new definitions of gender roles and reductions in gender asymmetry. For instance, the categories 'successors' and 'children' were associated not so much with family as with the revolution, so that men and women were frequently referred to as 'revolutionary successors' or 'sons' and 'daughters' of the revolution. Soon these new terms of address and androgynous titles were to be adopted nationwide and it became rare to hear old forms of gender-specific address.

New modes of address were accompanied by the widespread adoption of unisex dress in the form of the blue trousers and jacket of peasant and worker worn now by all men and women. Male and female bodies were similarly clad with minimal stylistic modifications in an attempt to reduce or negate gender-specific difference. The new dress was accompanied by new images or visual representations of women. A new female image replaced that of the traditional woman who, slight of build, reticent and restrained of body, had been characterized by an aura of feminine restraint and resignation. In the past she was often to be found positioned within an interior or courtyard, delicate of stance and preoccupied with 'feminine' pursuits such as the embroidered needle, inked brush or musical instrument, or poised on a threshold – seen and not seen – seeing and not seeing, or insignificantly positioned at the margins of both the inside and the outside. Now decorum and temperance were to be replaced by boldness of bodily gesture. The new female images appeared on billboards, on posters and in magazine or newspaper pictures portraying women central in space, large in size and strong, assertive and heroic in stance. She stood singly within groups or alongside her male peers, with arms reaching out to an outside world, assertive in her embrace of the future. In these new and powerful images, women were most often depicted as workers alongside sickle, tractor, factory machine, train and aeroplane or poised high above the ground amid high-tension wires. Uniformly they proudly occupied new roles hitherto denied them that seemed to place them equally alongside their male peers. Smiling, rosy-cheeked and wide-eyed, 'Iron Girls' wore the unisex blue trouser suit and displayed strength and gesture no different from their male peers. Like language, images inscribed sameness and equality for women, rejecting sexual difference, divisions, asymmetry and hierarchy. Women might be said not only to have stood up, but to have crossed a threshold, to stand tall alongside and in imitation of their male counterparts.

To end the reign of Confucian adage and homily that had succinctly and memorably condensed the secondariness of women, new adages or slogans that were also succinct and memorable but advocated female equality were introduced to punctuate official speech and text. Slogans such as 'women are a great revolutionary force', 'let both men and women take part in our revolution' and 'women can do revolutionary work and contribute their share to the strength of the country just as men' were aimed at changing the image, self-image and expectations of women by associating them fully with their male peers in the revolution and in production or work. As 'daughters of the revolution', women were newly exhorted 'to unite and take part in production', to fill 'half the world of production' and to make up a 'vast reserve of labour power'. Slogans, such as 'women are the equal of men' or 'anything a man can do a woman can do also,' were also used to summarize a new rhetoric of female equality and a reduction of gender difference. Even the term *funu* (woman), adopted formally by the state, was a pejorative term denoting a single category of women which, incorporating little of the female, overlapped conceptually instead with the male other. To prepare women to live the new rhetoric, conceptual and practical questions were placed on a national agenda for discussion. An open letter addressed to the readers of one national Chinese magazine listed the questions facing women in this new age. Published in 1956, it noted that the women of China had:

> won the right to dignity and equality only recently, after long years of tremendous struggle. Now they are energetically trans- forming these rights into deeper reality. In every walk of life, in cities and villages all over the country, they are asking: how shall we act to use our freedom well for our children, for our country and ourselves? With steady purpose, they are expunging the effects of age-long feudal oppression from their lives and learning how to take their new position in society.
>
> Such knowledge does not come of itself. Discussion, analysis and exchange of experience show the way forward. Serious ques- tions which affect great numbers of women are debated in the national press and in women's magazines, in forums and in meetings large and small. Should housewives go out to work? Should educated women stay at home and care for their children after they become mothers? Is a weekly nursery better than a day nursery for children of busy parents? Should women try to do men's jobs? What should be the grounds for seeking and granting a divorce? What is the best way to bring up children to be good citizens of the new socialist country that is coming into being? Even simple everyday problems like 'What shall we wear?' have come up for wide discussion and men as well as women have joined in. For this is a new age and the old standards of women's duties and women's rights no longer prevail. The liberation has opened all roads. The new standards have to be thought out and established by women themselves.[2]

Androgynous women

To encourage women to live the new rhetoric, an important role was assigned to the promotion of model women displaying in their daily lives exemplary words and deeds. The promotion of models that were both descriptive and prescriptive continued a longtime Confucian tradition of journeying towards worthy or virtuous behaviour in emula- tion of model daughters, wives and widows. Now new life stories, similarly written and published for edification, became vehicles by which the new prescriptive policies, goals and behavioural standards were made known to women as they witnessed models who were both translating rhetoric into new daily behaviour and thought patterns and acquiring new skills and accomplishments to the benefit of themselves, their family and society. The efficacy of the models as exemplars on revolutionary pedestals rested on the practice of emulation or on the willingness of the audience to replicate desirable and emancipatory gestures. With an almost Confucian belief in the example of virtue to instil new forms of behaviour, it was assumed by the new government that contemporary women would begin to comply anew after comparing and contrasting their own lives with those of the models and narrowing the gap in attitudes and behaviour. The attitudes and behaviour of female models most emphasized in the new narratives were androgynous or overlapped with male attitudes and behaviour in a way that was most evident in definitions of work.

The Communist Party had long predicted that improvement in female status would closely follow participation in social production or work. The expansion of the national economy and the reorganization of industry and agriculture had been planned on the assumption that China was uniquely rich in labour power and that women formed one of the most underdeveloped of China's economic resources. In the mid-1950s Mao Zedong said that women 'form a vast reserve of labour power which should be tapped in the struggle to build a great socialist country'.[3] However, government policy assumed not only that the involvement of women in social production was necessary for the economic development of the country, but that involvement in production was of the utmost importance to women themselves as a precondition to their emancipation and equality with men. After Engels, the government and the women's movement emphasized that the first premise for the emancipation and equality was the introduction of the entire female sex into public industry. In support of this premise the following passage from Lenin was often quoted:

> In order to emancipate women thoroughly and to realise real equality between women and men, it is necessary to have public economy to let women participate in joint production and labour, and then women would stand in the same position as men.[4]

Through employment, women were to acquire an economic independence and access to social resources that they could use in bargaining to improve their position. From the mid-1950s the recommendation of Mao Zedong that women 'unite and take part in production and political activity to improve the economic and political status of women' was widely quoted.[5] On these grounds successive government policies of land reform, the collectivization of agriculture and the expansion of the industrial and rural sectors of the economy were supported by the women's movement. It encouraged women to take advantage of the new opportunities to take a full and wide-ranging role in production after the examples of new model women.

One of the earliest of female models was Tien Kuei-ying, a young girl of 20 years who became one of China's first woman train drivers. Her life story was written up in the national press for others to learn from.[6] Her first job had been selling meal tickets in the workers' dining room at the Dairen City Railway depot and for a long time her sole aim was to find a husband and thereby escape this menial occupation. She had even begun to embroider a trousseau in anticipation of setting up a new home in the very near future. However, there was a turning point in her aspirations following her attendance at a lecture on the role of women in the new society where she learned of the traditional oppression associated with confinement to the household, with the result that 'her dream burst.' She had always thought of marriage as an escape to a newer and happier life, but she then realized that 'it had all been a dream, nothing but a dream of slavery in another form.' She remembered the theme of the lecture 'to become really free, women must take part in social labour, for only when women are economically free can they find true political and social freedom.' She began to change her attitude towards work, and after visiting an exhibition illustrating the role of women train drivers in Russia, she made up her mind to follow their example.

Tien Kuei-ying thus applied for entrance to a new training programme that had been set up for women. It was then that she began to face strong opposition, beginning with that from her father. He objected to her chosen occupation, saying 'Remain where you are a little longer and then it will be time to marry you off.' Her father's reaction was duplicated in the varying responses of the men of the factory. She was said to be handicapped by her lack of physical strength and stamina, an attribute that seemed to underlie much of the explicit male prejudice she experienced. 'The locomotive section must be making a joke' said the doctor who gave her the prerequisite medical examination. 'Well if women can do this work, why should there be men at all?' said an experienced engine-driver. 'If you women wait until you break down from exhaustion before you give up this crazy notion, it will be too late then,' a stoker said with mock concern. Kuei-ying and her classmates were not to be deterred and they vowed not to give up before their training was completed. Many were the times they were reported to remember this vow as they suffered perpetual exhaustion from continually stoking their engines and struggled with their limited education to master the technicalities involved in their new occupation, in which they were to become very successful.

One girl who was influenced by Tien Kuei-ying was Li Chen-yung, a young woman tractor driver, who in turn too became a model woman worker.[7] An educated girl, Li Chen-yung became one of the first group of students to attend the Peking Agricultural Mechanized Farming School. She too faced much prejudice on entry and in the course of study she met with a host of obstacles. In particular, she had difficulty in taking notes, drawing engineering charts and plans and following the technical lectures. She worked very hard to overcome these handicaps with but one thought in her mind: 'We must overcome these difficulties so that other girls can follow us.' When she went to neighbouring farms to practise the peasants were sceptical: 'How can they allow women to drive a machine?' 'Next year's harvest will certainly not be so good as this year's.' With a strong will, she finished the course and went on to prove her capacities to become a woman tractor driver of national renown.

New national models not only comprised younger single women making first life-choices, but also included examples of married women who, hitherto preoccupied with domestic duties, stepped beyond these to take part in production or politics. Pu Chun-sheng was a graduate of Yenching University who had taught a little, got married and had two children.[8] She had shut herself up in her home and turned house-keeper. 'I only looked after the children, put the house straight and made it a cosy home.' She did not bother with outside events until she saw what other women were doing in the community. Additionally influenced by her children, she began to take up her studies again and resume teaching. She and her husband were both drawn into the community and political activities and began to share many outside interests as well as their home and children. She summed up her experience: 'Three and a half years ago, I led the inactive life of a hibernating insect, buried deep in the soil and quite unaware that spring is near.' Chao Sung-chiu, a housewife with six children who thought that women had too much housework to attend meetings, also thought on hearing of the model women train drivers that 'We house-wives musn't lag behind others. We must step out and learn to serve our country.' She entered political and community work and was elected a deputy to the local people's congress, although she found it difficult to combine the care of her home and children with learning how to do her new job as people's deputy properly. Eventually, with the help of child-care facilities and training classes, she no longer feared for her children's welfare and increased both her abilities and confidence in contributing to the welfare of her community.[9]

Chu Chin also previously limited her attention to her home and was only vaguely aware of the changes taking place in society. When she began to attend meetings or study sessions her mind wandered: 'Are the children all right?' 'What will she cook for dinner?' Yet when she returned home, she would catch herself feeling lonely and left out. She would stand still and wonder to herself:

> Is this all there is to a woman's life? You grow up, get married, have chidren, cook and then you grow old and just die. Other people seemed to have time for all sorts of jobs. Will my life ever be different?[10]

When a neighbourhood factory was established near her home, however, she trained for a job, earned wages, met other women and had an outside interest that she now shared with her husband while her children attended the local nursery. Wang Wen-lan was a 38-year-old woman with five children who was thought to be a greatly stressed mother. Once she went to work with her husband in the commune fields, she often went out in the evening and learned to read and write 700 Chinese characters. Her children attended school and the commune nursery and kindergarten, and the family often ate in the public dining room of the village. She became cheerful, busy and confident: 'The commune has given me a bigger world, now I am beginning to know lots of things besides babies, nappies and pots and pans.'[11]

For all the model women workers, living became defined as working and the defining moment or rite of passage to adulthood was not so much marriage but entry into the workforce so that becoming a man or woman became synonymous with becoming a worker. The usual biological differences between male and female centring around reproduction were recognized but these were rarely permitted to translate officially into the social. The chief area that overlapped for male and female was work, so the female life story was divided into before and after entering the workforce, with model women denying any specificity of female experience in marriage or reproduction, or at the very least relegating it to a minor place in their lives and reducing if not rejecting gender difference.

Before marriage, model women workers like Tien Kuei-ying were shown rejecting marriage as the predominant goal of their lives, and their expectations broadening to include entry into the public sphere with the domains of politics and production becoming desirable goals in themselves and as the basis for independence of esteem and material support. The saying 'Marry a man, Marry a man, clothes to wear, food to eat' was no longer to hold true for the new woman. After marriage and the birth of children, androgynous or overlapping male/female productive rather than female reproductive functions constituted activities most relevant to the revolution. Encouraged by the rhetoric, the model woman worker thus commonly worked long hours, acquired new qualifications, solved technical problems and overcame male prejudice by being capable and resourceful and never asking for leave for 'trivial matters'. Instead of taking full maternity leave, most women sent their children to live with relatives or to board in weekday nurseries in order to give their entire energies to work. Like her male colleagues, the model woman made no concession to reproductive roles despite numerous institutional concessions to reproductive roles including nurseries and breast-feeding breaks. Whenever any of these model workers was faced with a choice between breast-feeding and work, between continuing to work and looking after a sick child for a few days or undertaking a distant work assignment and leaving a very young child for several months, they opted for the job, regardless of whether it was really necessary or whether another colleague might equally well have substituted for them. In one such narrative, a model chief engineer and deputy director of one of the refineries in a large petrochemical complex became highly trained and highly skilled in her job. After the birth of her daughter, she and her husband, also an engineer, decided not to have any further children so as to devote their lives to the petrochemical industry. After their young daughter was ill for three weeks, her parents decided that it would be better for her if she lived with her grandfather, aunt and uncle some distance away – and there she stayed for twenty years! Such decisions seem to be made with complete single-mindedness and with little reference to other factors. It was as if women workers were to be the same as men and both were assumed to be free of responsibilities for reproduction or the domestic and of emotional desire as they single-mindedly pursued unidimensional androgynous roles.

Representing lives

Both to encourage the belief that change in female lives was possible and to shape change in the direction of the new androgynous rhetoric, new slogans, images and life-stories redefining womanhood were popularized via all forms of the media including billboard, newspaper, magazine, broadcast, film as well as in study and political campaign. From the very first days of the new government, there was a tremendous importance attached to the role of education in popularizing new definitions of womanhood as well as in introducing broader social changes. Indeed, what was particular to China's revolution was the importance attached to education on the premise that new knowledge presupposed new thoughts, beliefs and actions. On this premise, the government assumed the right to redefine the boundaries between public and private, bringing not only individual thoughts and attitudes into the public arena but also chanelling desire, will and emotions in the direction of the new images. What is distinctive about this process of imaging in China during the thirty years of revolution was its self-consciousness. Indeed, one of the factors distinguishing the continuous

Chinese revolution was the importance attached to capturing the consciousness in introducing and maintaining social change. Each individual's thoughts and actions became the subject of consciousness-raising, a process requiring constant and extensive monitoring of thoughts, words and actions. Obstacles to change were generally perceived to be more internal than external; thus, the appropriation of new thoughts and beliefs was perceived as pivotal or as the most important and difficult of stumbling-blocks to ending gender inequality. A slogan of the early 1960s emphasized the importance of a new conscious learning process: 'without self-awareness women would be unwilling to fly though the sky was high.'[12] The sky was assumed to be high so that what was missing was the willingness to take advantage of the new opportunities. To encourage self-awareness, the government purposely set in motion specific consciousness-raising programmes to draw attention to the ways in which the notions of female inferiority, dependence, secondariness and incapacity had long limited or circumscribed both society's expectations of women and women's own expectations of themselves.[13] The process of consciousness-raising and thought reform, its more concentrated and intensive form, were above all attempts to instil ways of seeing and ways of speaking so that the thoughts of individual women became indistinguishable from the new rhetoric. It is a measure of their success in capturing the female consciousness that for much of the thirty years of revolution women publicly spoke almost exclusively with the tongues of rhetoric.

At first new and quite novel titles of address took some getting used to. In one village in the early 1950s an old woman, on first hearing the term 'comrades' at a village meeting, was heard to ask 'Who is comrades'? On being told that 'we all are' she thought that the novelty of the idea was such that it definitely 'needed thinking over'![14] Peasant women, who were said to have first greeted the new slogans as they had the new androgynous titles with scepticism, began to agree that it would be wonderful if women were the equals of men. But what chance had they if from ancient times until now 'man has been the Heaven and women the Earth'? But increasingly for many women in the first years of the Revolution, the new rhetoric seemed to fit and reflect recent changes in their roles. Did not they themselves have new opportunities to enter the labour force and community politics? And was not the society in which they lived transformed? Professional, peasant and working women could constantly compare and contrast their lives before and after the revolution, and in the first decade, many rightly perceived that the conditions in which they performed their productive and reproductive activities were much altered and improved by the new revolutionary government. They justifiably contrasted the poverty, political and economic insecurity and glaring inequalities that had affected the majority of women from the early twentieth century with the more adequate and equal provision for basic needs increasingly advocated for much of China's population. In terms of achieving basic literacy, wider access to education, a more stable family food bowl and basic health provisions, the new government had begun to institute substantial new programmes and women had begun to benefit from these basic measures. Chinese women proudly began to draw attention to the contrast between the customs and practices common in China prior to 1949 which had penalized daughters, wives, mothers and employees and which were now to be phased out by new marriage, labour and land legislation, which all emphasized women's rights and female equality.

Chinese women had also begun to expand their economic and political roles in society, and in particular they were entering a new range of employment opportunities in both the cities and the country-side. By the end of the first decade of revolution, it was estimated that between 80% and 90% of urban and rural women between 16 and 60 years of age were employed,[15] either full-time or part-time and season-ally, thus earning their own cash incomes however small and however indirectly. Women, albeit still as a small minority, began to be elected to local political leadership bodies. Women also drew attention to the institutional and political presence of their own nationwide organization, the All-China Women's Federation, in overseeing the implementation of policies and programmes designed to improve the position of women. Above all, they contrasted Confucian text and folk-saying, which em-phasized gender difference and hierarchy, with new Communist law and slogan, which advocated both the redefinition of female roles and equal status with their male peers in the family and in society. Women increasingly began to represent themselves in report and conversation as able to benefit from the new possibilities. As one grandmother said to an Australian journalist in the mid-1950s, not only was her daughter one of the new female train drivers, but in the new society her grand-daughter would grow up 'to do anything she liked'.[16] Many began to liken these changes to a reversal of heaven and earth,[17] to a world turned upside down or to the attainment of 'half of heaven'. Not only did the changes seem to many women to be very considerable in the 1950s, but henceforth periodic popular campaigns in favour of gender equality not only educated and exhorted women, but also began to celebrate their liberation as if it had already been achieved. Pictorial images represented women as workers already the equal of male counterpart in size, stance and value. Texts in booklet, periodical and newspaper continuously proclaimed the emancipation of women and the equality of woman with man. Women and not just the models began to speak, write, recall and repeat a rhetoric celebrating emancipation or equality, the very appropriation of which came to constitute an achievement in itself. However, this appropriation proved to be something of a disservice and the achievement sometimes hollow, for the dominance of a rhetoric prematurely and continuously celebrating equality and sameness had the effect not only of separating the rhetoric from female experience but of denying women's experience and eventually of silencing the very language of experience.

One of the most striking of initial impressions on any first acquaintance with revolutionary China, be it in the 1950s or the 1970s, was the contrast between the rhetoric of women's equality and the sexual division of labour, which allocated women to certain occupations and spheres of activity and denied them access to others. What disappointed most observers of the revolution was the degree to which the sexual division of labour within production and reproduction remained unchanged despite popular and public representations of change and equality in text, speech and image. When Margery Wolf, long experienced in the study of Taiwan, went to China to conduct a field study in the 1970s, she was prepared for the fact that women's lives were not going to be the miracle of liberation as presented. What she was not prepared for, however, was the frequency with which she would be told of this miracle in the very presence of women's continued oppression.[17] In her field study, she concluded that the power of the rhetoric had frequently shaped perceptions to the degree that the new images substituted for experience. Again the authors, Emily Honig and Gail Herschatter found that their female Chinese friends usually insisted that men and women were equal despite the blatant examples of inequality around them and continued to do so even after these had been pointed out to them.[18] In my own field work, women were simultaneously said to be the equal of men in society, yet almost without exception they were presented as secondary or subservient to another, whether as daughter, wife, mother or female worker and revolutionary comrade.

At every point in the public and domestic arenas, the rhetoric of equality belied women's separate and secondary experience of the revolution. It was not so much that women did not see the juxtaposition or discrepancy between rhetoric and experience, but that there was no place for this experience or even a language in which to express their experience of daily secondariness. With the gradual exclusion of semantic or visual variations of image and text, the rhetoric of equality and language of celebration soon became the only language officially tolerated in public and increasingly in private spaces. It was as if voice and eye were held and increasingly bounded by the rhetorical. There were no images of or words for representing the inequality of experience.

Symbolically, too, the eyes of billboard- or poster-women overlooked the foreground as if it was of no importance, and it frequently was blurred in pictorial representations. Rather it was as if the shining distant dream-like gaze, the stare of the clear shining bright eyes was fixed, stretched and focusing pointedly on some distant objective that was undefined and beyond the horizon. If we combine this long-sighted distancing revolutionary gaze with its semantic equivalent, that is the language of rhetoric, which, too, was fixed, removed and bounded so that the foreground of immediate experience was blurred, masked and confined, then we have what might be called a 'rhetorical glaze'. The main characteristic of this rhetorical glaze is that it is separate from the experience of the body and its senses and it ultimately denies it. In these circumstances women began to represent their own experience or permit their experience to be represented rhetorically in speech, picture and text as if the rhetoric constituted their experience.

The process whereby imaging became a substitute for living or experience is repeatedly exemplified in the words of the role models who *par excellence* had learned to speak or write in the tongues of rhetoric. They spoke, wrote, recalled and repeated their experience in words or pictures of celebration and achievement that were devoid of the ambiguities of private feelings and body senses. The substitution of image for experience is memorably captured in the words of a woman peasant painter in a conversation with the French writer Julia Kristeva. In depicting a profusion of colour, products and people in her paintings, Li Fenglan displayed all the hallmarks of the new rhetoric of profusion and plenty in her paintings. Describing her source of inspiration as that based exclusively on her own experience: 'I can only paint what I see and what I have direct contact with.' She went on blithely unaware of the shift:

> In fact I don't paint things I see, but I paint them from my dream, often I dreamed of them when I came home from the fields a bit tired. My dreams are mostly in colour ... One must rise above what one sees ... Now we are happy, but I am happiest when I pick up my paint brush'.[20]

It was this way of seeing, speaking and writing that masked the experience of Chinese women during the revolution.

Masking experience

For much of the revolution, the question of how Chinese women perceived their experiences beyond the rhetoric remained something of a mystery. For both Chinese and foreign fieldworkers there were not only severe constraints surrounding entry and time in field study, but an explicit, well-developed masking rhetoric causing informants to be more concerned with what 'ought to be' rather than 'what is'. Anthropologists of the status of Lévi-Strauss have identified the problem of an all-pervasive rhetoric as constituting one of the most difficult of barriers in ethnographic enquiry.[21] In China during revolutionary years, even the simplest of enquiries elicited a coded or rhetorically bounded response. Few informants used the word 'I', thus denying any individuality of experience or any emotion that was not generalized into the range of permitted responses. The very language deployed bounded their experience and reflexivity, and the official certainty that rhetoric expressed experience also rendered any internal Chinese sociological or anthropological investigation of social issues, including gender, superfluous. Thus, the disciplines of sociology and anthropology in China were either disbanded or confined to narrow fields of investigating non-Han 'others' for close on thirty years. Nor did there seem to be any personal narratives that could communicate the experience of women behind the rhetorical mask or the female living of revolutionary rhetoric.

Exceptionally, there was one debate in the Chinese press in the early 1960s that hinted at the inadequacy of the range of permitted representations of women's experience. Then, an editorial in *Zhongguo Funu* (Women of China) admitted that 'Though the broad masses of women have taken part in production, they still have many special problems in production, living and thought.'[22] It went on to point out that women's reproductive functions and the traditional definition of women's roles meant that they would continue for some time to face a number of difficulties if they wanted to enter production and at the same time continue to be women and that these difficulties and tensions would not go away if they were neglected or simply swept under the carpet. More importantly as a beginning in attending to some of these difficulties, an important article in *Zhongguo Funu* recommended that women be encouraged to 'begin with themselves' and look at their own individual experiences.[23] In reply to the question of in what ways women should be conscious of themselves as women, it suggested that though men and women workers could be said to view many questions in the same light, there were also questions specific to women such as the continuing influence of the traditional idea that men were superior to women, different physiological conditions and different social obligations inherited from the past. Subsequently there were criticisms of those who were 'not bothered' or impatient with what they labelled 'complications of the personal lives of women'. The case of woman cadre, Chen Yunjing was quoted. Apparently she was even reluctant to hear the two words *funu* (woman): 'While in school I would get angry with those who referred to me as a woman. I believed that a woman was one who had married and had children ... How could I be called a woman?'[24]

In acknowledgement of such difficulties and denial, *Zhongguo Funu* established a national forum in which it invited readers to write in and relate their own experience on two separate but linked questions: the more general question asking 'What do women live for?' and another more particular question 'What should be the criteria in selecting a husband?' Underlying both these questions was a debate about what definitions or concepts of happiness are appropriate for revolutionary women. Women readers were invited to make their contributions and many different views were expressed in letters published in *Zhongguo Funu* in 1963–64.[25] Some women wrote that they thought that their biological functions determined their primary social roles which were thus the main foundations of their 'personal happiness':

> Women's peculiar physiological structure determines their role of taking up the natural and sacred duty towards society that is bringing up the next generation and to support husbands – these are women's inescapable functions in addition to doing the job well and gaining promotion.[26]

In this view, children and the cultivation of 'warm and enjoyable small families' were considered to be full-time jobs for women and the loving relationships and the sense of well-being generated were the main sources from which they were said to derive their happiness. Others felt that the quality of their personal and family happiness was very much dependent on the material standard of living which their husbands were able to provide and thus chose a husband accordingly. As one writer said in considering the economic standing of her would-be husband: 'I always felt that happiness consisted of a good economic condition and a comfortable and happy home, for is not living well materially the foundation of happiness?'[27] Another thought that:

> a woman will find her life the happiest, the most joyous and the most amusing if she can find a husband who works in the city, if she lives in a modern industrial city, does a little light social work and leads a rich diversified urban life with her husband.[28]

Some correspondents criticized those who put such 'personal happiness above all else' or the 'interests of the small family above revolution', advocating instead an alternative view linking individual happiness to collective or social well-being. As one correspondent argued it was 'absurd to think that a good material life meant happiness or a nice little family constituted happiness' for it was:

> only with the liberation of their country that most women had the opportunity to even think of or enjoy a secure livelihood and family life so that any present happiness was due to the form of the new society and not to the individual situations within it.[29]

If women did not take advantage of new opportunities then they would never see themselves as equals in work and in society, but regard themselves as men's 'auxiliary belongings', adhering to a concept of happiness 'way behind the thought of our times'.[30] There were those who wrote in to the magazine wishing to counter the view that the greatest source of happiness was to be found in love. They suggested that it was selfish to live for love and pleasure alone, for surely pleasure was to be found in working together. These and other such questions reflecting opinion and experience were raised by discussion in this national forum, which was primarily designed to provide women with an opportunity to exchange their individual experiences as part of their own consciousness-raising process *as women*. It was anticipated that such discussions would lead on to serious consideration of such questions, but the Cultural Revolution intervened with the substitution of a rash of articles on the purpose and importance of work and political study for women. Their publication marked a renewed and exacerbated emphasis on common and overlapping class consciousness and on the interests of men and women workers who were called on alike to make an even greater commitment to the revolution.

> In the past I thought a woman worker was a good one if she
> fulfilled her eight hours and then went home to her family. Now
> I think differently, and am involved in factory activities such as
> political study meetings.[31]

In the Women's Federation much of this political study took the form of criticizing the publication of the forum on 'How the Problem of Women should be Viewed?', primarily because it had distinguished and focused on female-specific issues based on discussions of women's own experiences. In this way it had turned their attention away from political and revolutionary issues and encouraged them to personalize and individualize their problems. As a result of these trends, the publication of *Zhongguo Funu* was suspended and the Women's Federation disbanded during the Cultural Revolution on the grounds that women should be enjoined to participate directly in economic and political affairs on the same terms as their male counterparts.

This discussion in the pages of *Zhongguo Funu*, brief as it is, stands out because it was somewhat exceptional during the years of revolution. For more candid or extended personal narratives it is necessary to turn to the writings of women who either left China for one reason or another or who retrospectively constructed such narratives during the more liberal years of the 1980s. It was only after the change of leadership and the onset of the reforms that the discrepancy between rhetoric and experience has been openly admitted by a number of Chinese women. Only in recent years and in retrospect has it become possible for them to begin to give voice to and construct the dimensions of the discrepancy between revolutionary lives and revolutionary rhetoric. For me one of the most important sentences written in the past few years, and one which has underlain some of the thinking for this book, was that uttered by Chen Yiyun, a sociologist with the Academy of Social Sciences who also worked on Beijing's first psychological helpline on sex, love and marriage. In an interview reported in *Newsweek* in 1992, she noted that 'Many Chinese women feel alienated by the rift between the government's official policy of equality of the sexes and the day-to-day reality.'

For an amplification of the insiders' view of this 'day-to-day reality' we have to turn to some of the writings, fictional and autobiographical, published within and outside of China during the past decade or so. They suggest some of the main ways in which revolutionary women experienced discrepancies between what they heard and said and what they saw or sensed.

Writing lives

The growing awareness in China of an increasing discrepancy between what people saw and what they heard in revolutionary times seems to have been particularly acutely felt by the young from early teens onwards. There was an important correspondence on this very phenomenon published in 1980 in the pages of *Zhongguo Qingnian* (Youth of China). It was generated by a letter written by a young woman, Pan Xiao, who wrote of her disillusionment at the discrepancy between sights and sounds:

> I'm twenty-three this year and should say that I've just begun my life, but none of life's mysteries and charm will ever again exist for me. It seems I've already reached its end. Looking back on the road I've travelled, it has been a passage from crimson to gray, a journey from hope to disappointment and finally to despair.[32]

She describes how the long river of her thought began with the excited reading of the good works of Lei Feng and other models, which she then attempted to put into practice in an effort to truly 'make other's lives more beautiful'. Soon however she also experienced an ill-defined discomfort:

> This arose from the fact that what I saw before my eyes was in sharp contradiction to the education my mind had accepted ... I began to feel that the world around me was not as alluring as the descriptions I had previously read in my books. I asked myself

whether to believe in my books or my eyes, whether to trust my teachers or myself. I was extremely confused. But at that time I was still young and unable to analyse these social phenomena. Moreover, my past education had given me the rather strange ability to close my eyes, convince myself, recall my quotations, and retreat into the lofty world of my own soul.

But later on this wouldn't do ... As for living for the revolution, that seemed too empty and off the mark, and anyway I never wanted to hear those sermons again. Living for fame again seemed too far from most people's experience ... I acquired a dual personality. On the one hand I came to despise this vulgar reality; on the other I learned just to drift with the tide.[33]

Other young people responded to this letter, some agreeing and others adopting a different view. Those who agreed with Pan Xiao emphasized the discrepancy between ideology, rhetoric, image or even 'empty dogma' and experience or reality. A predominant theme was the regret and anger that 'our schools, books and magazines, often present a single and perfect picture of our society' that did not match with experience or the evidence of their eyes.[34] Many would have agreed with the correspondent who wrote that: 'The social education I received during my youth left me with a sort of childhood colour-blindness in which all of the outside world appeared to my eyes in rose-coloured hues.'[35]

Several young women who left China have also written more extended accounts that recall, albeit with the benefit of hindsight, a similar scepticism towards an all-pervasive rhetoric. Schoolgirl San San, who told her story to Bette Bao Lord after leaving China, related how she was constantly urged in and out of school to become more 'progressive'. She describes how she became adept at following directions and maintaining a good political record, although she 'hardly lived only for the goals and politics of the state' and seriously doubted whether anyone could. This scepticism made her approach the life stories of the models with some ambivalence:

At school, in the movies, on the radio, in magazines and in newspapers, I heard about these people who were ideal citizens and honoured as folk heroes. Every time I learned about their lives I only laughed to myself. Their stories were absurd, too ridiculous for even a baby to believe. Of course, I kept my opinion secret. At political discussions in school, I was dutifully extravagant in my praise and sincere in my wish to follow their examples.[36]

She could not take their feats or their devotion to tractor, furnace or Mao Zedong as serious, realistic or indeed even sensible. Yet when she did give them more serious thought she would invariably become

depressed. 'These people and their attitudes personified the characteristics and qualities that would succeed and find happiness in our society.
What then would become of me?'[37] After participating in the many
political campaigns during the eighth and ninth grades and witnessing
their consequences, she drew her own conclusions:

> I knew I had to be always watchful of my words and conduct in
> and out of school. I knew I must say and do just enough to satisfy
> my political obligations, but never so much as to attract attention
> ... I couldn't explain in words how I knew what to do to keep
> within the safe areas of a political campaign. I understood in-
> stinctively how far I should criticise and how much to keep inside
> me. I don't believe this sense can be taught, for it is something
> one learns through experience.[38]

It was a lesson also learned early by Jung Chang, the author of *Wild
Swans*, consisting of the best-selling life stories of her grandmother,
mother and herself. In her school-days, she too read of the models and
although at the time she attempted to emulate their behaviour by
'serving the people' at suitable opportunities, with hindsight she observed that it seemed to her that 'the whole nation slid into doublespeak
with words that had became divorced from reality, responsibility and
people's real thoughts.'[39]

Lies, she thought, 'were told with care because words had lost their
meanings and had ceased to be taken seriously by others.' She early
learned to live with the ubiquitous loudspeaker blaring for up to
eighteen hours per day in a perpetual hubbub of chanting and de-
nouncing. 'Quite apart from the content, the noise level was unbearable,
and I had to develop a technique of forcing myself to hear nothing to
preserve my sanity.'[40] As a young person she thought it was hard to get
behind the rhetoric, particularly when there was no alternative view-
point emanating from the colluding adult population. She realized that
her own parents, like virtually every parent in China, never said
anything unorthodox to their children. She recalls that she early learned
to live with 'contradictory thoughts and realities' and became accustomed to compartmentalizing them.[41] Although she lived, and watched
others live, the concrete demands of the exaggerated rhetoric, she
concluded that this had resulted in ordinary people having difficulties
in retaining 'confidence in their experience or own knowledge'.[42]

Many of the autobiographical narratives in the past few years also
record how older women felt when they were exhorted to place revolution before family and production before reproduction. Jung Chang's
mother recalled her sentiments on leaving her four children in different
nurseries once she was busy as a medium-ranking official 'racing towards socialism':

In the early 1950s, a Communist was supposed to give herself so completely to the revolution and the people that any demonstration of affection for her children was frowned on as a sign of divided loyalties. Every single hour apart from eating and sleeping belonged to the revolution, and was supposed to be spent working. Anything that was regarded as not to do with the revolution, like carrying your children in your arms, had to be dispatched with as speedily as possible.[43]

At first Jung Chang's mother had found this difficult to get used to and the charge of 'putting family first' was constantly levelled at her. Jung Chang remembers how her mother was eventually drilled into the habit of working non-stop and only watched them as they slept. Many years later, her mother, sent to the countryside away from her family for correction, lay on her straw mattress and, thinking back over her children's early years, realized 'that there was not an awful lot of family life to remember'. Had she not been an absentee mother when her children were growing up, giving herself to the cause of the revolution at the cost of her family? Now reflecting with remorse on the pointlessness of her devotion, she found that she missed her children 'with a pain that was almost unbearable'.[44]

In an account of her own revolutionary odyssey, which had required periodic prolonged absences from her children, Yue Daiyun also later had regrets: 'Sadly I recalled how little I had been able to care for my son, not even able to nourish him with my milk when he was an infant.'[45] Anchee Min remembers how her mother, on coming home from the hospital with tuberculosis and lots of medicine bottles, was in a way 'pleased to have the disease because she finally got to spend time with her family'.[46]

One of the first, widely popular and much talked about short stories that reflected on a similar sense of feelings shadowed by rhetoric was the moving story *At Middle Age* by Chen Rong, published in 1980.[47] Although the story is well known to China specialists and has been told before, it featured so largely in city conversations during the summer of its publication that it is worth briefly repeating it here. It concerns a middle-aged woman doctor who has to combine the many demands of home and hospital life although it might equally well have been those of any institute or enterprise. In the bid for modernization, the demands on the middle-aged skilled professional person during the revolution had been considerable and it was not for nothing that they had been called the 'backbone of the country'. The central character of the story had worked to the point of exhaustion and serious illness. Interestingly, it is only when women are sick or dying in hospital, a space and time placed outside of work or home that they seem to have time to pause, reflect or think of the burdens placed on women: 'Now that all physical and mental burdens had been lifted she had plenty of time to experience her past and explore the future.'[48]

Here is a woman who is perhaps seeing herself for the first time. The story is partly about the course of an illness from which she eventually recovers and partly about her thoughts as they flash backwards in a state of semi-consciousness. This narrative strategy enabled the doctor to describe retrospectively the conditions of her revolutionary life and work. She had long been totally committed to her work as an eye specialist, and to her patients and the hospital. Yet she was never promoted, she had a low salary and she was abused during the Cultural Revolution. All was hustle and bustle at home too, where the needs of her two young children and her husband, also engaged in research and trying to make up for 'the lost years', meant that the burdens of keeping house were considerable.

For years she returned home every day at noon after a morning in the operating theatre so exhausted that it was a great effort to stoke up the fire, prepare the vegetables and be ready to serve the meal in the fifty minutes or so before afternoon school and clinics. Frequently she came home to find no leftovers or stores in the cupboard that could be used. When her daughter was sick with feverish pneumonia, she allowed her patients to delay her from going to see her daughter at the nursery and only the child's extreme agitation caused her to take her home, where she immediately left her with a neighbour while she went back to the hospital. The family all lived in a small room 12 metres square, and the doctor described what it was like to live in a room so crowded with cribs, beds, children's clothes, pots and pans and books that they could hardly move. The one desk was used by family members on a shift basis – first the son to do his homework, then herself for her work and much later in the evening or early morning it was her husband's turn. Another recurrent theme of the story is the guilt and regrets that the doctor felt as a working mother too busy to attend to her family and home. She might have been a good doctor, but to be so 'I've messed up the whole family. The fact is I'm neither a good wife nor mother.' Had she not thought 'only about her work'?: 'I have a home, but I've paid it little attention. Even when I'm not working, my mind is preoccupied with my patients. I haven't been a good wife or mother.'[49]

Although she had lived the life of a model worker, it was not so much guilt as regret at the sacrifice of so much that was precious that saddened her as she lay apparently dying. She dwelt on the fact that she never had time to plait her daughter's hair into the desired pigtails with ribbons or find the time to get her son the much wanted and needed gym shoes. Her relationship with her husband had afforded her much pleasure, but when had she got home at a regular time to prepare supper or let him have the desk before the late hours of the evening and early hours of the morning? The author allows the doctor to voice her regrets and uncertainty as to whether she had made the right choices or indeed if she had had any choices at all. In a memorable line towards the close of the story, the author contrasts the present thoughts of the doctor with the words of one elderly woman whose platitudes were such that she is described as merely 'spouting revolutionary phrases'!

Characteristic of so many of the retrospective accounts of living with revolutionary rhetoric is the commonly remembered difficulties of 'holding back' or avoiding saying anything that was known or thought, felt or seen. In public speech and text, women recalled their 'living' devoid of reference to any multi-dimensional selves. The simple slogans and the presentation of black-and-white moral imperatives were allowed to deny and invalidate much of a woman's individual experience of familial roles in the interests of androgynous productive and public roles. In consequence, becoming a new woman became synonymous with becoming a worker, requiring the appropriation of new androgynous forms of behaviour and attitudes, although in practice androgynous became synonymous with male.

Not only was the revolutionary rhetoric deployed to silence certain aspects of living in the interests of effecting new public roles for women, but the rhetoric itself was characterized by a certain reticence. There was no official or public language to refer to female experience, largely because so much of women's experience lay outside or beyond the rhetoric. The female life was shrunken to a single fragment, that of the working woman, which excluded most categories of non-working women and in particular daughters.

Living as daughters

As the rhetoric largely directed women into production and the public arena, it ignored the growing up of daughters in all aspects but their preparation for productive roles. One of the most pertinent features of the thirty years of revolutionary programmes to promote female equality was the omission of references to daughters in families. Despite enormous government effort in China to formulate and popularize the tenets of female equality, perhaps unmatched by any other government, daughters rarely constituted a category of rhetorical relevance. Not only did the rhetoric of equality rarely encompass daughters, but education in the new rhetoric was rarely directed either at daughters, at families with daughters or at teachers of girls. Socialization was confined to educating pupils for being workers rather than girls for womanhood. Even the campaigns of the Women's Federation focused almost exclusively on the needs and interests of working women. In schools very little attention was given to girlhood as opposed to childhood largely because it was assumed that as revolutionary successors, girls would henceforth be welcomed into the school, the work-force and society on an equal basis with their brothers. Yet in schools, it could be observed that girls continued to be differently and differentially categorized and encouraged to take 'soft' rather than 'hard ' subjects and manual rather than mental activities. Did these activities not suit 'their nimble fingers'? In all my visits to Chinese schools over the years, teachers and pupils seemed quite oblivious to the assumptions underlying such categorizations and their implications for sexual divisions of labour or the social status of women.

Again there are few records documenting girlhood experience of the revolution, but those who have left records of their revolutionary girlhoods rarely refer to a female-specific rhetoric or experience, to sexual difference or to 'girlish things'. The schoolgirl San San remembers how in primary school she:

> was a child who didn't know the difference between the sky and the earth. I only knew about being popular in school and making up dreams. My dreams were usually about dancing and the theatre, but in others I was someone else, a person about whom I had read or heard a lovely story. One of my favourites was of a white-haired girl ... I loved this story and others of unhappy people whose lives were completely changed by fate. In many of the stories I read, 'fate' was the Communist revolution, but the new government affected my life very little during my elementary school years.[50]

She was not particularly aware of calls for gender equality except during the Great Leap Forward (1958–59) when 'it was shouted in every newspaper.' Then there was a sustained campaign to encourage women to enter the workforce. Not surprisingly, she associated improvement in women's position exclusively with employment. She recalled how some women were happy to avail themselves of the new opportunities to enter employment while others only worked because of fear of criticism. At the time though it seemed that it just did not make sense for them all to work for a salary which just covered the expenses of putting their children in nurseries. Many preferred to stay at home and take care of their own. 'While no one spoke out, the dissatisfaction with this phase of the campaign was obvious.'[51]

Jung Chang also noted that although one of the popular slogans was Mao's saying, 'Women can hold up half the sky,' 'women also knew that when they were given the privilege of this equality, they were in for hard physical labour.'[52] Perhaps the association of equality with work was not surprising given the symbolic importance attached to work in revolutionary China. In a very perceptive study of the cultural construction of emotions, the anthropologists Jack and Shulamith Heins Potter concluded from their long-term field work that villagers assumed a persons's significance to be a product of the social and to be particularly associated with and affirmed by work rather than derived from individual emotions within. They wrote:

> When the Chinese wish to affirm and symbolise relationships, they must utilize symbolic forms that do not draw on emotional expressiveness, but on other means of social action. The critical symbolic dimension for the affirmation of relationships is work ... in every case the capacity to work rather than the capacity to feel was what was significant ... work is the symbolic medium for the expression of social connections and work affirms relationships in the most fundamental terms the villagers know.[53]

Just as model workers exemplify commitment to the revolution and society, so the villagers used the capacity to work with or on behalf of people or institutions as a measure of closeness or distance in describing a wide variety of relationships. As one of their informants directly admitted: 'We Chinese show our feelings for one another in our work, not with words.'[54] The anthropologists thought that nowhere was this emphasis on work so pertinent as in the liminal family–daughter relationship where the prodigious effort made by young unmarried women to work hard and earn more than their brothers despite discriminatory wage rates was particularly noted. This, they concluded, must be interpreted in the context of an age-old attempt by transient peasant daughters to work to affirm more completely their relationship with their parents and validate their status within their families. This familial attempt by daughters was ratified now that it seemed that societal emancipation, liberation or equality had come to be equated with the assumption of work. The fact that the rhetoric of equality rarely embraced daughters in any other capacity meant that there were few official messages to counter the messages of subordination that they continued to receive from their families.

Peasant daughters, perhaps more than any other social category during the revolution, received a dual message: while in revolutionary rhetoric, daughters might be the equal of sons as 'revolutionary successors', in family rhetoric as family successors, daughters were nowhere near the equal of sons. For them, marriage as well as or even rather than work remained the rite of passage to adulthood and so long as there was no attempt to reduce differences in the male and female experience of marriage this inequality would remain. It is true that the new Marriage Law, passed in 1950, had far-reaching consequences for women. It opened with the unequivocal statement that the arbitrary and compulsory marriage system based on the idea of superiority of men over women was to be abolished. It was to be replaced by a new marriage relationship between husband and wife as full and equal partners based on the recognition that women had an equal right with men to develop their knowledge and skills, an equal right to independence and to the freedom of full participation in economic, social and political life. First and foremost, its intention was to abolish arranged marriage, that is the rights of kin groups or persons other than the bride and groom to negotiate the passage of women between households, and to abolish the elaborate negotiations and transactions that reflected the dependence of women on male kin.

The redistribution of power involved in the substitution of free choice for arranged marriage had implications for the traditional authority exercised by elders and kin groups and thus for their rights over the circulation of female kin. The placing of the negotiations of marriage within the control of the individual parties, the basing of free-choice marriage on the congenial bonding of the partners, and the strengthening of the marital bond as opposed to all other familial and kin bonds invested marriage with a new significance for the younger generation and especially for women. Brides were to enter into freely chosen contracts as equal partners to their grooms who, it was assumed, would have none of the traditional rights over women's labour, fertility, chief ritual attachments and persons. However, no new rules of post-marriage residence were formulated to challenge the long-established practice of virilocal marriage or the recruitment of brides to the household of the groom.

Patrilineal messages

Virilocal marriage, or the recruitment of wives to the domestic group in which the husband resided prior to marriage, was widely practised in China before 1949 and nowhere were new rules of post-marital residence explicitly stated. Rather, the domestic group or household was said to stem from the marital bond, for either it functioned to establish a new household completely or it perpetuated an old household for a further generation. There was one occasion when it was recommended that uxorilocal marriage (the recruitment of the groom into the bride's household) should exist alongside virilocal marriage. During the campaign to criticize Confucius and Lin Piao (1973–75), the population was encouraged to emulate those Party committee members who had promoted uxorilocal marriage as a normal form of post-marital residence. They had supported any groom who chose to live in his wife's family after marriage on the grounds that then the birth of a daughter could be as advantageous to the future of the rural household as the birth of boys. Parents of daughters would need no longer to fear for their future, for the new practice would break with the traditional idea that only wives would be recruited into the household on marriage. The establishment of this new residential pattern was designed to break the dominance of the old virilocal post-marital residential patterns that had so penalized daughters in the past, but it failed to take hold in any sustained way. In the absence of any campaigns for change, peasant daughters were thus still transient and continued to be the recipients of a very different message that testified to the continuing importance of sons who exclusively continued the patrilineal line and ensured the future of the family. So long as marriage remained unreformed and daughters continued to marry out and be groomed for and exchanged in marriage, sons continued to be the most important and only permanent members of the family and essential for the continuation of the family line and support of family elders.

In my own field work, one of my most potent memories over the years has been of the contrasting status accorded to sons and daughters within the family, constituting an unmistakably clear message for daughters. Although it was no longer the practice during the revolution to reckon daughters of so little account that they were omitted from tallied lists of family members, in hundreds of household interviews over the years, sons were without exception enumerated before daughters whatever the birth order; many sons were the cause of congratulations, only daughters the occasion of commiseration. On the unique occasion I can remember when the son was listed second, he had been adopted. Interestingly, the father felt more proprietorial towards his daughter-in-law for whom he paid 'good money' than towards his son with whom he had no blood ties. It was only this very unusual reversal of sex order that alerted me to question further. Family planning was not even considered to be a viable option until after the birth of a son, and the exchange of daughters in marriage with the payments of betrothal gifts for rights over a young woman's fertility and labour openly continued despite official advocacy of free-choice marriage.

In households with several sons there was a degree of confidence and investment in the future of the domestic group that was not characteristic of families with no sons and only daughters. In villages there was a close correlation between the number of sons per household and the number of new houses that were built. Those with sons built for a future; those without sons had no future. I can remember so very clearly the exact and stunning moment when I directly felt the differential value of sons and daughters in relation to the future of the household. During one of my first field experiences, in 1977, I visited a succession of households in a southern Chinese village: those with sons were hustling and bustling, building houses, storerooms and new kitchens, anticipating and planning for future expansion following marriage and births of children and grandchildren; in those with only daughters there was no house-building, no storeroom and no new kitchen, all signifying silence or lack of anticipation, an absence of plans and the foreshortening of the future. Here within one afternoon and in practice was the visible and audible evidence of the continuing efficacy of the old adages likening daughters to 'goods without profits' or those on whom the future is lost.

Within the peasant family then, sons, positioned between ancestors and descendants of past and future and bonded permanently into the chain of generations and the source of support in old age, continued to receive messages denoting privilege and preference. Sons also received a message of preference and superiority from their mothers who, though not chained into the generations to the same extent as their male counterparts, nevertheless continued to rely on sons not only to increase their prestige within their husbands' families but also because they too were her only source of long-term protection and security. For men and women then, sons continued to embody the family future, indeed without sons there was still no certain family future. Son preference continued to be expressed by each and every family and confirmed their position as permanent members of the family.

The messages a daughter received were very different. During the revolution a daughter was born within but still distanced from her natal family by virilocal marriage, which meant that all daughters were still destined to become daughters-in-law and wives in other families. In the absence of any sustained policy or movement for change, numerous sayings remained in place. They emphasized this very important gender difference apparent from birth: 'a son is born facing in and a girl is born facing out,' 'men rear sons just as they grow trees for shade,' 'a daughter married is like water poured out the door,' 'a daughter belongs to somebody else's family,' 'investing in a girl is a loss' and 'a family with daughters is a dead end family.' As temporary members of their parents' household, daughters were in no position to compete with sons, who were permanent and long-term sources of support and certainty. Daughters even in their younger years were taught that they were temporary, passing through or ultimately belonging to another family; their presence was transient and their future lay elsewhere. They could neither substitute for sons nor compensate for their absence. In comparison to sons, who received a congruence of messages as both revolutionary and family successors, the revolutionary and familial messages for daughters as successors were discordant. In one they might be said to be deserving of equality, but in the other there was no attempt to even suggest that they were the equal of sons. The reticence of the new rhetoric of equality with regard to girls of daughter age meant that for them the revolutionary rhetoric promising gender equality did little to counteract age-old and inherited family rhetoric.

Marriage choice

The Marriage Law, which initially was designed to pass the initiative to sons and daughters to choose their own marriage partners independently, became so associated with female rights that it too was soon de-emphasized in favour of the pursuit of androgynous productive and public worker roles. A number of campaigns following the promulgation of the Marriage Law had popularized women's right to new forms of marriage and encouraged them to live according to the new marriage law. The Women's Federation had been responsible for the widespread advertisement of the provisions of the Marriage Law and it played a supportive role in counselling and practically assisting women to exercise their new rights. This was a responsibility that they took very seriously. As one of the vice-presidents of the Women's Federation wrote: 'We must use and are using every possible means to implement the Marriage Law thoroughly. We regard this as a constant, serious, political task and are determined to achieve complete victory in this important social reform.'[55]

She wrote that the main purpose of the publicity drive was:

> to make the fundamental spirit of the law – equality of men and women, and freedom of choice in marriage – known to every household in the city or village, from the centre of the country to the remotest areas, so that every man or woman should abide by the law and observe it as the new social morality.[56]

Numerous new stage plays, films, folk-tales, rhymes and songs were centred around the themes underlying the new law. In one village, for example, one young girl whose own free choice of a husband had aroused her family's anger, encouraged the girls in the village to act in a play called 'This Way is Better.' It was about a village girl who made her own choice of a husband and had a very happy life.[57] One of the new operas was based on a story of an 18-year-old girl who had been forced to marry a 10-year-old boy. Following the Marriage Law she had been able to get a divorce and marry a young man of her choice. Many new folk-songs and rhymes reversing older versions were substituted during these early years. Thus a rice-planting song suggesting that 'Only a horse [widow] that accepts two saddles is a good horse' and 'If a woman marries eight times she is still virtuous' was written to replace 'A good horse won't accept two saddles and a good woman doesn't marry twice.' Another from Hunan province, advocating resolution in the face of opposition to free marriage, opens with the line: 'If a boy is resolute and the girl is resolute, why fear the mountains being high and the rivers deep?'[58] Another on the same theme originated in Shandong province:

> The water bubbles in the stream
> I ask you, who will arrange your marriage?
> Will it be your father, will it be your mother?
> Will it be your elder brother or his wife?
> It is better to choose for oneself, arrange the marriage oneself!
> There is no need for the go-between and her boasting to
> both parties.[59]

There were also articles specially written for the press; periodicals, wall newspapers and copies of the Marriage Law were widely distributed with pamphlets on the subject published for discussion by study groups held in factories, villages, organizations, government agencies, army units, school and street committees. With the support of these groups, many women found the courage not just to talk, but to act and struggle for the right to choose their own marriage partner, to remarry if they had been widowed or to divorce. In many cases it was the Women's Federation that acquainted women with the new legal procedures. Nevertheless, the initial implementation of the Marriage Law was not easy.

The new Marriage Law affected each family, and in much of China new practices were introduced that were totally at odds with the long experience of generations of the majority of the population. This was especially so in the newly liberated provinces of southern China. A woman leader in a southern Chinese village told the Australian author, Dymph Cusack, that change did not come easily in their village, that there was much opposition from the older generation and that the village was often deeply divided on many of its provisions.[60] The free choice of marriage partner, the remarriage of widows and the practice of divorce particularly seemed to have aroused suspicions and caused bitter struggles not only between older and younger generations but also between men and women. The older generation felt their control of family affairs to be threatened by the ending of the old practice of arranged marriages. Many a story from villages reported parental opposition not so much to the new partner as to the fact that they had not been reponsible for the match. When one girl told her family that she had chosen her own marriage partner, her father had replied: 'What is this free love business – it's losing face business.'[61] Although women were still forced into marriages not of their own choice, many arrangements became a form of compromise where parents might introduce the young couple who now met and gave their consent before the ceremony. In areas where continued segregation of the sexes tended to reduce the chances of mixing and mating and where cadres continued to support the old ways, there was little in the way of reform. The negation, sometimes brutal, of the freedom of widows to remarry was not uncommon, but the problem arousing the strongest social resistance was that of divorce which was often necessary before free choice of a new partner could take place.

The stability of the family institution seemed to be at stake as the number of divorce cases brought before the law courts increased and formed the largest proportion of all marriage cases brought to the courts in the early 1950s.[62] Many of the cases were initiated by women, the significance of which was not lost on village populations. Indeed, women claimants used the new law in the support of their cases so often that the Marriage Law was dubbed 'the divorce law' or 'the women's law'. However, although the new Marriage Law in theory, and sometimes in practice, gave women a new weapon with which to bargain to improve their position *vis-à-vis* their families, the fear, suspicion and outright opposition to women that abounded sometimes resulted in female death or suicide, particularly in the most conservative rural areas. Violence was not only common where there was misunderstanding or family opposition, but also in cases where cadres or local officials, mostly male, suppressed or ignored the new marriage demands of women or otherwise actively abused the provisions of the law. In a report from southern China it was said that to get a divorce there were the three obstacles of husband, mother-in-law and cadre to overcome and, of the three, it was the behaviour of the cadres which was responsible for much of the suffering of women caught between the old and new forms of marriage.[63]

These problems caused the government to investigate the implementation of the Marriage Law towards the end of 1952. It was found that that nation-wide, the law had been uneven in its implementation: only in a minority of localities had the implementation of the law been satisfactory. Rather, in many localities both people and cadres had misunderstood the law, made many mistakes in its practice or resisted it to the extent that the large number of suicides and murders warranted serious investigation. The widespread problems involved in introducing reform in this intimate area of family life prompted a new government campaign in March 1953. Again, the publicity and heightened attention to the law caused such disruption of family and village and particularly conflict between men and women that the government began to halt its programme of marriage reform. A government directive criticized the disruptive methods used in support of the law's implementation, its association with women's rights and its deployment as an 'unequal treaty against men', which the report said had resulted in 'inevitable disruption of family and village which was not acceptable given the degree to which new productive policies rested on family and village cohesion and social stability.'[64]

The government in recommending that henceforth the establishment of new forms of marriage take second place to encouraging the entry of women into social production alongside their male peers and holding up 'half of heaven', set a precedent whereby campaigns for female-specific interests were relegated to a secondary position in favour of policies that directed attention to the androgynous or overlapping male/female categories of work. What is perhaps only apparent with hindsight too is that for much of the revolution, not only did the new rhetoric omit references to categories of needs, interests and experiences that were daughter- and female-specific, but female-specific revolutionary rhetoric also, summed up in the slogan 'half of heaven', itself contained within its own definitions the germination of a rhetorical defeat.

Half of heaven

Attractive as the alliteration is in the English translation, the revolutionary slogan 'half of heaven' may not have been as comfortable conceptually for Chinese women as its popularization or international appropriation suggested. In and out of China during the first thirty years of revolution, attention centred on the rhetorical feat of associations of female with heaven and on 'the half' or equal entitlement of the female population. While analysis was so concentrated on the half, less attention was directed towards the notion of heaven and recognition of its conceptual incompatibility with the female half of the population. It was this incompatibility that was to fracture the very association of heaven with the female half and this may offer some explanation for the shortfalls in achieving women's full entitlement to knowledge and power incorporated into the notion of 'standing up'. At a very simple level and given its association with yang, the male, the public and the outside, heaven was far from being an asexual or gender-free space. Attaining or shouldering 'half of heaven' thus became synonymous with the appropriation of public male roles in production and politics, with few concessions to female roles in marriage, reproduction or the family. There had been a recasting of sexual difference into sexual resemblance, of which the male-styled unidress was perhaps the most potent symbol. It has already been stressed that there were few concessions to the female body, female dress or adornment.

The female was largely defined in terms of the male, and measures of success were largely male with access to the public domain correlative with the assumption of values usually ascribed to the masculine yang. In the binary of hierarchical oppositions, the domestic, dark, secretive, private yin spaces remained outside the definition of heaven (especially when it came to the allocation of resources), so that achievement and entitlement came to consist almost exclusively of the possibility for women to be permanent guests in a space defined, constructed and hosted by men. Model women crossed gender boundaries to become 'male' in construction and address. As 'Iron Girls', women penetrated male spaces hitherto denied them to become men of women or as one of Mao's poems would have it, young female militants were likened to 'sons of China'.[65] One young girl working to bring about land reform in north China found her presence in the village was only tolerated because she was so novel that she was perceived as belonging to a different species from the village women. Men and women of the village refused to accept her 'strange behaviour' as a living example of an ordinary girl who had changed her life so dramatically as to 'come out of the kitchen'. Did she not come from Shanghai, which might be another planet where the natural laws were thought to be so different that 'it was almost as if I was a man myself'?[66]

Women had to deny the feminine, the female or that distinctively different from the masculine or male. At the very least, in a male-hosted space, the female as guest became by implication the invited, the outsider or the stranger. The concept of estrangement would seem to be especially apt. The notion of the stranger has been particularly well defined by Simmel for whom the stranger was

> fixed within a particular spatial circle, or within a group whose boundaries are similar to spatial boundaries. But his position in this group is determined essentially by the fact that he has not belonged to it from the beginning, that he imports qualities into it which do not, and cannot stem from the group itself ... His position is thus composed of certain measures of nearness and distance.[67]

Subsequently, sociological literature on stranger-host has centred on spatial and social distance, the acquisition of host qualities by the stranger within processes of accommodation, assimilation or incorporation and the resilience of stereotype and myth in mediating persistent socio-economic discrepancies between host and stranger.[68] The literature up to now on Chinese gender relations has also been primarily concerned with the appropriation of male roles, status, attitudes and behaviour by the female stranger in public places. The usual explanations given for shortfalls in assimilation have to do with continuing official and folk prejudice undermining female access to productive and political bodies, lack of resource allocation to reproduction and family discrimination and failure to invest in daughters. What these explanations have in common, is that they primarily attribute failure of accommodation, assimilation or incorporation to the qualities of the male hosts, be they conscious, unconscious or even conspiratorial. However, Simmel's original definition offers another set of explanations that have to do with the qualities of the stranger, ambiguous and combining nearness and remoteness of concern with indifference, thus constructing the notion of the ambivalent if not willing stranger with female qualities separate from definitions of overlapping gender qualities. Could it be that, as strangers to heaven women, were also estranged from revolutionary rhetoric and thus from the revolution?

Strangers to heaven

Field work suggests that women, and especially married women, could be seen to be somewhat estranged from revolutionary activities. What has constantly surprised participant and observer alike has been the reluctance of many women, especially after marriage, to take advantage of the unprecedented opportunities for the acquisition of new roles, statuses and attitudes afforded by the revolution. Before marriage women might be energetic in their support for productive and public service, while after marriage women tended to drop out of community, public affairs and sometimes less than full-time economic activities. In Chinese texts too, it was apparent that the revolutionary fervour of women or their commitment to the revolution was seen to fall off after marriage and not just because they had new or added domestic responsibilities. As a Chinese saying had it, they had proved 'unwilling to fly though the sky is high'.[69] One example from Margery Wolf's book, *Revolution Postponed*, stands out in my memory. She observed that although peasant women were still excluded from most positions of decision-making in the villages, the significant point was that, because the rhetoric had constantly and persistently told women that they could do these things, they were less impressed by the fact that only men did them: 'Perhaps these important things of the men's world are not so important after all.'[70] This passage directly calls to mind the ambiguity and ambivalence already referred to in Simmel's notion of the stranger.

In rural China, the female stranger was one who was not so intimately and personally concerned with the socio-political life about her and who had a relative detachment that freed her from the self-consciousness, the concern for status and the divided loyalties of marginality; instead, even at the centre, she retained a duality based on different qualities imported. In this case, the distinctive qualities imported and distinguishable from the male host include those most obvious or those associated with reproduction. However, there may

also have been a female-specific experience or conceptual understanding of space and time and, most particularly, of the present in
relation to the future, which, arising from the peculiarly female experience of marriage, may have had the effect of estranging women in
China from the concept of heaven which, distancing the present, also
privileged the future.

The most important and immediately identifiable of the qualities
imported by the rural female stranger and distinguishable from those of
the male host, aside from reproductive capacities, derived from the
uniquely female experience of peasant marriage. An original term used
exclusively for female marriage had the meaning of 'going out'.
Although after the revolution the term was not used so widely, many
local terms with a similar meaning continued to be appropriate given
that peasant girls almost uniformly moved to the groom's household
after marriage. The significance of this transience for daughters and
their families was that girlhoods continued to be lived in uncertainty
and in anticipation of change or rupture. For analysts of the process, as
for women themselves, the moment of marriage has been primarily
conceived as constituting the movement of peasant women in space,
that is from one household and village to another, so that women
experienced both spatial remoteness and nearness before marriage (in
their natal family and village) and after marriage in their husband's
family and village. It has become almost commonplace to note the
ensuing failure to invest in the education and training of daughters by
families and villages before marriage and to note the lack of political
participation, power and influence of daughters-in-law in their new
villages. It might be said that during the revolution, the experience of
female marriage continued neither to entitle nor empower daughters or
daughters-in-law, and that it also gave them a gender-specific construct
of time.

There have been many analyses of the economic and political
implications of virilocal marriage for women in rural China and particularly of the concept of woman as bearer and marker of property and
status in marriage.[71] Not surprisingly, female forms of marriage have
been identified as one of the most important obstacles to realizing their
claims to 'half of heaven'. This spatial dimension is an important factor
with implications for female experience of family and society, but it
may be that there is another equally important factor arising from
marriage and that is the bearing and marking of time embodied in the
female anticipation and experience of marriage. The female-specific
conceptualization of time may be almost as significant a gender-specific
marker in ultimately estranging them from the concept of time embodied in the revolutionary notion of heaven that dominated official
discourse during the revolution and may have estranged them from a

rhetoric that appeared increasingly irrelevant and in particular from the notion of Heaven.

'Heaven' was a term or concept that had a multi-faceted history in China and a tradition of thought, imagery and vocabulary that asserted hope for an era of harmonized and equalized unity, or of heavenly order on earth through a sudden but prophesied change.[72] The concept differed from that deployed in Judaeo-Christian and Islamic notions in that, paradoxically, despite being other-worldly and outside of everyday experience, it was central to this-worldly imagination, neither making promises of an after-life nor having any transcendental significance. Rather, it was a state attainable on earth. Much, although not all, of this idea of heaven as the earth's other was a necessary part of the construction of the dream and perception of the future. If meanings are often born of contrasts, then the most significant contrast was that between heaven and earth, and out of the scarce resources and vulnerable conditions of the Chinese earth was born the image of heaven.

Although symbolically and practically it was the earth that was the most durable source of food, wealth and security, for centuries Chinese farmers had lived precariously on the margins of subsistence, suffering insecurity of life and property in the face of climatic uncertainty and scarcity of cultivable land. For the majority who had little or no land and had to pay exorbitant land rents, borrow at high interest rates against their land or in extreme circumstances sell their land to survive, it was not surprising that equitable, sufficient and secure land resources were for dreaming. Heaven then was differently characterized – by limitless possibility, by prosperity, plenty and profusion and by equity in distribution with equality and security for all. The contrast between heaven and earth partook of that most fundamental of contrasts between yin and yang so that heaven was mostly associated with yang's light, positive, strong, bright and open qualities. In addition to representing desires, the dream can also be seen as a potent means of adaptation, promoting toleration of the present by compensating for its shortfalls. Traditionally, in Chinese Buddhism dreams were perceived as excursions of a duplicate soul into regions otherwise unseen. Moreover, the bliss of regions unseen, the imaginary regions of heaven, were popularly thought to represent the collective future so that heaven also became the map of the future, not unlike Heidegger's 'time that offers possiblity'[73] or Bordieu's 'field of possibilities to be explored'.[74] In China of the revolution 'heaven sees only what is distant.'

Privileging the future

The emphasis on the future in revolutionary rhetoric placed the future at the centre of consciousness as an image to be desired and dreamed, and privileged it in relation to the present – not unlike Bordieu's one 'context of meaning', which both formulated the future beyond the present moment and enclosed it within the present.[75] Indeed, the idea of revolution can be said to privilege time over space and the future over the present. The long-sighted distancing eye of the revolutionary gaze is exhorted to 'look towards the future'. Cross-cultural conceptualizations of time and relations between peasant cyclic time and imposed linear time, with their implications for the separation of past, present and future has been the subject of anthropological interest for several decades.[76] In China during the revolution, the emphasis on heaven as opposed to the earth, the dream as opposed to experience can be said to have placed the future at the centre of consciousness. After 1949, not only was 'Look towards the future' the essence of countless slogans, but privileging the future functioned to shift attention away from the present and make it more tolerable. The denial of importance of the present, except as an extension of the past and *en route* to the future, was already an integral part of Chinese cultural constructions of time. One of the first Europeans to reside within a large Chinese household has described how the keeping of time and the recording of events reduced the import of the present, emphasizing its ephemeral place between the long narrative of the past and the blank scroll of the future.[77]

This liminal state was reinforced by Marxist theory in which the present is largely conceptualized as a state of transition to a socialist future. Again, the idea of a trade-off between the present and the future with rewards or gratifications deferred to the future explained and legitimized the deprivations of the present. To make the present more tolerable, slogans such as 'Three years of hardship for a thousand years of happiness', common in the first revolutionary years, reiterated the message that tomorrow would always be better than today. In practical terms, this deferral of gratification largely meant delayed consumption not just of the conspicuous kind but also for comfortably meeting basic needs of much of the population. If dreams of the future legitimized present deferment by providing imaginary means of adaptation, then it was but a short step from image or dream as compensation to image or dream as substitute for experience. The process whereby imaging became a substitute for living, which it can be argued occurred increasingly in China's revolution, primarily took a form of visualization, as if what was imaged or envisioned was already in a state of being. Thus the present was not only perceived through the eyes of the future, but the present began to be experienced as if it was the future.

If the rhetoric celebrated the future in the present, it did so by distancing individual and direct experience of the present from the collective and desirable image of the future. This is in line with the concept of continuing revolution that distinguishes the Chinese from other revolutions which can above all be seen as a *sustained act of will* to change the earth to pattern heaven by leaping historical stages and catapulting landscape and person into the imagined future inclusive of female equality and sameness. In this schema, women were invited to enter and share not only male space but also male temporality or male-constructed and male-hosted time, privileging the future and directly linking investment in present with future rewards. However, in accepting the male invitation it was the female-specific experience and construction of time, particularly the anticipated foreshortening and early arrival of the future, that may have estranged women from the notion of heaven or future incorporated into the slogan 'half of heaven'.

Female futures

The female-specific experience and apprehension of time can be linked explicitly to women's unique experience of transience, uncertainty, rupture and discontinuity occasioned by marriage. If before marriage daughters experienced transience in the present, they also experienced uncertainty of future, with present and future divided by the anticipated rupture of marriage. Although the significance for daughters of the sudden change that virilocal marriage and removal to another family normally entailed has been well studied, there has been little attention directed towards the bearing and demarcation of time embodied in the female experience of marriage and women's consequent conceptualizing of time, which may be an even more significant gender-specific marker. For males, marriage in the ordinary course of events posed no break either spatially or temporally, for all dominant forms of marriage made for a spatially continuous chain of male generations between ancestor and successor. Marriage and the assumed consequent birth of sons was thus the most important act of ensuring linkage and the gravest of unfilial acts continued to be the absence of sons. For males, then, time stretched continuously and linearly from past to present to future in a sequence with continuity and normal certainty of narrative, so that the quality of future could be perceived to derive directly from investment in the present and from past inheritance. Lineage time had its own modes of time-reckoning incorporated into kin-naming, denoting generation and sequential order within generations. With sequential shifts from past to present and from present to future, time-frames were assumed to be continuous and linear, with investment in one assumed to benefit the next.

For women, in contrast, time continued to be broken or ruptured by marriage, making for discontinuity, separation and dislocation of present and future, with no direct correlation necessarily ensuing between investment in the present before marriage and the quality of the future after marriage. Unlike sons, peasant daughters had long been taught that their only future was to marry and that its quality was dependent on husbands (another family): 'a husband he is heaven.' For women still, their 'rice was cooked' not so much at birth but at marriage, marked by movement and appropriation by another household. Old repeated sayings such as 'a daughter married is as water burst its banks,' 'marriage for daughters is as a slammed door,' 'obey heaven and follow fate' and 'when you marry a chicken live with a chicken, when you marry a dog live with a dog' continued to remind women of their approaching separation from the present and of the fact that their future lay somewhere else and was irrevocably linked to the circumstances of their future husband and his family. Before marriage, then, the present for women continued to be shadowed by uncertainty and by the anticipation of discontinuity and dislocation. To compensate for the temporary nature of their positions, to mediate nearness and remoteness and to anticipate eventual estrangement from their natal family and an unknown future, revolutionary daughters, in common with daughters of the past may have dreamed, continued to visualize a marriage and alternative future for themselves that assumed qualities if not of limitless possibility at least of romance or fantasy. Establishing a relationship with time in the imagination that co-exists with measured time but puts it at a distance is thought to be a particular female strategy cross-culturally utilized to escape the constraints of external time.[78]

In the China of the revolution, two young town girls left records of such thoughts while young. One, San San, wrote that as a young girl in Communist China she knew only about being popular in school and making up dreams: 'My dreams were usually about dancing and the theatre, but in others I was someone else, a person about whom I had read and heard a lovely story': the transformation of unhappiness into happiness.[79] Only during the famine when arduous daily living and the search for suitable food took precedence did the present outdo the future for attention. Another schoolgirl, Jung Chang, recalled how she spent her childhood 'racing towards the future, hurrying to be an adult and always day-dreaming about what I could do when I was older'.[80] For peasant girls escape was occasioned by the anticipated movement in marriage from all that was familiar. In the face of approaching separation on marriage, imagined time or a future full of 'all possibility and desire' continued after the revolution to be nurtured by story-telling, folk-tale and teasing. Imagined time too went some way towards allaying their anxiety in the face of uncertainty and discontinuity. Before marriage it also enclosed and even substituted for the present. Marriage not only separated the present from the future or even substituted the future for the present, but after marriage too, women lived the future as visualized or dreamed in the past. This foreshortening or 'early arrival of dreams' – not shared it seemed by males – had important implications, for the future lived was seldom as good as that imaged or dreamed.[81]

This unique female experience may have effected the removal of much of the mystery and efficacy associated with the invented collective heaven or future as imaged and striven for within the revolution. As to the present, it too was shadowed for women both before and after marriage. Before marriage, it was shadowed by discontinuity and un-certainty of future, and after marriage, it was shadowed by the absence of familiar dreams imaging a future of limitless possibility to sustain or colour it and generate will or agency in its anticipation. This dislocation of time sequence with ensuing enclosures of the present by the future and of the future by the present may have had unique implications for female constructions of both present and future, thus separating gender conceptualizations and experience of time.

Recent hints as to the signification of marriage in this female-specific experience of time can be found in short stories that draw attention to the generation of female dreams before marriage, and after marriage to the demise of female dreams and the subsequent 'down' of living the present without the image of a future to compensate for its short-comings. In one short story, entitled 'Age of Maturity for Women',[82] a 30-year-old woman looked back over the previous decade contrasting the sweet dreams of limitless possibility or 'hopes colourful and sweet' of 20-year-olds, centring on the meeting of a husband handsome, strong, rich and capable, with dreams common at the age of 30 years. These are in contrast 'just like beautiful bubbles, broken one after another and disappearing'. Now at 30 , albeit embraced by strong and tender arms, she usually has a 'sense of loss and solitude' and likened being 30 to 'ripe apples on a tree hanging on the branches heavily'. Did not, she asked, an 'age of heaviness' ensue for women deriving from the sense of loss and deprivation subsequent to marriage? In another more subtle short story entitled 'On the Other Side of the River',[83] the girls in one poor village customarily went to the 'other side of the river' to be married. Only women and not the men of the village crossed the river, which in the short story was portrayed as 'wide as a lake, an ocean or a plain'. One young girl, who had been living in the shabby old village for seventeen years listening to stories and watching and waiting for marriage, had long nursed dreams of a fantasy future sustained by stories of riding off in a red cape once a husband had come on a white horse and with stories to transport her to a land of markets, riches and light (electric lamps), tractors and husband once the river was crossed. She eventually 'crossed the river' after her father had found her a family reputedly rich. For long it had been the ' other side of the river' that had constituted 'a sacred place in her mind', and the remainder of the story describes her disillusionment with 'the other side', an allegory likening the impoverishment of life after marriage to that of the mind after marriage.

This shifting emphasis in time-frames during the female life was reflected in the widespread admission within and outside of China that women after marriage so often lost interest in the revolution or gave revolutionary activities less time and attention. It was as if peasant daughters of the revolution outgrew the revolution and moved on much as daughters did of their natal families. Thus women's experience of the separation of the present from the future rather than sequential movement from one to the other contrasted with the continuity, certainty and commitment envisaged by males via the concept of heaven. And it was this contrast that may have transformed women into ambivalent strangers less inclined to believe in or *will* a better future. This nearness and concern for the common future was also mediated by a detachment generated by their unique experience of the future, which made them feel less of a commitment 'to these important things of men's affairs'. Although daughters may have most immediately felt both remoteness and nearness in their families of birth and marriage in spatial terms as a result of their physical movement, it may have been their conceptualization of time that became a more significant gender-specific marker in the long term, differentiating female from male experiences and images of the revolution.

Living the revolutionary rhetoric, characterized by a substitution of rhetoric for female experience, by a discrepancy between representation and experience and by an inherently flawed rhetoric, may have contributed to a many-layered rhetorical defeat. Despite enormous efforts by the revolutionary government in China to introduce a new rhetoric of female equality and to establish new androgynous categories reducing gender difference and hierarchy between comrades, revolutionary successors and workers (perhaps unmatched by any other government), the very experience of women estranged them from the rhetoric and reduced its efficacy in reaching its desired ends. If the revolutionary period could be said to be marked by a discrepancy between (albeit flawed) revolutionary rhetoric and female living, it was only during the more recent reform period that events were to detonate the rhetoric itself in favour of experience and focusing on living.

PART III

Not the Moon

Gendered Difference and Reflection:
Women of Reform

What then is the image of modern woman?' *Women of China*, 1984
Difficult or Not, to be a Woman?' *Women of China*, 1992.(1)

With the onset of Reform in the late 1970s, a single nation-wide image of women in blue receded to be replaced by a plurality of female images in the China of the 1980s and 1990s. In the first decade of reform visitors to China were frequently surprised by the variety of colour, style and fabric, the array of jewellery, cosmetics and hairstyles and the interest in fashion that contributed to the emergence not only of the 'young and modern miss' but also of the 'smarter older woman' and not only in the cities. Nowadays any crowded shopping street reveals the availability of a wide range of goods to fashion the female body and furnish the home, both increasing evidence of mass consumption and individual consumer choice. In shops and on market stalls, a plethora of popular magazines are devoted to fashion, beauty and life-style; above, the billboard images are overwhelmingly female portraying wide-eyed and smiling women not as producers but as retailers or customers in the company of washing machine, cooking pot, watch, television and toothpaste or cosmetics. Alongside, on billboards advocating family planning, attractive baby girls are shown cherished between parents and smiling as befits the desired single child. The poster presence of females of all ages in the absence of their male peers is important, intentional and of rhetorical significance.

In the first instance, the new era of Reform, as of Revolution, was greeted as a new age 'creating unprecedented opportunities for women to explore their potential'. It is by now well known that the overall aim of the Reforms of the past fifteen years has been to transform China rapidly into a powerful and modern nation-state by reforming and developing all sectors of the economy, altering the balance between plan and market, production and consumption and public and private forms of resource allocation. To this end, policy programmes have emphasized the importance of education, professionalism, skills, scientific and technical knowledge, profitability, the operation of economic incentives and the demands and interests of the consumer. In formulating and implementing the reforms, the government also frequently refers to women as 'half of heaven' or 'one of two hands' again deeming them as necessary to the success of reform and of revolution. Policy statements not only commonly began with the injunction that reform and development would only succeed if women participated, but also that women needed the opportunities provided by the new reforms in order to become truly equal. If such injunctions continued to sound familiar, there was also a marked and contrasting characteristic of Reform distinguishing it from Revolution and that was the gradual and increasingly open acknowledgement that the rhetoric of equality did not match with female experience of inequality either in the past during revolutionary years or now in reform.

This discrepancy between rhetoric and experience was retrospectively seen to be a major characteristic of the Revolution. In a personal interview reported in Honig and Hershatter, a teacher could ask but a few years into Reform, what the point had been of teaching ideals that were totally divorced from female experience during the Revolution?

We were taught that women and men were equal, that women could do what men could do. And then it took the entire Cultural Revolution, and almost ten more years after that, to realize that reality was totally different. What was the point of teaching us ideals which had no relation to reality?[2]

At about the same time a poem entitled 'Four Questions' published in 1983 in the *Renmin Ribao* (People's Daily) cartoon supplement repeatedly juxtaposed the differing qualities of the rhetoric and experience:

Times have changed,
Men and Women are equal.
Then why, in a certain production brigade,
Are men and women not treated equally?
They get different pay for the same work.
So men and women are different.

Times have changed,
Men and women are equal.
Then why in a certain factory
That is recruiting workers are they not treated equally?

If a man is hired the terms are flexible,
If a woman is hired the terms are strict.

Times have changed,
Men and women are equal.
Then why in a certain family
Do they respect boys and look down on girls?
If a baby boy is born the mother is happy,
If a baby girl is born she does not like it.

Times have changed,
Men and women are equal.
Then why is it that when a certain school
Admits students they are not treated equally?
To admit women they look at the score,
To admit men the score can go down.

Times have changed,
Men and women are equal.
It is natural to have both men and women.
The old feudal thinking
Must be eliminated to the core!'[3]

Again in interviews, a number of women have spoken of the alienation that many Chinese women had begun to feel as a result of the rift between the government's official policy of equality and 'the day-to-day reality'.[4] During the first years of reform, 'day-to-day reality' was increasingly and openly characterized by discriminatory actions against women, and state policies too were marked by an increasing and open acknowledgement of all forms of female discrimination. This more explicit acknowledgement of discrimination in both female experience and policy was a direct result of the greater incidence of female infanticide, which was almost single-handedly responsible for detonating the rhetoric of equality.[5]

Female infanticide

The billboard image of the cherished girl infant was increasingly at odds with the experience of many daughters, for a recurring trend in the Reform era has been continuing daughter discrimination and death, due not so much to the economic reforms, although these have strengthened the household as the most important units of production and consumption, as to the one-child family policy which, introduced in 1978–79, was to reinforce anew the age-old secondary status of daughters. With the introduction of the one-child family policy, the sex of the single child became a very important question: 'the question of having boys or girls is a common social problem that at present faces most families.'[6] In 1981 a survey from Hebei province had revealed that 95 per cent of the population wanted two or more children of which one at least was to be a boy, and if only one child was to be permitted then a mere 2.2 per cent wanted a daughter.[7] Surveys and my own interviews in Beijing in 1983 revealed that parents of single daughters were more reluctant to support the policy, took longer to sign the single-child family certificate and constituted a majority of the couples defying the policy and proceeding with out-of-plan births.[8] In rural areas, this son preference was so marked that there were reports of female infanticide. The practice was not uncommon before 1949 and since that time there had been occasional reports in the media of female infanticide, and the figures obtained from some localities on the sex ratios at birth or in the first year after birth had produced some puzzling results.

However, the first serious suggestion that female infanticide might be a factor to be reckoned with came in a research report on population forecasts based on detailed data gathered in 1978 from three counties in Zhejiang province, which suggested that the lower proportion of females born in 1978 should attract attention since this reflected the 'recurrence in recent years in some places of abandoning and killing infants, for the most part girls'.[9] In 1980 it was noticeable that the new Marriage Law continued to incorporate prohibitions against infanticide even though reference to other traditional practices that were thought to be no longer relevant had been dropped. By 1981 however, it came as something of a surprise to most observers within and outside of China when female infanticide became the subject of emotive headlines in the Chinese press.

At the end of 1981, the national youth newspaper ran the headlines 'Save Our Baby Girls' because it deemed it necessary to draw attention to the numbers of baby girls abandoned and the sharp increase in female infanticide which had occurred in China in the 1980s.[10] Once reports in the media indicated that the first years of the new decade had been marked by a sharp increase in female infanticide, the government charged the Women's Federation with ascertaining the scale of the problem of female infanticide throughout China. It initiated a nation-wide survey designed to investigate and document cases of female infanticide and other forms of discrimination against female infants and their mothers. In inland Anhui province, where the history of infanticide had given rise to large numbers of unmarried men over the age of 40 years, there was now reported to be a disproportionate number of newborn and young female infants who had died in the last few years. In some areas the ratio of female to male infants had dropped to a low 1:5, in one production team more than forty baby girls had been drowned in 1980 and 1981, and in another brigade, of the eight babies born in the first quarter of 1982, the three boys survived, three girls were drowned and a further two had been abandoned. Further comparisons with nearby villages had revealed that these patterns were not unique. In one of the counties, the percentage of male over female infants had risen from 3.2 to 5.8 per cent within one year, so that in 1980 the percentage of males born was 53 per cent compared to 46 per cent male. In another county, the problem was shown to be yet more serious, for the percentage of males born had risen from 112.6 to 116.4 per cent between 1980 and 1981 so that in 1981 the percentage of males born was 58.2 per cent compared to 41.8 per cent female.

The national newspaper *Renmin Ribao* (People's Daily) published these results of the Women's Federation survey and drew attention to them in order to emphasize that the intolerable behaviour of drowning and forsaking baby girls 'is still rampant in some rural areas' and 'a major problem worthy of serious attention'.[11] There were also reports in the media from Henan, Hebei and Hunan provinces, where maltreatment and deaths of female infants occurred on a fairly large scale. In these inland provinces, the sex ratios of the newly born children showed a higher proportion of males, frequently as high as 111 or 113 to every 100 females. These figures above the national average of 108.5:100 estimated by the State Statistical Bureau in 1981 did seem to suggest a degree of female infanticide, female neglect or at least under-registration of female infants.[12] The system of registration did not itself take account of babies dying within three days of birth, and in cases of acute disappointment, the registration of a baby girl did signify that the parents were relenting and accepting the child. However, most demographers within and outside of China agree that any tendency to under-register female infants could only exaggerate and certainly not alone account for the higher ratio of males to females among the new-born in some regions.

The nation-wide survey conducted by the Women's Federation not only suggested that female infanticide was an increasing problem, but also suggested that there was a whole range of less tangible, but nonetheless serious, forms of prejudice and discrimination against female infants which could not be quantified. For instance, the results of their surveys in two rural communes on the outskirts of Beijing revealed that, while there had been no cases of female infanticide or untoward maternal deaths, a strong preference for sons still existed and was sometimes explicitly or symbolically reflected in patterns of behaviour surrounding the birth of the first child. The birth of a son might be the occasion of much rejoicing by parents and their kin, with the mother en-joying special foods and the son the focus of joyful celebrations and chat.

In contrast, there had been occasions in these communes where disappointed relatives had precipitately left the hospital on hearing that the new-born infant was a girl so that there were no celebrations and no special food. Grandparents were particularly likely to show their disappointment and there had been instances in one commune where the grandmother had taken a little time to be reconciled sufficiently to order milk for her baby granddaughter and special food for the mother. In another suburban commune, the worst case of prejudice against the mother of a baby girl uncovered by the Federation during its recent investigation concerned a typist in the commune office. While she had been pregnant, a fortune-teller had predicted the baby would be a boy and expectations surrounding the birth were high. Once a girl was born however, relations between the mother and the disappointed mother-in-law, who felt extremely let down, rapidly deteriorated.[13]

In the circumstances of the single-child family policy, the birth of a daughter could give rise to open tension within a family by setting husband against wife and mother-in-law against daughter-in-law. Such cases were not confined to the countryside, but also were reported to exist among city workers and cadres' families. In the delivery room in a large city hospital in the north-east of China, there were instances where parents refused to accept that they had given birth to a daughter, so convinced were they that the hospital had made a mistake; where husbands were said to have fainted with worry prior to the birth, so anxious were they about the sex of their first born; where voluntary abortions took place on the mistaken advice of the fortune-teller that the expected baby was a girl; and where mothers were verbally abused on the birth of their daughters. At another hospital, the degree of post-partum complications was found to be significantly higher among mothers of daughters and this was attributed to their fall in spirits immediately after birth.[14]

Following on from investigation into infant female discrimination and death, the Women's Federation embarked on an intensive campaign to persuade the population that it was as good to have a girl as a boy. This was probably the most extensive campaign in China's history to upgrade the value of daughters, as there has been little previous or sustained attention given to investigating and redefining attitudes towards daughters. In the early 1980s, women's organizations published a number of pamphlets designed to show that girls were the equal of boys and daughters as valuable as sons and that it was demeaning to women of all ages to discriminate against female infants. In one important pamphlet, entitled 'It's as Good to have a Girl as a Boy', the Beijing Women's Federation explained that it was the current wave of violence against female infants and mothers of female daughters that had made it necessary for them to publish such a pamphlet:

The question of how to regard having a boy or a girl is an important part of socialist morality and not to be ignored. These materials on the sameness of boys and girls and on protecting women and female infants should be widely studied to promote feudal education and to teach people about the legal system. They set out to convince people that boys and girls are equal and that we should oppose actions which harm women and which lead to loss of life.[15]

In many regions the Women's Federation had also found there to be an absence of knowledge of the law so that infanticide was not necessarily conceived of as a criminal offence. To counter such ignorance the Women's Federation initiated an educational campaign to convince families that females did not determine the sex of a child and that daughters could participate in economic and political activities on a basis equal to sons, to the advantage both of themselves and of their households. If daughters were seen to care for their parents more attentively and satisfactorily than sons, and if sons-in-law could be persuaded to marry into their wives' households, then daughters could also remain as permanent members of their parents' households and their value henceforth be equally recognized. Although it was recognized long ago that virilocal marriage caused girls to be conceived of as poor forms of long-term investment, the government has sometimes suggested in the past that the recruitment of the groom to the bride's household in a form of uxorilocal marriage might be one means of promoting the equality of daughters. It did so again, but in the circumstances of the single-child family, it is much less likely that peasant parents of single daughters will voluntarily give up their only son.

The booklets and pamphlets published in the early 1980s were full of stories in which grandparents were won round first to accept and then to welcome their granddaughters, in which disappointed parents accepted their daughters and reluctant husbands eventually supported wives who were mothers of new-born daughters against the opposition of other members of the family. Posters in the streets on the commune and factory walls advocating the one-child family almost all uniformly depicted infant girls as the single child alongside her smiling mother or parents. Cartoons illustrated the long-range problems that would result if daughters were devalued and infanticide occurred. In one, ten fond mothers watched proudly as ten sons play; years later, ten fond mothers were seen searching far and wide for ten daughters-in-law. Much of this literature and the visual materials was also aimed at women, who were not only the victims but also themselves frequently colluded in the violence against infant girls. As the Beijing Women's Federation emphasizes in the introduction to its booklet, 'It's as good to have a girl as a boy':

We also hope that young women who give birth to girls will not feel a loss of self-esteem, will value their own rights and life, will rely on various organisations and will struggle resolutely against backward, ignorant ideas, and stand up for their own rights.[16]

Although much publicity has been given to the neglect, abuse and death of infant daughters and their mothers, the scale of such practices may never be fully known. It is my own view that while the disappointment and the lesser expression of this disappointment at the birth of a daughter was certainly widespread, female infanticide was most likely to occur in families where the birth of a daughter marked the end of the family line and in poorer inland regions of China where there was a tradition of infanticide, so that it was consequently scarcely thought of as a crime. Although it has been argued by some that female infanticide might still have been practised during the years of revolution, there is no doubt that the attention it received in the media and from the state in the early 1980s suggested that there had been a marked increase in violence against daughters. As with so many practices in China, it is difficult to ascertain the scale of their incidence, but in the case of female infanticide, as important as ascertaining the extent of its practice is the recognition of its importance as a watershed redefining the relationship between the rhetoric of equality and female experience. As several mortified and perplexed mothers of daughters from Anhui province wrote to a national newspaper in March 1983: 'We simply cannot understand why thirty-two years after China's liberation, we women are still weighted down by such backward feudal concepts ... We long for a second liberation.'[17]

Indeed, if parents were at all prepared to forfeit the lives of their daughters in favour of sons, nobody could pretend that the rhetoric of equality accurately reflected the experience of women. There is no doubt also that it was the incidence of the visible and more extreme forms of violence against daughters that led to new investigations into the experience of women and a new interest in all forms of discrimination against women. As one of the vice-presidents of the Women's Federation explained in an unusually strong-worded statement in September 1983, it conceived of infanticide and violence as 'only the visible manifestation of the invisible patriarchal partiality that persists in spite of all the rules and laws written since liberation incorporating political and economic equality'.[18] Ironically, it was the visible and extreme forms of violence that led to more open recognition of the degree of discrimination suffered by women that had not been possible to acknowledge when discrimination against women was largely and officially disguised by the prevailing rhetoric of equality.

It is no accident then that in the early years of reform and of disillusionment with rhetoric, women's experience of sexual discrimination in education, employment and politics received more attention than at any time during the entire revolution. This is not just because of the legacy of the revolution that had left the experience of women lagging behind the rhetoric of equality, but because many of the new reforms themselves led to further discrimination against women and exacerbated their secondary position. As the gap between the rhetoric of equality and experience of inequality widened and was increasingly acknowledged, there was a shift in the focus of attention from rhetoric and images of equality to experience and problems of discrimination. A number of bodies including the Women's Federation, social scientists at the Academy of Social Sciences and other groups of women scholars all became newly interested in understanding the multi-faceted dimensions of women's lives based on investigation of their experiences. The validation of women's experience as a topic for research and field investigation was brought about by the revival of sociology and anthropology as academic disciplines. Using their own distinctive techniques of field research, social scientists set out to investigate lives as opposed to rhetoric in a variety of social settings and in relation to a number of social problems, many of which drew attention to the special difficulties experienced by women during the early years of reform. Their discussions and research particularly focused attention on the split between the rhetoric of equality and women's working lives.

Urban working lives

One of the main characteristics of revolutionary rhetoric was the practical and symbolic importance attached to work, especially for women, for whom it also provided a measure of emancipation, liberation or equality. During the revolution women had expanded their economic roles in society with the result that almost all women between the ages of 16 and 60 years were economically active in some form of employment. As in any other society, the measures of women's participation in production very much depended on what definitions of work, employment and production were utilized, but even allowing for the usual factors that lead to the undercounting or underestimation of female labour in agriculture and informal sectors, it was estimated that on the eve of reform, the economic activity rate of women in China was higher than in any other Asian society. In China several years into reform it was estimated that women made up almost 40 per cent of the total labour force and that the female participation rate was rising[19] (see Table 1). In 1987, national statistics suggested that women continued to constitute a significant portion of the measurable work force in most sectors, making up 40 per cent of those employed in commerce, industry,

Table 1 Employment of women in 1982 and 1990 (in 10,000)

	1982	1990	No. increased	Rate of increase (%)
No. of employed women	22,784	29,101	6,317	28
Professional/technical	1,012	1,556	544	54
Department/ Organisation Leaders	84	130	46	55
Clerical	166	289	123	74
Commerce	432	909	477	110
Service	551	801	250	45
Farming	17,566	21,901	4,335	19
Factory	2,953	3,501	548	19
Other	20	14	-6	-30

Source: The Report of the People's Republic of China on the Implementation of the Nairobi Forward-Looking Strategies for the Advancement of Women, Beijing, China, 1994.

the public service, the professions and in education[20] (see Table 2). By 1990 in the fields of health care, sports and social welfare, the proportion of female employees surpassed 50 per cent and in public utilities and commerce, the proportion had risen to more than 45 per cent. Although the opportunities for women in employment seem to have expanded and become more various during the reform years,[21] the nature and conditions of that employment had undergone substantial changes and not all to women's benefit.

Work could no longer be represented rhetorically as an androgynous activity overlapping male and female categories of worker and conditions of work, for the openly acknowledged degree of discrimination against female workers drew attention to the increasingly differentiated experience of male and female workers that was undermining notions of sameness and equality characteristic of the androgynous worker in revolutionary rhetoric. Although revolutionary rhetoric had long negated the sexual division of labour in which working women had predominated in the lesser skilled, the lighter though not necessarily less physically demanding jobs and the least specialized, mechanized and well-paid sectors of the Chinese economy, it was not until the reform period that practices of discrimination penalizing women workers reached such proportions that their experience of discrimination eroded the rhetoric itself. This erosion largely came about as the result of enterprise reform in which state, co-operative and private enterprises assumed primary responsibility for the recruitment and organization of

Table 2 Female employment by occupation 1992

Form of employment	Total	Female	% Female
All occupations	147,919501	55,855797	38
Farming, forestry, fishing	8,179148	2,906107	36
Industry, mining	66,214336	27,413712	41
Geological	1,000865	243,903	24
Construction	10,359421	2,087009	20
Transportation, communications	8,188727	2,027527	25
Commerce	19,463842	8,735789	45
Housing, public services	4,397427	1,993673	45
Health, welfare	4,209342	2,268890	54
Education, culture	12,129680	4,648748	39
Scientific, technical	1,592200	547,423	34
Finance, insurance	2,229375	830,945	37
Party, government	9,961138	2,152073	22

Source: The Report of the People's Republic of China on the Implementation of the Nairobi Forward-Looking Strategies for the Advancement of Women, Beijing, China, 1994.

their labour force alongside the procurement of their own resources and markets. They became accountable for their own profits and losses with new controls over the disposal of profits which, while permitting the enterprises more autonomy, also made enterprises more vulnerable to market forces. This vulnerability disadvantaged the female labour force in a number of important respects.

The most serious problem to emerge in the past ten years has been the reluctance of employers in the state sector to recruit and retain women workers. In cities and towns, new and greater discriminatory practices derive directly from the contraction of the state sector employment and the costs of employing working women. There has been a decline in the privileged state sector of employment in which workers earn higher wages, have more fringe benefits including health insurance and greater opportunities to acquire training in new skills. In 1987 it was estimated that women constituted a third of the labour force in state-owned enterprises, and in light industries, the textiles and food processing up to 90 per cent of the workforce may be women.[22] The proportion of the female labour force employed in state sector enterprises has declined largely because of the contractions in the state labour force and the introduction of contract work. Recent reports and surveys suggest that enterprises may either directly refuse to accept women assigned to the enterprise or unit or individually refuse them by artificially raising entry requirements for women recruits. In a survey conducted by the All-China Federation of Trade Unions of 660 factories with 15,000 workers, only 5.3 per cent of the employers indicated that they were willing to have women in positions that could be filled by men or women; of the 89 textile mills surveyed, 75 per cent said they preferred to hire males; and in the 66 financial enterprises and 77 commercial enterprises women recruits were required to gain 12 to 13 points more in the entrance tests.[23] These practices appeared to affect women graduates in particular, a high proportion of whom continue to have great difficulty in finding employment. Of those awaiting employment in 1986, an estimated 61.5 per cent were women and in 1992, 70 per cent of the young people awaiting employment in urban areas were women.[24] As you might expect, given the difficulties in defining and counting the unemployed, there is some variation in these estimates. More recently the Women's Federation has suggested that the proportion of women among unemployed youth is slightly lower at 57 per cent.[25]

Women employees have been the first to have their employment contracted or terminated in enterprises engaged in some reorganization or streamlining of staff. Surveys by the Women's Research Centre and the China Managerial Science Academy in 34 enterprises in eight provinces confirmed that the percentage of women who have been made redundant has been higher than their proportion in the workforce. It is estimated that 70 per cent of all workers losing their employment as a result of job rationalization are women and it is anticipated by some that of the 20 million workers who will lose their jobs, as many as 15 million will be women.[26] There is also the problem of under-employment for women workers in the 2 to 3 million factories and enterprises not in full production; women have usually been the first to be laid off, either part-time or temporarily by urban enterprises contracting their labour force either due to efficiency measures and restructuring or economic strictures.

Married women workers, older women and women with young children are particularly at risk from dismissal. Although all the evidence suggests that women preferred a maximum of six months paid maternity-leave in the interests of retaining their income, skills and promotion prospects, there have been reports recently of enterprises encouraging women to take a long, sometimes up to seven years, maternity-leave at 50 to 75 per cent of the pay in order to save on the costs of benefits and providing nursing and child-care services.[27] Some enterprises have provided home-based work to offset the cost of providing nurseries and other services for mothers of young children. Women workers are now also encouraged to retire earlier, in some cases up to 20 years less than the official retirement age for women or at the age of 40 years. There is also some evidence to suggest that a disproportionate number of older women workers in state factories aged between 40 and 45 years may be at greater risk from the termination of their contracts at a younger age than male workers. A survey of more than 400 enterprises in Shanghai in 1989 showed that 6 per cent of women workers (of whom 80 per cent were between 24 and 40 years) were forced to stay at home either because the enterprises had all the workers it needed or did not have enough work for its labour force. One factory had a policy that when there is not enough work to do, women over 45 had to go home.[28] Nationally, a survey of 660 enterprises showed that only 5.3 per cent of directors wanted to take on women workers,[29] and in Shanghai a survey of more than 100 large and medium-sized enterprises showed that 92 per cent of the directors preferred to dismiss female workers because there were more of them than male workers. The directors said that if the decision was up to them they would discharge one fifth of their women workers and in contemporary China it is the directors who are increasingly likely to make such decisions.[30]

One of the main reasons why women are discriminated against is the high costs of providing for maternity leave, child care and other related benefits. The importance of these was reiterated in new special regulations for the protection of labouring women issued in 1988 updating those first issued in 1950[31] (see Appendix 1). The costs of pregnancy, childbirth and breast-feeding were estimated in one survey to cost an enterprise more than Y1,259 per worker; another survey showed that a male worker could earn Y10,600 more than his female counterpart who was pregnant and involved in childbearing and caring over the same two-year period.[32] There was also the cost of providing nurseries and other services. Since the reforms, these costs have to be borne by the enterprise, and they are reluctant to accept the higher costs and lower profits involved in employing female workers. Several measures are under consideration to solve these problems. There has been some considerable effort to persuade the population that reproduction has a social value and that its costs should therefore be borne by society and not just by the individual work units. Experiments have been conducted in cities whereby each worker contributes for example Y20 per year to a city-wide fund for meeting such costs; these have been successful and are expected to be more widely emulated in the future. The Trade Union movements would like to see a nationwide tax levied for this purpose, but they also acknowledge that to organize such a nation-wide solution in the absence of full-scale national social security reform has its difficulties. At the present time, such measures have not yet succeeded in stemming the discrimination against employing women in the state sector. In contrast, women are predominantly employed in the plethora of new private and smaller enterprises that are less likely to protect their labour or safeguard their maternal benefits.

In cities and towns women predominate in the services, the textile, the food-processing and other light industries and perform the least mechanized, the more repetitive and lower-paid jobs. From the mid-1950s the collective sector of the urban economy consisted mainly of small street or neighbourhood factories with a subsidiary and secondary place to the state sector that was reflected in the lower levels of wages, fewer fringe benefits and the absence of political and social status associated with employment in the state sector. Due to the informal origins of most of these enterprises, the labour processes and types of products, women formed a very high proportion of the workforce of this sector. The reforms have expanded the number of collectively and privately-owned small street, neighbourhood and individually operated enterprises many times over. Many of the enterprises already established have been expanded and managed by new owners, and many new enterprises have been established by units, families or individuals and run by company managers, groups of workers or household heads.

The current expansion of textiles, high technology, handicrafts, light and service industries ensures that a high proportion of new workers recruited into such enterprises are women and not just in cities and towns but also in smaller townships and larger villages. In November 1988 it was reported that 35 million women were employed in the fast-developing township and village enterprises and made up 41.2 per cent of the 80 million or so workers in these industries.[33] In these enterprises, especially the smaller enterprises operating with low profit margins in a competitive market, there are frequent complaints that there is no concept of a minimum wage in China or laws preventing arbitrary increases in working hours, summary punishment or dismissal of workers and that the supervision of existing labour protection regulations is lax.[34] Where the labour process is fast, fragmented and repetitive, with payment calculated according to piece-work, there is evidence to suggest that women work for longer lower-paid hours, conditions of work are cramped and there are few provisions for the implementation of new and improved labour-protection regulations. In 1989 a national survey found that about half of the country's enterprises and units investigated did not implement the women's labour-protection laws and regulations effectively. More than 44 per cent of the surveyed factories did not reduce the heavy work of pregnant women or take them off night-shift. Although in 90 per cent of the factories, women received their full wages during maternity leave, their bonuses and other benefits were not guaranteed, leading to a decrease in income by one third.[35]

Women have also constituted a high proportion of the new casual labour force, much of it migrant, contracted to produce electronics, textiles, clothing and automobile components and other light industrial goods primarily, but not only, for the export market. These factories may be financed by foreign investment, make use of imported raw materials and assemble foreign parts, but the labour is Chinese and a high proportion of that 'sweated' labour force are women. Various estimates from informal sources suggest that up to 80 per cent of the labour force in the foreign or joint foreign–Chinese enterprises is made up of young single women whose health and safety may be jeopardized. Those thought to be particularly at risk include young women who are migrant workers from the rural areas in small manufacturing enterprises, many of which are funded from Hong Kong or Taiwan where workers are likely to be forced to work overtime, sometimes between 12 and 16 hours daily, and on piece-work payment. After surveying 914 foreign-funded enterprises, the all-China Federation of Trade Unions released a report in summer 1994 on the 'appalling working conditions' that women suffer despite their 'increasingly vital role in foreign-funded enterprises'. The survey found that women were hired and fired at will, had no legal contracts, did not receive equal pay and that many enterprises paid no attention to labour-protection regulations safe-guarding women's health or safety. In view of the harassment of female workers, the report recommended that women, without channels to voice their complaints, should form women workers organizations which were 'badly needed to safeguard their rights and interests'.[36] Recently during a visit to Beijing, I heard of a meeting of women's provincial representatives at the national Women's Federation to discuss the recent spate of factory fires in which numbers of women had lost their lives.

After an interval of nearly thirty years, urban residents in the past decade have again been permitted to set up their own individual or family-based enterprises to make available a wide range of small goods, foods and services to urban inhabitants. Many of these individual- or family-based enterprises are managed and operated by women who take advantage of neighbourhood employment, flexibility of working hours and some individual control over the labour process. According to the Chinese Individual Women Workers' Association, the number of individual traders with licences has reached 21 million from 13 million households, and 5 million of these are women mostly with licences for hairdressing, sewing, commerce, handicrafts and household services.[37] There is no government department charged with the supervision of the employment of labour in privately-owned enterprises. Although home-based work has been a permanent feature of some rural villages, it is a newer phenomenon in the cities, where now many women may expect to work at home rather than in factories or enterprises as a result of expansion in the putting-out or contracting out of work to women in their own homes. For those outside of established units of employment, that is those in small-scale neighbourhood, household or individual enterprises where the labour process is unregulated and unsupervised, the insecurity and isolation must be deemed considerable in an urban economy where the status of the unit of employment is still an important source of benefits and social security. There is some evidence that female entrepreneurs or heads of individual enterprises may have difficulty in gaining access to raw materials, credit, technology and markets. Recently a spokesperson from the newly-formed Female Entrepreneurs' Association stated that its members received little support in their economic activities.[38] At the same time as some of the most successful urban individual enterprises are managed by women often earning tens of thousands of yuan per year, female workers in family-based urban enterprises may become de facto employees of the male head of the household with all the attendant disadvantages deriving from the structure of familial authority reproduced in production.

Rural working lives

In the rural areas of China, where around 70 to 80 per cent of the female population lives, agriculture is still the main source of employment for women (see Table 3), although the proportion of women exclusively or predominantly engaged in field cultivation is declining as a result of changes in the organization of agricultural production during the economic reforms. The government introduced a number of new economic policies including the rural production responsibility system, the diversification and expansion of agricultural and nonagricultural on- and off-farm economic activities and the establishment of a rural market. Each of these reforms had wide implications for the location and the range of peasant women's on- and off-farm activities, the organization of peasant women's labour, the sexual division of labour and forms of resourcing and remuneration. One of the most important dimensions of the recent rural reforms that directly affected the location of peasant women's economic activities was the decline of the collective and the emergence of the peasant household as the dominant unit of production with new responsibilities and new demands on its material and labour resources. The peasant household now takes primary responsibility for agricultural production from the acquisition of inputs to the processing, transporting and marketing of the product. The peasant household has become an increasingly complex and autonomous economic unit demanding new skills in production and resource management of its members, including women, to maintain it as a diverse economic unit responsible for production, processing and marketing. Rural women both benefit from and are penalized by the new economic

Table 3 Employment composition of China's working women 1990

Form of employment	% of women in occupation
Professionals	5.35
Government, party, organization officials	0.45
Clerks	0.98
Commerce, business	3.12
Service personnel	2.75
Agriculture, forestry, fisheries	75.26
Industry, transport	12.03
Other	0.05
Total	100.00

Source: The Report of the People's Republic of China on the Implementation of the Nairobi Forward-Looking Strategies for the Advancement of Women, Beijing, China, 1994.

reforms with the well-being of women now primarily dependent on regional location, the labour and material resources of the household of which they are members, and the distribution of resources and rewards within that household.

The most important repercussion of changes in the organization of agricultural production during the economic reforms has been the reduction in the number of opportunities for women in field cultivation. It is estimated that, since the introduction of the rural economic reforms, the agricultural field labour force has been reduced by a third. Nationally at the outset of reform it was estimated that eventually the numbers of people engaged in agriculture would be reduced by about two-thirds, giving rise to surplus labour of some 200 million persons.[39] At the same time, the President of the National Women's Federation identified lack of employment for peasant women as one of the major problems facing Chinese women in the 1980s.[40] Finding employment for this surplus labour and developing new income-generating activities within the rural economy has thus become an important urgent problem for the present government and led to the recent expansion of on- and off-farm activities in rural areas and the migration of millions to towns and cities. The government has encouraged the peasant household to diversify its operations and expand its commodity economy to include animal husbandry, cash cropping, handicraft, industrial and commercial activities. Thus peasant households have expanded their range of on-farm activities to include the raising of pigs, poultry, and other animals, fish farming, fruit farming, and the expansion of small industries and services for which resources, labour and markets are required. Rural fairs and markets have been re-established so that goods, foods, local handicrafts and daily necessities produced locally can be exchanged and procured for wider distribution and export. At present it is estimated that women account for one third of the total of the 14 million rural self-employed.[41] Increasingly, rural farm workers are also encouraged to move outside of agriculture and into an extended range of off-farm activities including a new range of rural industries producing goods for the local, national and foreign markets and providing services in townships, towns and cities. All these developments have broadened the scope of women's income-generating activities both on and off the household farm.

On the farm, the majority of peasant women cultivate land and undertake a variety of economic activities ranging from vegetable production, the raising of livestock and the production of handicraft goods to the provision of services for their local community. It is one of the characteristics of domestic production that its scale of operation is predominantly determined by the household's access to female labour, given that occupations such as cultivating vegetables, tending livestock and producing handicrafts have traditionally been performed by the women of peasant households. At the outset of the rural reforms, the most important farm resource, land, was distributed to peasant households on a per capita basis and there have been some reports that women did not receive the same quantity or quality of land as their male counterparts, although in only one case of my many field studies was this so. The establishment and expansion of most other on-farm activities including livestock-raising require that peasant women have access to a number of resources including credit, raw materials and machinery for production and processing. All of these are still scarce in much of rural China, although recent data from rural villages suggest that it may be more difficult for peasant women who have little education or connections within or outside the village to obtain formal access to credit and other resources. Although certain types of sideline activities such as livestock-raising are traditionally undertaken by the peasant women of the household, the gender-typing of on- and off-farm economic activities is variable and much depends on the range and type of economic activities available within any one region. The gender-typing of some activities such as field cultivation, fruit farming, fisheries, forestry and many other activities may be either male- or female-typed economic activities depending on the range of alternative economic activities. Common patterns in the sexual division of labour in rural areas are several. Where there are no or few off-farm activities, males tend to undertake field cultivation and women other on-farm activities such as livestock raising, handicraft or small-scale food processing.

In the expansion or diversification of on- and off-farm activities of the post-reform peasant household, jobs tend to be gender-typed although definitions vary according to the number and range of economic activities available within the region. For instance, depending on the type of non-agricultural and other employment available, it may be either the men or women farmers who leave the fields to be recruited into non-agricultural occupations, leaving the other on the farm. In these circumstances a new division of labour seems to be established: not that between skilled and unskilled or lighter and heavier jobs within agriculture as before, but between agriculture and non-agricultural occupations and it is commonly the women and especially married women who are left in agriculture. Where there are a number of off-farm activities into which males are predominantly recruited, women undertake most of the field cultivation and sidelines. Peasant households exhibiting this pattern are commonly referred to as 'half-side families' where males reside away from the household, which is, for all practical purposes, female-headed and operated. Women who are to all intents and purposes the head of their household due to the absence or incapacity of their male counterpart may well suffer discrimination.

This is likely to be an increasingly important question given the scale of male migration, seasonal, temporary or permanent, that has recently occurred, especially from the poorer regions where the villages have become largely feminized at least for a portion of the year. It has never been clear what the proportions of female-managed households are in rural China and whether they have suffered any discrimination in the distribution of resources. This is a question that I have often been asked, given the degree of discrimination experienced by female-headed households in other agricultural societies. Recently in my own investigation of female poverty in south-west China, I was particularly interested in the circumstances of female-operated households which were referred to as female-'managed' rather than female-'headed' households. In Guangxi Autonomous Region, the investigation of their conditions by the provincial Women's Federation was an important initiative, for it is one of the first instances that I know of in which female-managed households have become a matter for official and specific concern. There it is estimated that a high proportion – 23 per cent of the households and 2.02 million households out of the 3.3 million or 61 per cent of poorer households – are female-managed in that the men are either absent or labour-weak. They were considered to be unduly disadvantaged not so much in terms of inputs, information and markets as due to the heavier demands on female labour.

Now that the peasant household is once again the dominant unit of production, the degree of independence and autonomy accruing to peasant women will be very much dependent on the sexual division of labour and their relation to the male household head. It is likely that the more separate the location of their labour and the greater their visibility as producers, the more individual their rewards and bargaining power within and outside of households are. It is also likely that their claim on resources within and outside of the household is very much dependent on the sexual division of labour and the visibility of their separate inputs. The rapid growth and diversification into on- and off-farm economic activities of the post-reform peasant household has had repercussions not only for the sexual division of labour but also for the intensity of and demand for female labour. One of the main means by which a peasant household could immediately maximize its labour power in order to rapidly expand its economic activities was to intensify demands on family and especially female and child labour. Although the economic reforms have altered the ways in which farmers structure their working day, many peasant women recognize that although they have greater control over production processes and more flexibility, their daily routine is even more demanding than before the reforms. In particular the diversification of on- and off-farm activities, the responsibility for procuring production inputs and arranging for the disposal or sale of farm products have taken more time than previously.

There may be more water, more fuel and more fodder to be collected now that their sideline activities have expanded, and there is also a worsening shortage of fodder and fuel reported in many rural regions, which means travelling longer distances for supplies. Marketing may also entail several hours of walking several times a day to dispose of the farm's produce.

In regions where all members of households are employed outside of agriculture, women who have moved into full-time waged labour off the farm may still be required to cultivate the fields and raise domestic livestock as part-time farmers labouring after work or on their days off. One of the ways in which a peasant household can recruit additional labour is via marriage and the recruitment of daughters-in-law. The demand for a daughter-in-law's labour has lowered the age of marriage and increased the expenses of marriage, many of which have led to reports of the sale and abuse of young peasant women. The demand for child labour in the countryside is one of the main reasons why female children are more likely to be spasmodic in their attendance at school and be withdrawn from education earlier than their brothers. In turn, one of the serious side-effects of the high rates of illiteracy and education drop-out rate among peasant girls is that entry into extension training schemes frequently have a literacy or educational requirement and, in turn, access to credit often requires prior attendance in training schemes.

Off the farm the main new sources of employment have been the expanded township and village industries with the proportion of rural women employed in any one of these industries very much depending on the type of enterprises with the number of women employed rising sharply in textile, light and clean industries. Recently it has been estimated that by the end of 1992, China's rural enterprises had employed more than 100 million persons, among whom more than 40 per cent were women producing 65 per cent of total output value in food, clothing, knitting, toy, electronics, traditional handicraft and service industries.[42] The female workforce in rural industries may be made up of women of all ages if they are within commuting distance of the village. If the enterprises are some distance, it is more likely to be made up of young unmarried girls who work and live away from their villages for short periods of time. Girls may acquire a specialized skill, and their wages plus bonuses are likely to be slightly higher than incomes from agricultural production. However, the skills they acquire may not be transferable, the conditions in which they work may fall short of acceptable standards in that they may work long hours for piece-work under physical conditions that may be to the long-term detriment of their health. Where there is surplus labour and there are few local opportunities for young women to find employment in the village or nearby township, they may become part of the expanding mobile labour force often migrating long distances from interior to coastal provinces, from the north to the southern provinces and to the larger cities in order to find employment. The fortunate of the urban 'floating' population, often numbering tens of thousands, may find employment in manufacturing or in the service sectors of the city including domestic service.

The recruitment of rural maids into city households became an increasingly popular response to China's most pressing rural employment and urban service problems. In December 1983 this privatized service sector was formally legitimized by the establishment of new channels for the recruitment and training of maids first in Beijing and later in other cities. In Beijing, when I conducted interviews with maids in November 1984, it was estimated that their number had trebled since 1966 and by February 1984 it was estimated that there were upwards of 30,000 maids employed in the households of Beijing alone.[43] The practice spread to other main cities and by the 1990s the scale of their movement is such that it is very difficult to estimate their numbers, but they must reach more than a million in all the largest cities. There are well-trodden trails that rural women take between Sichuan and Anhui provinces and Beijing or between Zhejiang, Henan and Shandong and Shanghai, Nanjing and Wuhan. Most village women follow friends and relatives either on their own initative or via agencies organized by the Women's Federation and other bodies. Some village women are forced by poverty and lack of employment to move; others, on their own admission, are lured by the city lights and opportunities and, away from their families, the control of their own wages and spending. Some stay but a short period, others leave on marriage and some return to or remain in city households for many years. One maid of my acquaintance has already resided in the household of one of my friends for the past thirteen years. She first returned to her village in Shanxi to get married and then brought her husband back to the Beijing household where she has since resided and where her son was born. It is not just city parents of small children who have employed maids to ease the child-care problem; increasingly older couples employ a maid to care for them in their old age. A series of interviews in households with maids also revealed there to be a third category of households in which resident grandmothers used their pensions to employ maids to relieve them of family pressure to care for grand-children – in order that they themselves might enjoy their retirement and new-found opportunities for leisure activities! Relations between maid and family can be mediated by neighbourhood service agencies run by the Women's Federation that have been established to monitor standards of employment and work, thus providing a safety net for rural girls at risk in a new urban environment far from home.

Many young rural women begin their urban careers as maids and then go on to find employment in more lucrative retail and service outlets, but these are frequently likely to be on a short-term contractual basis with all the potential risks inherent in such a position. There are many reports of exploitation and sexual harassment of such young women, both those employed and those stranded without employment, with young girls and women turning to prostitution, which has become a commonly observed and reported feature in the cities and towns of China. In fact, an important new area of official concern has been the increase in levels of violence against women. Both the government and the women's organizations have drawn attention to the physical abuse of women by men and there have been more cases of rape and discussions of rape reported in the newspaper than ever before with the struggle of women to bring accusations of rape and pursue the offenders through the legal system more openly documented. There has been a rise in the abduction of women and children either for adoption, as brides or in organized prostitution, with public trials of the offenders and sentences heavier than normal to deter others from following their example. Mobile rural women often return to their village to marry, and the problem of reintegration back into the countryside has been cited as one of the causes of the high suicide rate among young married women in the countryside.[44] Others marry in the towns and leave the countryside for good. Most begin with this fantasy. Their rags-to-riches dream was recently dramatized in a popular television series called 'Sisters from the Outside', which highlighted the ups and downs of country girls who had gone to work in a Shenzhen factory just across the border from Hong Kong.

In city and countryside the demands on the domestic and public labour of women remain considerable and may be rising rather than declining. In 1990 in their work alone it was estimated that 87 per cent of working women were physical labourers, and of every 100 working women, 75 are farmers, 12 are workers and only 6–7 in non-manual technical cadre or office work and 5–6 in service and trade (see Table 3). It is noticeable that despite years of official exhortation and encouragement for women to become technicians, clerks and officials, women fill only 6 per cent or so of these occupations.[45] Where women have conspicuously entered into new jobs hitherto occupied by men and in the many professions where women are increasingly employed and better represented than in most societies, they continued to be disadvantaged in terms of remuneration, pensions rights and promotion prospects. According to a survey on the social status of women in China, in 1990 an urban male worker received Y193.15 per month compared to female workers who earned an average of Y149.60.[46]

There is clear evidence that women are less likely to be promoted into managerial positions and the predominance of men in the leadership, managerial or administrative hierarchies, whether based on technical and professional skill or political attributes, can be easily observed and documented. Moreover, only 12 per cent of the heads of government, Party and people's organizations, enterprises and institutions are female. In political institutions and organizations, women have most obviously not entered into formal positions of decision-making in proportion to their representation either in production or in the population as a whole. One of the most striking impressions of any official visitor to China continues in the 1980s and 1990s to be the predominance of men in the leadership committees at all administrative levels of the government and the Party. It is reported that there are 8.7 million women leaders making up a third of China's total officials[47], although many of these will be the designated women's representative on various committees. Of the members of the National People's Congress, women make up 21 per cent and of its Standing Committee, the highest organ of state power in China, women make up 12–16 per cent of the members, while approximately 10 per cent of Standing Committee members of the Chinese People's Political Consultation Conference (made up of representatives of the Communist Party, democratic parties and mass organizations) are women.[48] Even after constant campaigns to increase the number of women members, they make up approximately

13 per cent of Party membership. At all administrative levels from the ministries, provinces, cities, counties and townships, it was reported in 1990 that women made up approximately 7 per cent of the cadres.[49] In the past few years these low proportions have been constantly acknowledged in the press with attention drawn to the continuing discrimination which women face in gaining access to employment and power.

Overall it is difficult to weigh up the repercussions of the economic reforms for the employment of women, for they are very mixed. Although it can be argued that women have generally shared in the increased income and standards of living of the majority of even the poorest households, differentials have risen in the past ten years, widening the gap between the richest of new women entrepreneurs and the categories of peasant women most at risk, including the young mobile unemployed peasant girls and women in poor health or those who are otherwise incapacitated and without full labour power. Initially observers and analysts were divided as to whether they emphasized the new opportunities that reform offered to women or the new forms of discrimination that were likely to cost them dearly. Several years into reform, it is not difficult to observe that with reform have come new opportunities, choices and expectations alongside increased discrimination, penalty and disappointment. It was recently admitted in *Women of China* that while many women were 'joyously grasping their opportunities, hundred and thousands of other women feel that challenge and crises are inevitable'.[50] As disappointment and penalty increasingly and more openly marked the experience of women, discrimination became not only a social phenomenon worthy of research, but also the subject of new policy initiatives. The first of these initiatives was to re-emphasize female self-improvement or the importance of encouraging women to take advantage of all the opportunities available for them and so give less cause for discrimination by acquiring an education, skills and vocational training alongside their male peers.

Educating women

As with each new decade of revolutionary development in China when women were encouraged to acquire education and skills in order that they maximize their participation in the workforce on a basis equal to men, so with reform and modernization, women were also encouraged to make a greater and more skilled contribution to production by increasing their managerial, productive and technical skills and their productivity in a new range of enterprises. In particular, women have been encouraged to raise the levels of their education and acquire new skills. It has been widely reported in recent years that female education and training shows much improvement compared to the past, and

Table 4 Women's education status, 1990

Level	% of Women graduates	% of Women enrolled	% Increase over 1980
Post-graduates	20	25	+13.0
Colleges and universities	33	34	+10.3
Secondary technical		43	+5.5
Secondary normal		55	+29.0
Technical		38	
Ordinary middle	42	43	+3.5
Junior middle	43	44	
Senior middle	39	39	
Secondary vocational	44	39	+13.9
Primary schools		47	+2.0
School age entrance rota		96	+4.2

Source: The Report of the People's Republic of China on the Implementation of the Nairobi Forward-Looking Strategies for the Advancement of Women, Beijing, China, 1994.

national figures in all sectors of education for 1992 show an increase over 1985.[51] (See Table 4.) However, it is also officially admitted that they have not participated or benefited to the same degree as their male peers. In a number of my own interviews in 1990 in Beijing at various levels of administration within Chinese ministries and other official bodies reponsible for formulating and implementing gender components of state policies and programmes, it was quite clear that for some years they all had thought that the single most important problem, priority and policy had to do with the education of women. This was not only perceived to be the priority of the State Education Commission but was of direct concern to other official bodies, the Women's Federation and those concerned with research. The main problems identified were the high illiteracy rates among young women of rural areas, lower female enrolment and attendance rates and high female drop-out rates in primary schools leading to low proportions of female students in higher levels of education. Alike, however, they all drew attention to the link between education and economic opportunity and income for women.

Women have entered higher education in greater numbers, but they are still represented nowhere near to the proportion of their numbers in the relevant age-groups. Presently the demand for higher and tertiary education outstrips supply and, now that the educational system has again become highly selective, competition for places is fierce. During the revolution, the numbers of students entering higher education increased from 20 per cent in 1949 to 25 per cent in 1980, with women making up 34 per cent of university undergraduates and 25 per cent of graduates in 1992.[52] Figures available for attendance at technical and vocational training courses show that female students generally accounted for some 30 per cent of the students, and it is generally estimated that women students currently account for one third of the total enrolments in institutions of higher education. There are wide variations between the major cities, Beijing (45 per cent), Shanghai (47 per cent) and Tianjin (51 per cent) and the inland provinces.[53] In Hubei province 29 per cent of students are female and in poor and remote regions even fewer of the students are women. There are also wide variations between disciplines with relatively few female students in science and technology (24.7 per cent) compared to medicine (53 per cent), teacher training (42 per cent) and foreign languages (53 per cent).[54] Despite uniform entrance examinations and rules instituting equality of opportunity, there have been frequent reports of higher education institutes discriminating against women students by demanding higher scores in the entrance examinations in order to limit their numbers. However the problem might be said to start much earlier, for at all schooling levels there are reported still to be more male than female students.

The State Education Commission has reported that the proportion of pupils enrolling in primary school has risen from 10 per cent in 1949 to 95 per cent in 1988,[55] but in 1992 of the pupils enrolled in primary school 47 per cent were female and in junior middle schools 44 per cent were female; in secondary technical schools, technical schools and secondary vocational schools girls account for 39, 38 and 38 per cent respectively.[56] However, at the primary school level, the most important entry point, field work suggests that enrolment rates are not the same as attendance rates and there is considerable evidence that the spasmodic attendance, drop-out and non-attendance rates of young girls are higher than for males of the same age cohorts. In 1988 the State Education Commission estimated that of the 2.79 million school age children not in school the previous year, 2.25 million or 81 per cent were girls, and in addition girls accounted for 70–80 per cent of the 3.69 million pupils who seldom attended school.[57] Although there have been campaigns to reduce illiteracy, it is estimated that 32 per cent of the female population and 13 per cent of the male population is still illiterate and that women make up 70 per cent of the illiterate and semi-literate in China today.[58] (See Table 5.) What is especially worrying to the government is that although the proportions are lower among females in the younger age-groups, they are still high,[59] which suggests that short-term gains from primary education are often lost, and indeed

Table 5 Illiteracy and semi-literacy among females, 1990, by age

	15–24	25–34	35–44	45+	Total
Percentage of population illiterate	6	9	18	52	22
Percentage of female population illiterate	9	15	29	72	32
Reduction in percentage of female illiterates in Population over 1982	-9	-23	-21	-16	-17
Female percentage of illiterates	73	78	74	68	70

Source: The Report of the People's Republic of China on the Implementation of the Nairobi Forward-Looking Strategies for the Advancement of Women, Beijing, China, 1994.

it is my own impression in villages that children had to be in school for at least three to four years for there to be long-term and useful literacy and that a higher proportion of girls than boys in many poor regions of China seldom had such an advantage.

Since 1988 much of the attention given to improving education standards of women has been concentrated on reducing the young and middle-aged illiterates by several million each year with the introduction of a number of measures to popularize the advantages of literacy and encourage women to attend long-term literacy classes. Government agencies plan that there should be a shown correlation between education and the acquisition of skills and between education and income so as to illustrate the advantages of literacy. The government has also imposed new sanctions against those not sending girls to school and against those employing child labour as part of the new measures to legally prescribe compulsory primary education. It is also planned to make special funds available to aid female education by establishing a wider range of local schools such as winter, seasonal and evening schools or schools with day-care centres for younger siblings and distance learning for women in remote areas, concentrated classes for busy and travelling women and segregated classes where appropriate for some minority nationalities. National figures showing declining female illiteracy suggest that generally it is not so difficult to persuade parents of the benefits of literacy or of sending their children to primary school, but it has been much more difficult to persuade rural parents that the advantages of long-term education for girls is the same as that for boys.

In the countryside, because of the temporary stay of daughters and new economic policies encouraging the expansion of family-income generating activities, some parents have shown themselves to be even more reluctant to send their daughters to school than before and the drop-out rate for girl pupils, even at primary school level, is now reported to be rather higher than in the past. In poorer rural areas girls may not attend school, and if they do, their attendance is not at all uniform; they frequently start school at a later age and it is estimated that 70 per cent of all those students who drop out are female. That girls are still seen to have less claim on the familial resources is important given that the costs of education have to be mostly and increasingly met by peasant families whose incomes are no longer rising to meet the increasing costs of agricultural and other inputs. The problems of resourcing education in villages in the face of reduced state allocations have not been solved in many regions, and there remains a heavy reliance placed on donations, fees and levies at the household and village level. The cost of schooling for households is rising and already prohibitive in some poor rural regions, which will continue to be disadvantaged by a policy heavily reliant on local resources. In these circumstances daughters are less likely to have a claim on scarce family resources so long as any investment in daughters will be lost to another family on marriage.

During the reform years, as in the past, much of the emphasis on the importance of education for girls and women had to do with their self-improvement or their acquisition of basic educational and vocational skills in order that they enter the workplace on an equal footing with their male peers. However, the emphasis on the female experience of education and the reporting and official validation of that experience, just as for employment, has emphasized that women alone cannot solve the problem of discrimination; rather, any solution also requires new societal attitudes towards women. It was this shift in emphasis from the responsibilities of women to those of society which led to the separation out of women workers' and more general female-specific problems, needs and interests and the formulation of female-specific demands or women's rights to protect these needs and interests. Indeed, the first decade of reform ended with the formulation of a new law solely devoted to the definition and protection of women's rights for the first time in China's history.

Women's rights

The increasing translation of the experience of discrimination into a plea for separate and legally-enshrined women's rights was the result of a growing demand by the Women's Federation that can be clearly seen in the reports and platforms of the four sequential national women's congresses held throughout the reform period. It is the deliberation of the national women's congresses, organized by the Women's Federation, that sets the direction of the women's movement for successive five-year periods, much as does the Five Year Plan for China's economy. The Women's Federation has long concerned itself with the role and status of women, albeit with varying degrees of success. The Communist Party from its very beginnings nurtured the separate organization of women in line with its early recognition of the special oppression of women (in addition to the general oppression shared by men and women of the same class) and of the importance for women of having their own organizational network that could take up women's issues and from which they could negotiate for new rights and opportunities. In practice, the government has required that the Women's Federation fulfil twin goals: the first required it to act as a mechanism of the Party apparatus extending its influence among a female constituency in a bid to gain its support for state policies, and the second required it to act as a separate pressure-group encouraging women to take an active part in defining and asserting their own needs and demands. In practice too, the two goals were not always mutually supportive and by the later years of the Revolution it became clear that the women's organization had come to operate within a very narrow prescription.

As a mass organization created by the government, the Women's Federation had been more effective in soliciting women's support for government policies than in getting them changed to take account of women's needs and especially those needs that did not appear directly to contribute to the prior goals of increasing production and promoting economic development. Given that the rhetoric of equality so masked female experience of discrimination, perhaps the Women's Federation itself perceived no need to redefine or further take up the cause of women's rights. However, once the rhetoric of equality could no longer be seen to represent female experience, then the Women's Federation lost little opportunity in taking up the cause of women's rights. My own view is that the turning-point came following the reports of a sharp increase in female infanticide when the government charged the Women's Federation to investigate the scale of the problem of female infanticide on the grounds that 'it would be a gross dereliction of duty if they should let this problem take its own course and not concern themselves with it.' The Women's Federation took this new responsibility seriously and, in turn, it was this special responsibility that precipitated a change in the role of the Women's Federation, culminating in the eventual formulation of its demands for a special women's law enshrining a wide spectrum of women's rights.

If the platforms of the four congresses for women held since 1978 are examined in sequence, it is clear that, after 1978, there is a gradual increase of interest in women's rights in ensuing congresses, with greater pleas that society should recognize women's rights to education, employment, property and person, and it was these pleas that culminated in the publication of a Women's Law in 1992. Twelve years earlier, at the Fourth National Congress held in 1978, the first for some twenty years, women had once more been exhorted to unite and forward their interests by encouraging the Communist Party to make work among women an important component of its work and to criticize the Party when it neglected women's interests.[60] At the Congress, a member of the Communist Party suggested to the Women's Federation that it should itself take more seriously the representation of women's special interests:

> The National Women's Federation and women's federations at provincial, municipal or autonomous regional level throughout the country should overcome the phenomenon of acting as a government organisation, forge close ties with the masses, gradually make themselves a mass organisation and become a better link between the Party and the masses of women. Women's organisations should do a good job carrying out investigation and study at the basic level and among the masses. Women's federations at various levels should be concerned about women's weal and woe and listen to their voices in order to really become a mouthpiece of the women's masses, an important representative of their interests and the home of women.[61]

The President of the National Women's Federation also urged women to speak out and assert their needs regardless of the consequences: 'In handling problems of immediate concern to women we should not fear giving offence or taking some risks, we must dare speak and be good at speaking in support of women.'[62] It seemed that the Women's Federation had the support of the government to speak out in favour of women's interests and, within carefully defined limits, it did so.

If the beginnings of a shift in rhetoric could be detected, there was also evidence of a continuing tension between the dual tasks of the Women's Federation to act both as a separate pressure group in defence of women's interests and as a mechanism for soliciting support for the Party and government. Indeed, the very definitions of the tasks of the Women's Federation as outlined at the Women's Congress in 1978 indicated that it should:

> resolutely implement the Party's general and specific policies and fully arouse enthusiasm among the broad masses of women, and how to mobilise the women to carry out the general task for the new period is the new problem for the women's movement.[63]

If the Women's Federation could and did speak out in defence of women's rights, it seemed that it was the Party that continued to decide which rights were legitimate and to circumscribe the independence of the Women's Federation. The single most important theme of the

National Congress in 1978 was still that the new line of the Party was to be the fundamental line of the women's movement and that the central task of the Party was also the central task of the women's movement.[64]

Perhaps the contradictions between the rhetoric of independence for the Women's Federation on the one hand and adherence to the Party line on the other was best revealed in a much publicized speech made by the Secretary of the Communist Party Central Committee two years later in 1980 which stated that:

> all the organisations of the Women's Federation should bring into full play the role of women in *working independently under the leadership of the Party, and according to the Party's line, principles and policies* and give full play to women's merits on the basis of their specific characteristics [emphasis added].[65]

The main assumption underlying such a pronouncement was that the Women's Federation fully represented both the interests of the Party and of women. Furthermore, these were assumed to be one and the same. It is as if a bargain had been struck: in return for supporting women's rights, the government expected the support of the Women's Federation for all its general policies.

It was this assumption more than any other that had characterized the work of the Women's Federation during its revolutionary history and caused it to implement general Party policies first and only then to study, analyse and draw out the practical implications that recent policies may have had for women. It was clear from a variety of sources, reports, formal interviews and informal conversations that the Women's Federation perceived its prior role as being to publicize and elicit support for the new policies and only retrospectively did it begin to spell out some of the likely repercussions for women. So women were encouraged by their own organisations to support the responsibility system, expand domestic sidelines, undertake outwork, work in the cooperative and service sectors of the economy, take out single-child family certificates and abolish the betrothal gift and dowry as if these Party policies could only be of benefit to women. However, these benefits were increasingly to be questioned as the Women's Federation was charged by the government with investigating many of the more obvious experiences of discrimination.

In contrast to the 1978 Congress, the balance in responsibility and accountability can be seen to have shifted when speeches at the Fifth National Congress of Women in 1983 primarily emphasized the role of the Women's Federation in defending and protecting women and their interests rather than primarily soliciting support for Party and government policies.[66] In her report on the work of the Women's Federation since the previous Congress, its President, Kang Keqing, spoke of the achievements of the past five years, but she equally emphasized the gender-specific demands of the Women's Federation and the necessity to strengthen its own organization, which would enable it to make and meet these demands. She called for the rights and interests of women and children to be protected:

> What demands attention is that remnant feudal ideas of regarding men as superior to women and traditional prejudices against women have re-emerged in recent years. For example, some localities and units have placed unreasonable demands and restrictions in recruiting or promoting women and women cadres. Some areas and units bluntly refuse to admit needed and qualified women; some neglect the labour protection of women in productive work. Parents interfering in their children's freedom of marriage, arranging marriage for money, marrying in order to extort money and other similar cases have become fairly commonplace.
>
> What is intolerable is the fact that some ugly phenomenon that had been wiped out long ago in new China have begun to recur. Criminal acts of drowning female infants, insulting women, persecuting mothers who gave birth to girls, and selling and harming women and children have occurred frequently. In some areas these have reached serious proportions.
>
> We women must unite with others in society and resolutely struggle against all acts harming women and children and vigorously help the public security and judicial organs crack down on these criminal activities ... and firmly protect the legitimate rights and interests of women and children.[67]

The main task of the Women's Federation in 1983 was defined as closely associating itself with women's interests in order that it might investigate, study and solve these problems. The proceedings of the Fifth Congress confirmed that the reappearance of infanticide and violence had done much to generate the gender-specific demands of the Women's Federation and to legitimize the open presentation of the Women's Federation in its role as defender and protector of women. In this, the Women's Federation had the full support of the state, thus fulfilling at least for the time being the prescription that the Women's Federation fully represented both the Party and women's interests and that these could be one and the same. Although there were no apparent conflicts between the two bodies voiced at the Congress, there were still some limits to the legitimacy of the Women's Federation's voice on many broader political and economic issues.

Similarly, at the Sixth National Congress in 1988, both representatives of the state and of the Women's Federation stressed that the legitimate rights of women were still far from universally recognized.[68] The President of the Women's Federation called on the whole of society to adopt a more civilized and progressive attitude towards women and fight against sex discrimination in new joint efforts to safeguard women's equality with men in political, economic and cultural fields as well as in their social and family lives. Likewise the President of China at the opening ceremony, after paying a warm tribute to Chinese women calling them a 'great force for the country's construction and reform', also stressed that 'the government and the whole of society should show more concern for women and better safeguard their interests and condemn sex discrimination and maltreatment of women.'[69]

He reminded the delegates that for various historical reasons, prejudice against women still existed and maltreatment and abuse of children and women happened frequently: 'Those behaviours are intolerable and those who encroach on the rights of women and children should be punished.' This was an important statement by the President, for it shifted some of the responsibility for discrimination to others and not just to the failings of women, as had been one of the predominant themes previously. Subsequent to this conference, there were two important initatives that resulted from these repeated and increased calls for more attention to the separation out and protection of women's rights. The first was the establishment of a new Women's and Children's Work Co-ordination Committee by the State Council in March 1990 and the second was the promulgation of the new Law Protecting Women's Rights in 1992.

The creation of the Women's and Children's Work Co-ordination Committee at the highest administrative level was an important symbol of the new importance attached to reducing discrimination against women and a recognition that such problems could not be solved by such mass organizations as women's federations alone, since the issues related to politics, economics, culture and other fields and 'should be dealt with by the whole society'.[70] A women's and children's group was attached to the committee and a permanent office for the committee was established at the All-China Women's Federation, while most provinces, autonomous regions and municipalities directly under the central government also set up special organizations for women and children. Its central committee, consisting of representatives from all the leading ministries and relevant organizations, was to have as its main task that of 'coordinating issues relating to women and children that should be settled jointly by the governments and units concerned'. The establishment of this coordinating agency marked an important step in an administrative system characterized by strongly demarcated vertical lines of authority and responsibility that had made any cooperation between Ministries difficult. It had also reduced the responsiblity of any one Ministry for gender issues, which then usually became the exclusive charge of the Women's Federation, not itself a Ministry but a mass organization. The name was later changed to the Women's and Children's Work Committee under the State Council in 1993 and its work so far has mostly involved researching regulations to protect women from abduction and prostitution, formulating laws to protect women's rights and the publicization and drawing up of this legislation. The second important initiative arising from the repeated and increasing calls for more attention to women's rights was the promulgation of a new women's law.

The Women's Law

The new law protecting the rights of women in 1992 (see Appendix 2) was the first law specifically defining a set of women's rights in China and was thus heralded as illustrating anew the importance attached by the government to women's rights and interests. Chen Muhua, Vice Chair of the National People's Congress Standing Committee and President of the All-China Women's Federation stated:

> The law on protection of women's rights and interests will produce a profound and far-reaching influence over China's efforts to protect women's rights and interests, raise the status of women, promote equality between men and women and arouse the support of women for socialist modernisation in an all-round way. It indicates China shows special concern for women and attaches great importance to women's rights and interests ...[71]

The Law set out the rights of women in political, economic, cultural and social life and with regard to property, marriage, divorce and the family. It protects the rights of women to life and health, outlawing infanticide, abuse or any form of abduction. When these lawful rights were infringed by others, women had the right to request and expect departments concerned to help remedy the infringement or to take legal proceedings with the people's court, and disciplinary action was to be taken against those who did not provide the requisite help. It has been stressed several times that 'the awakening of women to gender rights'[72] would be completely impossible without the strong support of China's laws and that 'more and more Chinese women will get accustomed to safeguarding their rights and interests through legal means.'[73] To accustom women to the idea of resorting to legal means, the promulgation of the law was followed by a month-long women's rights campaign to study and publicize the new law.

One of the very impressive features of the first revolutionary years in the early 1950s was the attention paid to educating people in the new laws in publicity campaigns following on closely after their promulgation. But legal recourse in appropriate conditions had never been institutionalized in China; rather less accountable local cadres mediated disputes and dispensed judgements within the units or regions under their administration. What distinguishes the reform decade is the new interest in the role of law and the establishment of newly available and accessible legal institutions, and the Women's Federation has played its part in acquainting women with their legal rights and providing help in obtaining legal redress in the face of discrimination. From its experience in the early 1950s, the Women's Federation had learned that legislation in support of women's rights and education in support of the law was not enough; there also had to be back-up legal institutions, personnel and individual support available to women to aid them in the exercise of their rights. Indeed, experience had taught grassroot women's organizations that 'the rights and interests of women and children are best protected by enforcing the laws and regulations designed to help abused women and by acting as their legal advocates and helping them exercise these rights.'[74]

In support of the various general laws and regulations published at the onset of reform in the 1980s, one of the main aims of the Women's Federation had been to set up a network of legal centres to advise female victims of violence, collect evidence and pursue offenders through the courts. These centres had been set up at provincial, city and county administrative levels to which lawyers and legal workers, most of whom were women, had been recruited to provide legal counsel and allied services to women.[75] To sensitize women to the protection provided by the new laws and to the availability of legal services, short and concentrated publicity programmes had been instituted in many localities during 1983–84. Classes were held to enable women cadres to study the pertinent provisions of the constitution, the Marriage and other civil laws and to follow the procedural laws on criminal cases. Public forums were held on the laws and legal counselling centres were set up on street corners and in parks where legal advisors made themselves available to answer queries and investigate grievances. It was reported that the most common questions on which help was sought had to do with the inheritance of daughters, the legal rights of the elderly to receive support and matters to do with divorce procedures.[76]

Publicity and practical campaigns such as these provided an infrastructure for a new campaign in support of the new Women's Law. During this campaign it was reported that the cases brought to the notice of the Women's Federation in a single month totalled that usual for half a year. In one case reported in the media, the Women's Federation in Beijing received an unusual joint telegram from 118 women employees of a power station in far Heilongjiang province outlining their refusal to be charged double levies in the fundraising for the factory's new living quarters. Instead of turning to their husbands, relatives or some sympathetic factory leaders, they decided to base their case on Article 23 of the new Law which stated that 'Women should be equal with men in the allotment of housing and enjoyment of welfare benefits.' This was widely cited as an example of the ways in which 'women are awakening to this new "legal shelter" and more women have learned to resort to legal means instead of swallowing unfair treatment.'[77]

The new law was also the main subject of discussion at the Seventh National Congress of Women held in September 1993.[78] Of the nine main goals outlined by the Women's Federation for the 1990s, four referred directly to women's rights as individuals, in society, in employment and in marriage and the family. The remaining three advocated an increase in female participation in politics and education and improvements in their health and reduction in domestic labour. If the promulgation of a Women's Law constituted a shift towards recognizing the responsibilities of society for seeing that women's rights were protected, it also marked a milestone in the separation out of women's separate needs, interests and demands. The redefinition of women's roles and status could not be willed by women alone however much they improved themselves; the validity of their needs and interests had to be recognized by society. The increasing awareness and investigation of women's separate problems and needs in living and work during the early years of reform not only led to a new interest in women's rights but also gave birth to more academic but policy-linked women's studies.

Women's studies

The initiative for separating out women's studies from other studies was spearheaded by a number of social scientists and scholars in institutions of higher education who had become interested in researching women's problems and by the Women's Federation which, seeking to reaffirm its legitimacy in representing the interests of women, commissioned numbers of popular and local studies of women's history. In 1980 the Women's Federation had taken a decision to establish local archives and research centres to encourage its members to write histories of the women's movement in their region or unit. The separation out of women's studies as a separate category of social studies was very much based on the rationale that understanding the history of women, their special problems and conceptualizing women's issues was only possible if women were separated out from the generalized definition of men and the study of men. According to Wan Shanping, the term *Women's*

Studies, introduced into China in a book review in *Studies of Social Sciences Abroad* of Shirai Atsushi's *Women's Studies and the History of Women's Movements,* was first seriously discussed at the first National Conference on Theoretical Studies of Women sponsored by the Women's Federation in late 1984.[79] Thus participants aimed at carrying out studies of women, researching women's problems theoretically and establishing various branches of women's studies in their specialized academic fields. In 1985 a women's committee attached to the Henan Institute of Futurology was set up and it led to the formal establishment of the Women's Studies Centre at Zhengzhou University in Henan in May 1987. It was the first special organization of women's studies in colleges, universities and institutes, and in the past few years the Research Centre at Zhengzhou has become an important academic base for Chinese women's studies and the centre of a nation-wide academic network in this field. It has compiled a women's studies series and essays and organized seminars and public lectures on women's studies.

In the past few years many other university discussion and research groups on women's problems have been established with a view to attracting broader attention to women's studies and women's problems. In March 1990 the Women's Studies Centre at Zhengzhou University organized a 'Workshop on Women's Participation and Development' to review women's studies and set up programmes for collecting systematic data on social attitudes towards women and female attitudes towards society for reference and for the long-term construction of a theoretical framework for women's studies.[80] Many other centres for women's studies have followed suit and have also collected data on women's experience and attitudes as a prelude to thinking about the problems of women both practically and conceptually. Although much of their new work in women's studies has reduced the influence of the Women's Federation and its domination of the discourse on gender issues, most of these new women's centres, institutes or societies work alongside the Women's Federation and are affiliated to it either because they were themselves initiated by the Women's Federation or because they took the decision that it was better to influence the organization from within. One of the most outspoken of the advocates for women's studies in China, Li Xiaojiang of Zhengzhou University, Henan, in critically analysing the Women's Federation has also paid tribute to its recognition of the importance of women's studies and to its establishment of women's institutes and research bodies in most cities and provinces. Attached to the Women's Federation, they have been encouraged to investigate and collect information about the experience of women in different fields and make this information publicly known via lecture, seminar and media report.

One of these research bodies, the Beijing Society of Women's Theory, founded in 1985, is made up of cadres of the Beijing Women's Federation who believed that this organization should not only help women to solve actual problems they encounter in their daily lives, but probe into and study women's problems theoretically.[81] Its members were made up of experts and scholars of the social sciences and institutions of higher learning who were interested in women's studies and cadres of the Women's Federation who have been specializing in women's work for many years. In the first few years after this society was founded, it set about 'studying the reality'. It did extensive investigation and research on women from different backgrounds in Beijing, and the results provided a basis for policy and laws concerning women that were beginning to be formulated at that time. In 1990 the Beijing Society of Women's Theory co-operated with the Guangzhou Society of Women's Issues and the Departments of Social Work at the University of Hong Kong to set up a research project on 'Comparative Studies on Women's Employment in Beijing, Guangzhou and Hong Kong'. The project set out to observe the employment conditions, the employment ideas and the views about equality between men and women in Beijing and Guangzhou and compare these with the views of women in Hong Kong by studying different social systems and different stages of economic development of the three areas. Also in 1990 the society took part in a large-scale survey called 'Social Positions of Chinese Women' organised by the All China Women's Federation. This survey specifically targeted marriage and family, education levels, self-recognition and social identification, lifestyles and the health of women in Beijing. In 1991 this society, along with the Beijing Institute of Social Investigation, also organized a survey of young female entrepreneurs who worked in private enterprises or individually-managed establishments in the Beijing area, acquiring data that investigated women's new outlooks on employment and trends in female employment in the wake of reform and the Open-Door policy.

In one of my own interviews, Professor Tao Chun-fang, deputy-director of the Women's Studies Research Institute in China also affiliated to the Women's Federation, emphasized that the role of her institute was to offer theoretical justification for women's studies, to provide advice to legislative bodies and to incorporate a training and educational element into projects that will widely benefit women. Combinations of these goals can be seen in its main areas of interest and research. The Research Institute has recently published a number of books on women's history covering the previous hundred years and is now conducting new research on the history of women during the past forty years of the revolution. In 1991 its members had undertaken a survey of women's status in twenty-three provinces in order to have 'an objective view of women's social status undertaken by women themselves'. Much of this work covering women's employment, education, political participation, family, women's health, women's rights and social ideology has been published already in report and statistical forms. Recently the Research Institute for women has turned its attention to the provision of reproductive insurance by cities and units to cover women's maternity and other benefits, the payment of which has hindered their recruitment and promotion in many enterprises. Some of this work is the result of a comprehensive study of reproduction and women's health undertaken by the Research Institute, which began in 1992 and is an interesting example of the inputs which women's studies can make in widening both the multi-disciplinary and the practical policy interest of important gender issues. In this respect one very interesting input of women's studies has to do with reproduction and female health, which was previously the sole responsibility of medical bodies.

In April 1992, the Women's Studies Institute, with sponsorship from the Ford Foundation, held the first conference on reproduction and health where, as well as the usual number of expert panels addressing topics ranging from menstruation to menopause, birth to ageing and contraception to sexual relations, reference was made to women's studies and the investigation of women's health by women. At the conference cadres from women's study institutes from each province were com-missioned to carry out their own investigations, discussions and studies of women's health and reproduction and were offered training in research methods. As a result there was a systematic investigation of women's health problems and a spread of information about women's health care with the establishment of consulting services or gynaeco-logical clinics, which also served as local centres for women's studies. A follow-up conference was held in January 1994 at which the study groups presented their findings. Some of the groups in the more developed regions where primary health care is already available had devoted their attention to ageing and menopause, while less developed regions concentrated on preventive health, the establishment of clinics, means of transport to hospitals and the funding of health-care pro-grammes for women and children.

One of the important findings was the widespread incidence of reproductive tract infections in the poor rural regions and the difficult relationships between women and doctors or gynaecologists, which led to delays in seeking treatment. This experiment in combining research, practical investigation and women's solidarity is seen to be an important precedent in both developing women's studies and meeting the practical needs and interests of women.[82] It is no accident that women's health is the mainstay of this precedent, as it is becoming one of the most important of women's problems needing investigation and is increasingly seen as the prerequisite to the success of most other contemporary programmes to benefit women and especially poor women. This was brought home to both Dr Mary Anne Burriss of the Ford Foundation in Beijing, which has provided much of the sponsorship for the programme, and myself when we visited poor villages in the south-west province of Yunnan in 1991 to investigate women's health and health-care among other topics.

The Yunnan villages were nestled in forested mountains in the east of the province near the Guangxi border; some were only accessible by mud road in dry weather and then for the majority of villagers without a mule only by foot; others could only be reached by a foot track. The houses were mostly of yellow clay or mud with natural wood beams and thatch, picturesque on the outside, but so very poor and dark and sometimes chokingly dusty within. Because there was little in the way of furniture, bedding, clothes or food beyond the barest of essentials, it was usually a case of crouching or sitting on slabs of wood a few inches off the ground, which made this stay and these interviews one of the most physically taxing of my many field experiences. There was no drinking water in the vicinity of the villages for much of the year, when villagers had to trek four hours to and from the nearest source of water, sometimes twice a day. There was no electricity in the villages and some of the villagers were so poor that they could not even afford the sticks, paper or matches to light their way from house to house after dark. The villages were located in one of the poorest 273 counties of China, so defined because their per capita cash incomes, per capita grain supplies and per capita land allocations were among the lowest in China.

In common with other poor, remote and mountainous villages in this region, they lacked sufficient available flat arable land to provide for their grain supplies and spent much of their hard labour cultivating steep slopes for very low returns. In addition to cultivating grain, the fortunate women of the villages raised a few animals, which in the absence of alternative economic activities in the village assumed prime significance in determining the wealth, cash income and welfare of a peasant household. Animals were the most important single source of cash income; however, they were not plentiful and, given the high death rate among chickens and pigs, they consituted a scarce and vulnerable household resource dividing village households into three categories which were referred to as 'not poor', 'poor' and 'very poor'. The poor and very poor households of the village, the majority, had in common a low per capita arable land allocations, a shortage of grain and few animals and they frequently suffered a shortage of labour through premature death, physical illness or disability and mental incapacity. Indeed, the most important factors determining the income, well-being and welfare of individual households, in addition to land allocations and the number of family members of labouring age, were the health and labour capacities of the male and female labourers. The very poorest households in the village had all suffered chronic disease, physical illness or disability, premature death or mental incapacity or had a high number of either elderly or young dependents. In a random sample of households, health profiles revealed that few households had escaped illness or death.

In household 1, consisting of five people, and 'not poor', the mother had suffered a serious illness some years before but had recovered in recent years. In household 2, with ten members , and 'not poor', there had been no serious illness in recent years. In household 3, with two people, and 'very poor', the widow was in a constant state of ill health with an eye problem. In household 4, with seven members, and 'not poor', two boys and a daughter had died: one son had died three days after birth from tetanus – he had been carried to hospital, which would not accept him once he was diagnosed as having tetanus; another son, 3 years old, died in hospital probably from pneumonia; the 7-year-old daughter also died from pneumonia, apparently 'very fast' before a doctor could be consulted. In household 5, with six people, and 'poor', one child of 2 years old had died rapidly within two days of falling ill with high fever; the husband had a persistent cough and was ill with frightening stomach cramps every two weeks during which 'he seemed to die'. In household 7, with four members, and 'very poor', one 2-year-old son had died from dysentery after a visit to the township hospital; the mother was mentally incapacitated and not in good health and one of the daughters was also mentally retarded. In household 8, with four people, and 'very poor', both parents were mentally incapacitated. Eight children had been born and five had died. This was not the only case in the village where such a high proportion of children in a single household had died. We learned of several others when we held what seemed to be one of the first meetings of village women to discuss reproduction and female health. Then we learned of the high incidence of debilitating reproductive tract infections among the women that did not even count as illness; the difficult conditions of home and hospital childbirth and the deaths of children; the desire of the younger women to limit the numbers of their children and their lack of knowledge of or availability of contraception; the expense of scarce paper making for difficulties in coping with menstruation and the absence of clinics and even medicines. It was said that the doctors were too poor to provide medicines, the villagers too poor to pay for them, and the village had no funds with which to provide a subsidy to pay for clinics or medicines. The village doctors had minimal training, difficulties in reading and writing and the hospitals demanded prohibitive cash deposits on arrival that deterred the villagers from making the arduous journey. Given that the township hospital had but a stethoscope and thermometer, even villagers who had the stamina or the money were reluctant even in the most extreme circumstances to attend their local hospital – a situation that had led to the common association of hospital with death and the depressing health profiles both in households and of women.

It was this visit that gave an impetus to the further investigation of women's health and reproduction sponsored by the Ford Foundation. One of the hallmarks of the new women's studies has not only been its emphasis on investigating the experience of women and combining practical with theoretical concerns, but also its focus on both the social and the personal. At the present time, women in a variety of urban venues are coming together with increasing confidence in the value of solidarity to understand and study their condition. As Li Xiaojiang has forecast, every class of women has its own pressing issues so that 'within a certain number of years the issues that will be defined as "female" will be of every hue and shade and of unprecedented variety, and their boundaries will be difficult to establish.'[83] Retrospectively, however, the women that I have interviewed in the past few years identify the main legacy of the revolutionary years as the 'coming out of women into society'. This phenomenon used to be referred to as the 'revolution within a revolution', but now women's organizations and studies have broadened their brief to draw attention to a third revolution or that within the female person as necessary, not only in order to take advantage of the new social opportunities offered by reform, but in order that they benefit and become modern women.

'The four selfs'

The Sixth National Women's Congress had first officially promoted women's 'self-development', which has been defined as 'the strengthening of the principles of women's four selfs – self-respect, self-confidence, self-reliance and self-improvement'.[84] Other phrases referred to at the Congress and in its associated literature refer to self-esteem, self-awareness, self-possession and self-love. What is new is not so much the notions of esteem, improvement, awareness, reliance, confidence and respect but their self-referential qualities. The shift in importance to the self that is also female and merits separate definition, discussion and deference is new. Instead of the 'we' of the factory, farm or family unit, there is the 'I' of the woman and a recognizable process of attempted or preliminary exploration or discovery as to who she is or who she might become in a new Chinese society. Now women are perceived as already having entered the social but at the cost of sacrificing something of their selves for socialism, the Chinese state, the urban enterprise or the rural collective, quite apart from their families, husbands and children. Currently then, it is their own self-strengthening that has become an important platform. The new emphasis on self-referential qualities has drawn attention to the distinctive qualities attributable to the female self or the feminine and to their difference from the male or masculine. The emphasis and reflections on gender distinction and difference grows out of the explicit rejection of the previous revolutionary 'masculinization of the female', 'female man' or 'super-women's masculinization' and marks the separation out of the female from the previous generalized androgynous definition of comrade or worker of predominantly masculine or male image. As Li Xiaojiang, like so many other women, has noted in retrospect, they knew they were women, but they knew less the difference between themselves and men.[85]

The Reform period is thus marked by a new interest in the image and presentation of the feminine, focusing first on physical appearance and adornment. This is not surprising given that one of the most important characteristics distinguishing reform from revolution is the new interest in consumption, in consumer goods and in their style, colour, material and brand name, all of which have generated a new phenomenon -- consumer desire. Eyes, and not just those on the advertising billboards, are firmly fixed on consumer objects to do with fashioning the individual and furnishing the home. Shopping has not only become a serious recreation and a sociable exercise with much noisy consultation; the new interest in commodities and lifestyles has brought about a new relation between people and things, so that persons have become classified not so much by their class background or 'work' or occupation as previously, as by the possession of objects or their evaluation, so that identity has become associated with lifestyle rather than class label. Adorning the body and the home has drawn attention to the persons and their immediate environments in a proliferation of style statements that is born of income generation and generates a sense of individual, family and gender difference. The desired and different qualities of the feminine are outwardly symbolized by choice of colour, style and fashion. One of the most noticeable features of recent years to long-time observers, and symbolic of wider shifts, has been the near disappearance of the uniform blue garb of the revolution and the subsequent and sudden swings in fashion. Gone are the days when I noticed the individual and stylish twist of the hairgrip that served to differentiate the modern young Shanghai 'miss' from her peers. Despite an interval of more than ten years, the visitor to China today is still taken aback by the great variety of and sudden shifts in fashionable colour, style and fabric. The all-pervasive interest in fashion is evident in crowded shop and market-place and the emergence of the fashionable young. Older women too are determined not to be omitted and are also seen to be 'eager to beautify themselves'.[86] Magazines now have at least some, if not all, pages devoted to fashion and the fashion show is now a routine event. In addition to dressing fashionably, there is a great interest in make-up, skin care, jewellery, cosmetics and hair-style, all accentuating the enhancement of physical appearance that is the new attribute of women who 'know how to be women'.

For role models too, the relation of working women to consumption is as important as their productive roles. In a new trend, the adornment of the role models may be as fully described in detailed terms of dress and other fashion accessories as their other attributes. An interesting example can be cited of the description of one such model in which the commentator also draws attention to the novelty of this apprehension.

When I went to the Shenzhen Daily Use Goods Factory to gather material, I found sitting in the office a dignified, beautiful young woman. Her hairdo was done quite tastefully, two gleaming ear-rings adorned her earlobes, a glittering necklace hung from her neck, suspended from her wrist was an exquisite small golden bracelet, and encircling the ring finger of her right hand was a conspicuous golden ring. Ah, one look and I realised that it was Fan Liying, deputy to the provincial People's Congress and pro-vincial model worker.

I could not help feeling stunned. So many stories about her tumbled about in my brain ... Originally she was an embroiderer ... her fingers were covered with needle marks ... two years ago, she happily took over the post of cashier, giving up her monthly income of about ¥300 without complaint and earning only a little more than 100 yuan ... and in the past two years has not made the slightest error ...

Yet I simply didn't quite believe my own eyes when I saw her. As if she saw my astonishment, she smiled gently, revealing shallow dimples, and said 'I am a twenty-three-year-old woman, and of course I like to dress up.'

Suddenly I understood. Model workers of the 1980s are good at creating wealth, and they also understand how to enjoy it. This is probably the charm of our times.

A model woman worker dressed in gold and jade? The way some people see it, perhaps this is a great outrage. In their eyes, a model worker who fits the image should be covered with grease and dirt, dressed in blue and black.

But nowadays in the Shenzhen Special Economic Zone, model workers no longer have that old appearance. There, the wage system has been reformed, and anyone who works hard has a higher income. Naturally, the income of model workers is higher than that of most and they live better lives than most. Not only do they dress in suits and leather shoes, they also have money to buy gold and jade. So why be astonished that model women workers are dressed in gold and jade? Rather we should say that if model workers live better lives than most, they will have greater appeal and will encourage more people to work diligently. If model workers only get 'a suit of blue and black' for their work, I'm afraid no one will want to be a model. From the changes in the style of dress of this model woman worker, we can catch a glimpse of the economic development of our nation and the change in people's concept of consumption![87]

The adoption of new fashions, make-up and jewellery by women is not only part of a new interest in consumption; it also marks a new emphasis on the feminine or female as separate and different from masculine or male.

Uniquely female

This interest in and new reflection on gender difference can be seen as a reaction against the enforced female appropriation of a male-defined world during the revolution when women are now seen to have responded to the call of the Communist Party to a point where they lost a sense of their female selves in the pursuit of gender sameness with a consequent loss of image, demeanour and perceptions distinctive to women and different from the male other. In emphasizing sexual difference rather than the sameness of revolution, attention had to be drawn to the qualities unique to women and female. In my own recent interviews, the quality that women most often thought to be uniquely female was 'softness', which together with nurturing qualities contributed to their uniquely female capacity for caring. However much attention might shift to definitions of the female self and the process of becoming a woman, it is also the case that definitions of the female take as their reference point the male other and separation from or 'othering' in defining of the female self. Although meanings are so often born of contrasts, with self-definition mainly resting on othering or demarcation from the other, the search for what is different and distinctive from the masculine does not start with questioning assumptions about the masculine so much as with the identification of 'woman's own perceptual world', 'women's own outlook and world' and 'inner qualities unique to women'. There has been a number of articles expressing the growing view that there is a peculiarly female perception of the 'natural world' that extends say from sexuality to tourism. For instance one article, entitled 'Women are the Natural Masters of the Perceptual World', argued that there are peculiarly female perceptions based on women's distinctive and different perception of nature and a rich perceptual world transcending and enriching male language and logic:

> I suddenly came to realise that the happiness derived from the perception of beautiful things is a true happiness in real life, a satisfaction, and confirms the perceptual world. Females are not as dull, shrivelled and abstract as males, who pretend to be serious all the time ... How can women protect their original clear rich and moving perceptual world?

Having established that women had a stronger claim to a superior natural pleasure, the writer goes on to translate this claim into a stronger claim for female sexual pleasure. The writer reveals that, although it was not until very late that she realized that the pleasure of sexual life not only belonged to men, she now thought that one of 'the happiest things in life is no doubt sexual pleasure for women'. Indeed, she thought:

> The female's longing for pleasure sometimes is stronger than the male's. However because of various reasons, mainly social reasons it seems, the females' strong desire and need for this pleasure have been depressed and hurt or even buried under social traditions that centered on men for thousands of years. They were crushed by various erroneous concepts, thoughts, customs and norms, which have caused many females to lose their chances in life, not knowing they should realise or demand to realise their own natural instincts. It seems that in the female's sexual pleasure, the rational is also mixed with perceptual ... The rational is not those concepts, thoughts, language and standards that can be recognised ... it has become one with the perceptual. Therefore they can get that unexplainable feeling and pleasure. Men can get their warmest and most delightful life in sexual contact with females ... [88]

The pursuit of contrasts in gender perception has led to some interesting reflections on gender difference. In one article, the author reflects on the different approaches distinguishing male and female tourists: the men rush round, with cameras, wanting to tour all the sights at rapid speed while women lingered taking in intensively the small, the hidden and the incidental at a more leisured pace. This contrast thought the author reflected and distinguished more generally female from male qualities:

> Nature has bestowed different gifts upon men and women. Men are usually impatient. For instance, when getting on a bus they

tend to elbow their way on, although they know everyone can have a seat. But women usually receive their gifts by lowering their heads.

Women are not like men, who seem to hunt hard after mountains and rivers. Compared with men's shining eyes, they usually half close their eyes to enjoy the scenery. Men value form, but women stress content ...

Men with education have created the phrase 'touring the scenic spots'. They play politics and war, so certainly they can do a good job of sightseeing mountains and rivers. Women with no education often have no chance to enjoy scenic spots, so they can only take it as a blessing when they can view green mountains and trees from their windows.[89]

Some women have even been heard to say (perversely?) that they wanted a girl not a boy child because of her capacity to appreciate the natural, emotion and experience:

A girl is more sensitive, has more capacity to feel everything – happiness, sorrow, all the sentiments. A girl can appreciate new experiences much more than boys. So the world is always a new world for her. That's why I want my baby to be a girl.[90]

Not surprisingly perhaps, the search for difference has once again led to an emphasis on those qualities thought to be traditionally and uniquely female such as gentleness, refinement, restraint, modesty, shyness and reserve or attributes, all requiring some degree of restraint if not submission in deportment and demeanour. Indeed, the rejection of sameness and pursuit of difference has led to an appreciation and cultivation of images based on the traditional definition of the feminine so clearly reminiscent of the first section of this book. However the search for what is female-specific cannot be seen merely as a reiteration of past qualities, for a prevalent theme of the new literature on female attributes includes female self-sufficiency and independence of person.

Independently female

Female independence now has a much wider definition than the notion of economic independence so commonly heralded during the revolution. Now it is something more that is advocated or an independence of personality and spirit that is now seen to have been previously inhibited in women by a 'spiritual footbinding' that 'deformed our souls'. Unfortunately, as one article stressed, 'many women do not know how to be women' in that, in limiting their horizons to appearance and adornment, they do not realize that independence of personality plus charm and elegance is the most seductive combination appealing to men and the most appropriate for the new society. 'Keep to this road' says the author 'and be true women.'[91] Noteworthy is the example of five young women students who, on establishing a successful campus candle-lit café, were irked when they were dubbed as 'the five warrior attendants'. They would have much preferred to be known as the 'five golden flowers', a more feminine image, although they also wanted to be appreciated for their 'strong determination' of which they were inordinately proud.[92] The most powerful and popular metaphor for the acquisition of a new feminine independence is that captured by the phrase 'not the moon'.

The phrase 'not the moon' was first used in a contemporary play to denote the realization of the heroine that she need not depend on the light of another, as does the moon, to make herself shine. The metaphor was afterwards adopted widely both to criticize women's dependence on men's reflective light and to advocate female self-reliance in developing 'their own brilliance'. Many writings including a television series have taken up this theme. An article in *Women's World* in 1985 entitled 'Woman is not the Moon' exhorted women to treasure this phrase:

> Woman is not the moon. It is true, woman is not an appendange of a man. As a member of society she has independent qualities; she has all the behaviour, morality, intelligence and ability of a human being. She can work and be creative ...
> Women is not the moon. She must rely on herself to shine. These are words that many pioneers of the women's liberation movement, valiant women, and heroines have inscribed with their their own actions, tears and blood. Let us treasure these words, remember them, and act on them. Hopefully each person can find her own path in life and develop her own brilliance.

The author argued that what most obviously stands in the way of female independence and individual shining-brightness is the continuing influence of old ideas subordinating woman to man:

> They believe that as women, we don't have to be strong. They think that as long as one finds a good husband to depend on, it will be enough to just live out one's days. Old ideas such as 'Woman is one of man's ribs,' 'If a woman does not have a husband, her body does not have an owner,' etc., still influence some people. Many believe that man is the supporter of the family; the only thing that a woman can do is help him at home as a virtuous wife and good mother; getting ahead is something for men to do. History and present circumstances make many of us women comrades oppressed and constrained. This makes it

impossible for us to display our talents, intelligence and creativity. We just become men's servants and their burden.[93]

If women have been encouraged to be independent, they also find themselves, in their own words, 'burdened by the wide rivers and high mountains' of contrasting social or male expectations of women. Women in Beijing I have talked to about recent policies towards women had strong views on the subject of independence. One 40-year-old university teacher thought that independence for women should be stressed, because from her experience as a teacher most young women were not sure about their own ideas unless applauded and were very dependent on their families and others for validation and approbation. An older woman I also interviewed instantly came up with her definition of the modern woman as 'one who plans her life without reference to men' at all stages of her life be it dressing to catch, competing for or living with and keeping her man. But she also simultaneously added that she was 'not being very realistic'. Continuing and current male expectations of women are perhaps most visibly displayed in male definitions of preferred or desirable marriage partners. According to one recent account, the desired female personality could not have more accurately reflected traditional virtues:

> The increasingly fierce competition in modern society pressures men more and more. They need a warm and harmonious family life, and want to find a life partner who is beautiful, gentle and kind-hearted. She should be both a virtuous wife and good mother – the traditional charm of Oriental woman, very womanly.[94]

In a recent city survey, male images of an ideal wife were reported to be of one 'who is beautiful, tall, healthy, soft, kind, well-mannered, loyal, virtuous and one who is skilled in domestic crafts (e.g. sewing, cooking and so forth) and can take care of children'.[95]

Much discussion centres around the conflict between socially approved qualities of 'virtuous wives and good mothers' and the ideal of the newly independent modern woman. A popular television series entitled *Women are not the Moon* centered on this female dilemma. The heroine, a beautiful young woman, is torn between pursuing a career 'after hard training' in the city as a fashion designer with 'a grand future in front of her' and marriage to a long-time sweetheart and now well-known entrepreneur who wants to marry her but keep her at home 'like a good wife'. The heroine however, believing that a woman is 'not the moon' and can shine without reflection from men, knows that she need not depend on a man, and thus she finally says goodbye to her young man in favour of pursuing her career – an ending that aroused much discussion among young viewers informally and in the press. Such tensions between the ideal of independence held out to women in their own literature and social expectations still surrounding female attributes and roles is most evident in interviews, letters and short stories written by older young women or older single daughters after the age of around 30 years.

Older 'single' women

Given their professional status it is just such older single daughters who have the potential for leading independent lives, but this they are not permitted to do formally or informally. These single women are often referred to as *da guniang* (big daughter or big girl), which reflects the importance still attached to marriage in becoming a woman or an adult. From their mid-twenties, these young women come under pressure to be married and it is their difficulties in finding husbands or men who will have them that has brought their plight to public attention. They find themselves in an anomalous position. Officially, the older single woman has no existence separate from or independent of her family. For instance, she cannot have a registration separate from her parents' household and therefore has no individual right to separate housing or other benefits. The young women themselves say they not only come under pressure to marry from others, but they themselves say they feel 'incomplete', 'without a future' or lacking self-determination without a marriage partner. One short story illustrates the plight voiced again and again by such older daughters. Entitled *Hopes Worn Away*, it charts the feelings of an unmarried woman whose hopes for a married future had little by little worn slowly away so that at 30 years of age, she described herself as 'old, shrivelled, dying' as she plucked up the courage to stare in the mirror and look at the 'shell of her body' or 'the sad remains of her life'. 'I'd made a fairy tale for myself but now found that I'd entered a nightmare, with me as the fairy tale's old hag – an old hag that everyone called "Old Maid". I felt a chill spreading over me.'[96]

An older woman in her late thirties thought that gossip was the worst feature of a single life. 'If you're different,' she said, 'there can be a lot of gossip and you're different if you're not married, especially if you are of a certain age. People start asking "What's wrong?" as if there is something peculiar about the single state.'[97] One older single woman described what women like her go through, 'day in and day out':

I still have strong desires in my heart. But I hate the prejudice that I have to suffer. I don't know if I can put up with it for ever. As a single woman in China, it is very hard to stand up. There are three kinds of us – the unmarried, the divorced, and the

widowed. It's hard for all of us, but the worst is to be unmarried.
Once you're over thirty – and I am – people think there is
something strange about you if you're not married. They think
you have bad relationships, that you're not friendly, or are eccen-
tric. If you work in an office as I do, if one day you talk with a
man, immediately there is gossip that you want to marry him ...

Married people keep wanting to give advice to you – they
mean well but they make you very uncomfortable. They say,
tomorrow, I'll bring a boy. Every day they ask have you a boy-
friend yet? What aren't you married? Why don't you like this boy,
this man?

It makes an unmarried woman like me very tired of this
problem ... Some people; decide in the end, they'll take any man
– not because she really loves him, but to get rid of all this
rubbish and the questions that go on and on. If you live in this
society, it's easier to be married, no matter to whom.[98]

Indeed the status of lone woman still carries with it such difficulties that
most daughters are said to 'want to marry even if they have no desire'
because marriage still gave them the best chance of social recognition
as a person.

If it was far easier for women to get married rather than not, it is
also, many felt, easier for them to stay married rather than divorce.
Divorced women too find it difficult to obtain housing or receive any
individual respect for their newly single status. Although the new
Marriage Law of 1980 made divorce easier to obtain, and the divorce
rate has increased, especially in the cities, the divorced woman still
finds that, although she might be treated as more adult in that she has
been married, she is also a lone female without rights or status. In 1992
a woman journalist, herself divorced, reported on her talks with other
divorced women and her surprise to find that they were still far more
interested in men's position, achievement and other material conditions
rather than their own. She felt quite indignant that these women were
without sufficient self-respect and could only think of depending on
men.[99]

The trauma associated with divorce is certainly the theme of many
a short story and in accounts of divorce in the media over the past ten
years. It is one of the most common topics of discussion in the media
and in conversation in the cities. My own interviews in 1994 with
several women who were divorced and struggling to bring up their
daughters after a tumultuous parting suggested that their situation was
not a happy one. They were in educational occupations and fortunate
that their housing was secure although sometimes hard won, but they
also mostly found it a very lonely state in which to survive socially and

emotionally. They thought it was much more common to look for love outside of marriage or alongside marriage, and I was certainly surprised to hear of the number of extra-marital liaisons that seemed to be an accepted or even preferred solution to the common lack of or end of love in marriage and certainly those so attached did not experience the loneliness felt by lone women in their thirties and forties.

This trend is confirmed by the popularity of Shen Rong's short story, entitled *Divorce, Why bother?* or *Too lazy to divorce*, in which the material and emotional cost of divorce was deemed so great as to suggest alternative solutions. An older woman, a social scientist, twice married herself, proffered the opinion that she knew of 'no women happy in marriage'. Given all the changes in recent years, she thought it had been difficult for any relationship to survive such 'twists and turns'. Although divorce was much talked about in Beijing, she thought that most 'just let it go' and led their separate lives as far as possible. She herself had managed to swap a four-roomed flat for two flats of two rooms each on separate floors of the same building which allowed her and her husband to live separately – although sharing a housemaid, they ate together. In this way women had fought to acquire some independence without the trauma of divorce, and given that the status of a lone woman, be she unmarried, divorced or widowed, has never been recognized as independent and worthy of individual esteem, this had seemed to be a sensible solution to some in towns and cities. In the countryside too movement to new places by both men and women may well offer something of a similar solution. However, although the marriage relationship may be seen by all to be still a most desirable state for women, falling in love is increasingly seen to be at some cost to female independence.

Love and the female self

With marriage still a well-nigh universal goal, there is much evidence of a new and prevailing idealization of romantic love in contemporary Chinese literature with more than 500 magazines focusing on romance, love, dating and marriage. Recently though, the literature on women's independence has suggested that women are most likely to lose their personal independence in love: it is both the most desirable and the most vulnerable of states. Young women, in dreaming of love and romance, are said 'to get carried away' and 'give up everything to someone'. To use a now common Western phrase, 'women love too much,' and in doing so in China they are similarly seen to lose something of themselves 'as a kind of surrender'. In a recent short story, one young woman muses: 'I thought to myself: love is such a simple word, but no one escapes it. When a person's life really begins, when they become mature, they all search for it and make sacrifices for it.'[100] In an interview, another young woman more ruefully commented:

When we love a man, we do everything for him, but we lose ourselves in the process. Love becomes a trap for women. It's not the same for men. They get a lot from a relationship. Whether or not one is married we women should never lose touch with our own needs never forget about ourselves.

So intense is the experience of merging one self with another in love and romance, that the literature is also full of references to the devastating anguish of lost love. A 28-year-old city woman summed up the feelings of her gender and age cohort when she noted that, because dating was a monumental experience, getting over the loss of a loved one was very difficult: 'You put everything into it. So that the other person becomes your life. For him to leave you when you are involved with him is crushing. It is an abandonment that is difficult to get over.'[101] The intensity of attachment and magic of romance is such that it seems to be difficult to sustain such an attachment following marriage with its daily routines and domestic life. The first few years of marriage are commonly thought to be the most difficult for a couple to traverse and their common lack of success in doing so happily is one of the reasons why marriage is often referred to as 'the grave of love'. One personal history after another illustrates that the risk of losing one's identity by being entirely preoccupied with another is a major characteristic of romantic involvement in contemporary China.

This preoccupation of young woman with male other is seen also to transfer itself to mother with child. A 38-year-old knitting-mill technician writes 'My love for my daughter surpasses my love for myself' and another mother writes 'to bring up a son, a sixth-grade pupil, I'm willing to sacrifice myself.'[102] A woman manager of a shirt factory office concluded with a heavy heart that 'women around the age of 40 are almost oblivious of themselves,'[103] such are their emotional investments in their families. In such cases not only were women seen to lose their identity and their dreams for themselves, but the children were also seen to be denied their own identities as they became dependent on and lived out their mother's dreams. Thus, in relation to both men and children, women have been increasingly exhorted not to lose their independent sense of their own needs and interests and to 'not surrender the female self' by wholly identifying with or receiving validation from another. As one young woman emphasized, their sense of value derives from the love of another: 'When you are really loved by one person, you can discover your own value.'[104] Frequent reference to notions of dependence on and validation of another and abandonment and incompleteness without another have worried counsellors newly charged with attempting to help the modern young. As one counsellor with experience of listening to young women's problems has said: 'Compared to a man, a woman must have more psychological preparation to venture into society alone ... In a strange world a woman tends to look for a shelter.'[105]

It was this search for shelter, she thought, that reflected the difficulty women had with the concept of independence. Unusually too, she also had a message for parents of daughters, admonishing them not to forget to tell their young daughters to 'Keep true to yourself no matter how rough life's road is.' This was an unusual message, for rarely at any time in China's history has it been suggested to parents that they might have a social responsibility to strengthen the independence, self-confidence or self-esteem of their daughters.

Female socialization

Although in the aftermath of the upsurge in reports of infanticide in the early 1980s, the Women's Federation had embarked on an intensive campaign to persuade parents that it was as good to have a girl as a boy, there has been little attention given to the socialization of girls or to the experience and lives of daughters during the revolution or in the 1980s and 1990s. This lack of attention to the socialization of daughters is an important omission given the evidence from cross-cultural studies, which show again and again that the most important prerequisite to redefinition of women's roles and status is self-esteem and that the origins of this self-esteem lies in their experience as daughters. There are the beginnings of such an acknowledgement and the development of such an interest in China, but it is still very small. An article written in *Zhongguo Funu* in 1985 was unusual in drawing attention to parental responsibility for early female socialization and to the importance of this socialization for becoming a woman with self-esteem:

> People often sigh at the feelings of inferiority of some grown women, and blame them for lacking self-confidence. It never occurs to them that much of this sense of inferiority is formed in childhood. This is mainly because parents do not understand how to cultivate a girl's self-confidence. So, in order to train strong self-confident women appropriate to a new era, it is necessary to begin in childhood.
>
> If parents pay attention to educating their girl children in self-confidence, giving them more encouragement, more support, more help, more opportunities to temper themselves, and help them to form a strong, brave character, then after they grow up they will be able to fully develop their own abilities and shoulder

the heavy task of constructing the 'Four Modernizations'. Conversely, if parents impose on their girl children the concept that 'males are worthy of respect and females are inferior,' this will cause them to form a sense of inferiority and a weak and timid character. It will limit them in giving full reign to their intelligence, ability, and wisdom, constrain their creativity, strangle their enterprising spirit and cause them to become weak people.

At present, many parents have not yet become conscious of the importance of fostering the self-confidence of girl children. Some even unconsciously undermine their self-confidence. For example, some girls are bright, like to study and have high aspirations, but their parents don't encourage them and even say that girls have low intelligence, that no matter how hard they work it will be a futile effort, and that they are better off doing more housework instead. Aside from doing housework, girls very seldom have the chance to temper themselves in other ways. Thus a difference is created in the abilities of boys and girls, which in turn becomes a reason for deprecating girls. Then there are some parents who often say in front of their girl children that girls are not as good as boys, causing the girls to feel they are second-class citizens from birth. The result is that in all respects they become careful and cautious, and are always shrinking back. With all of this, how could a girl's newly sprouted self-confidence not come under attack?

People often praise boys for their spirit of striving hard, seeking to outdo others, and swearing not to stop until they reach their goal. But this spirit, this self-confidence, this self-strengthening and courage, are by no means innate in their minds. They are the result of social education, and more important parental education. When a boy is easily upset and cries, his parents often say, 'Why are you crying? Men don't cry.' When boys retreat in the face of difficulties, parents often say, 'Be brave – it's not like a boy to shrink back.' This talk, these exclamations, are a form of education and encouragement. They bolster the courage and confidence of boys. If girls were given the same treatment, I firmly believe that a spirit of confidence and steadfast bravery would take root and sprout in the virgin soil of their pure souls.[106]

So far in China there is much less attention given to early differences fostered between girls and boys and much more emphasis given to physical, emotional and intellectual differences apparent at the onset of puberty. However, it is hoped that increasing attention will be given to the early socialization of daughters at a time when the fate of daughters is attracting more attention than at any time during recent history in

China. In particular, two phenomena drawing attention to daughters both resulting from the single-child family programme may have repercussions for the self-perceptions of young daughters. The first is the large numbers of daughters who are denied their lives at or before birth because they cannot substitute for sons and the second is the unusual experience of single daughters as the focus of parental expectations, who might be said to be newly substituting for sons. Both categories of daughters might be said to be 'missing'.

Missing girls

As the first decade of reform has drawn to a close, there has been increasing attention given to the phenomenon of missing girls, largely because of the rising discrepancy in sex ratios at birth. By mid-decade, trends in sex ratios at birth were estimated to be in excess of 110:100, which is 4 points above the international norm of 106:100. The 1990 census, according to both Chinese and foreign demographers, eliminated any doubt that sex ratios were high and rising in excess of 112:100; that ratios were higher for rural than urban areas and for poor or densely populated provinces such as Guangxi, Zhejiang Anhui Henan, Hunan, Shandong and Sichuan; and that ratios for higher parity births reached anywhere between 125 and 132 or even 149.4 if the first born was a girl.[107] All the evidence suggested a large and a growing number of missing baby girls. The latest figures released in China suggest that the problem is increasing as a result of pre-natal screening. The ratio in one city in Shandong province is estimated to have reached 163.8:100, which is higher than the norm reported for the surrounding rural areas which was estimated to be 144.6:100.[108] Altogether in China, the numbers of girls missing are reported to be in the millions, with foreign demographers persistently estimating that the numbers missing amount to around 40 million and one Chinese source estimating that this figure will rise to some 70 million by the end of the century.[109]

Explaining the causes of the imbalance in China's sex ratios and large numbers of missing girls has become the subject of many a demographic and social enquiry both within and outside of China. These enquiries commonly consider four hypotheses and their conclusions show some congruence. The first of the hypotheses is that female births are hidden by their parents either temporarily or permanently. There is certainly evidence of local instances of serious under-reporting or non-registration in order to evade penalties and to permit a second birth. Additionally, instances of temporary or permanent adoption by a friend or by family members would also raise the reported sex ratios of births. There is evidence that under-reporting of female births twice exceeded that of male births in most years between 1983 and 1988, and Chinese demographers have estimated that this factor accounts for at least half to three quarters of the shortfall in sex ratios.

This explanation implies though that the sex ratio of children at subsequent ages would fall to normal as the previously hidden or adopted children are enumerated in later population census and surveys.

While this was the main working supposition throughout the late 1980s, the 1990 census cast doubt on the degree to which under-enumeration or under-registration of females could have occurred during the previous years. Now Chinese demographers are inclined to concur that under-reporting can by no means wholly account for the higher than normal sex ratios, mainly because there has been little if any re-emergence of girls into the cohorts born in the last half decade. In their view this factor implies that, unless they have been concealed with a tenacity that is hard to imagine, they may never have been born or survived birth. The hypothesis based on under-reporting thus appears much weaker than it did several years ago. Another explanation is that female infanticide has increased either at birth at the hands of birth attendants or parents or some time later due to family neglect. Statistical and anecdotal evidence quoted in the Chinese press and in personal interviews and conversations suggests that infanticide, child sale and premature death of females has continued in many regions of China, giving reason to suppose that girls have less chance of surviving than do their male counterparts. However, there is general agreement that female infanticide is not likely now to be the main cause of the imbalance in sex ratios at birth, mainly because unwanted baby girls are more likely to be abandoned and placed in orphanages for adoption or to be aborted before birth.

Presently the most discussed and likely explanation for imbalanced sex ratios has to do with pre-selective abortion, for it has become increasingly possible for parents to determine the sex of the foetus and for the pregnant woman to undergo an abortion if she is bearing a girl. Improvements in medical technology in the 1980s have been responsible for the development and spread of various pre-natal sex-identification techniques, so that the now widespread availability of ultrasound B machines has made it technically feasible for sex-selective abortion to take place in many regions in China. In 1979 the first Chinese-made ultrasound B machine was produced; in 1982 a large volume of imported and Chinese-made ultrasound B machines began to enter the Chinese market; in 1987 the number of ultrasound B machines used in hospitals and clinics was estimated to exceed 13,000, that is, about six per county or enough to supply every county and many townships in China. A large number of the ultrasound machines were put in place for purposes of disease diagnosis, monitoring of pregnancy and checks on IUD placement. It is estimated that China now has a capacity of producing over 10,000 ultrasound machines per year, or enough to provide every county in China with four more machines every year, so that clinics and family planning centres at county and most township levels increasingly have ultrasound machines advanced enough to be used for pre-natal sex identification. Surveys show that ultrasound machines have been widely available in China since 1985, and widespread pre-natal screening for birth defects has meant that ultra-sound machines and technologies, such as amniocentesis, have become widely available and are used to determine the gender of the pregnancy in the period around 15 to 25 weeks after conception.

While government policy forbids the use of any of these technologies for ante-natal sex determination, their widespread availability makes real the possibility of misuse by officials open to bribes, the levy of fees to finance an otherwise under-funded local health service and the promotion of many forms of private and semi-private medical practices to supplement incomes an attractive option. Strong son preference, gifts and bribes make backdoor options more likely and the deployment of pre-arranged informal or unwritten signs such as a smile for a son and a frown for a daughter would suggest that the central government may have difficulty implementing regulations against the use of gender-determination technology. Despite government ruling against sex determination of the foetus, this explanation has the wide support of Chinese demographers and media, and what lends weight to this hypothesis is that even where birth surveillance is high, as in urban hospitals, medical records also show a high sex ratio, suggesting that numbers of women had undergone pre-natal sex identification.

Daughter discrimination, observed and recounted, has been an ongoing feature of my own field studies for many years. In addition to the features of household surveys I have outlined in Section 2 of this book, there are several memories that have haunted me on my many trips to China in the 1980s. For years many of those who have but casually crossed my path in taxi and train, not to mention colleagues and friends, have had stories and anecdotes of having seen or knowing somebody who has seen an abandoned and/or dead baby girl. For many years I have heard of the sale of baby girls and the under-registration of baby girls, depriving them of official record and facilities, but latterly in December 1992 the magnitude of the problem became more explicit with the publication of reports in *Nongmin Ribao* (Farmers' Daily), which estimated that there were 37 million more men than women in the population, and that by the year 2000, 70 million bachelors would be roaming China's countryside looking for wives.[110] Moreover, within the space of one week's stay in Beijing in March 1993, I had a number of telling exchanges and experiences. A colleague told of the orphanages almost exclusively caring for baby girls and disabled baby boys; another colleague was offered a baby girl for Y2000, a sum that was voluntarily reduced by the parents to Y500 upon his refusal to purchase; it was rumoured that, at an airport where three adopted girls and one boy were leaving the country, the boy apparently had to be dressed in girls clothes to distract an angry crowd; my hotel in Beijing was being used as a transit point by large numbers of Canadian parents adopting Chinese babies – all girls; the Chinese papers from the international seminar on China's 1990 census confirmed the widespread availability of ultrasound technology permitting pre-natal sex-selective abortion; and *China Daily* in that week ran the headline, 'More boys than girls – but no problem.'[111] It is particularly noticeable that any discussion of ensuing or potential problems has centred on the likely shortage of wives, problems of men unable to marry and fears for future social stability. What has not been defined as a problem, or even considered, is the possibility that the presence of such extreme discrimination and its widespread reports might affect the self-perceptions, self-images and self-esteem of China's surviving daughters.

It does not just have to be imagined how young girls might respond to reports that girls were missing in large numbers merely because of their sex. There are not the monograph-length autobiographical accounts featured in Part 1 of this study that documented the damage of close personal and familial experiences of discrimination, but there are shorter vignettes that suggest that girls continue to be fully cognizant of their secondariness and vulnerability to son preference. In one short account of her life so far, one very young schoolgirl wrote of how her birth had not only been unwelcome but also, she thought, the cause of her parents' estrangement and her mother's subsequent death:

I have a father, but I lost his love the day I was born. I experienced mother love for only a short time of six years. I was told that when I was born, Father came from another part of the country and asked loudly before he entered the delivery room, 'A boy or a girl?' 'A girl,' my grandma answered unwillingly. He immediately turned away with a snort of contempt, banged the door and went out without even coming near the bed to have a look at me. My father's love ended then and there. My mother lived in tears and misery. Father never came to see us. He occasionally wrote us a letter, only to irritate Mother. By now there was a pile of his letters kept sealed in Granny's paper bag. Mother got a serious illness because of her overtiredness and agony of spirit … She passed away when she was only 35 years old and looked so young. At that time, I was six years old, an age when mother love is the only thing you know and want, but I lost it forever. That I am a girl is the only reason Father left home for a faraway place and

Mother died. Since then, Granny and I have depended on each other for survival and every day I fear to lose her ...[112]

Another very young girl in less extreme circumstances wrote of how it felt when her mother seemed to prefer and privilege her brother:

My mom, no matter what happened, always considered my elder brother first and ignored me. At the table, she kept putting food into my brother's bowl and not mine, as if I were not her own child. This made me very unhappy. Except that he is a boy, my brother was nothing special. People often say that men and women each hold up half the sky. Mom would see sooner or later that I would grow up better than he, I thought. One day when I got home after school, I opened the newspaper and saw a cartoon. It showed a balance scale with a boy sitting high up on the left side, holding various fruits and foods in his arms, while a little girl was sitting listlessly on the other side being beaten and scolded by her parents. Under the cartoon the words said: 'Don't regard men as superior to women.' As I looked at it, I thought of myself and felt I was just like that little girl. I cut the cartoon out of the newspaper and put it on the wall so Mom would see it.[113]

When young girls were asked to draw their families in one of my own field exercises conducted in schools over the past few years, those with brothers, admittedly a small sample and mostly rural, thought that their parents preferred their brothers to themselves. However, where daughters were single children, a phenomenon usually confined to the cities, their experience of family life might be quite different.

Single-child daughters

More than any other policy, it is the single-child family policy that has been responsible for the differing familial values attached to sons and daughters in contemporary China although there is a major difference in urban and rural households. Whereas in rural families the second-ariness of daughters has been exacerbated in that they cannot substitute for sons, in urban areas, the picture is somewhat the reverse. There has never been the same degree of daughter discrimination evident in the cities largely because of the widespread availability of pensions and other economic factors that lay less stress on the importance of sons for economic reasons. Couples usually set up new households on marriage and later elderly parents may just as easily reside with a daughter as with a son. Indeed, some city parents would argue that a daughter's care for her elderly parents is likely to be more solicitous than that of a son. In larger cities, with the widespread stricter implementation of the one-child family policy, the majority of households have only one child and in these circumstances there is evidence to suggest that one-child daughters have become as important as sons and may even have become more important than at any time in the past, given their new status as substitute sons. City parents have thus invested in their only child regardless of whether it is a boy or a girl. In field investigations of household accounts several years ago, it was quite clear that the portion of family income devoted to the single child, boy or girl, was rising, whether for special foods, toys, clothes, recreation or education. In fact, meeting children's needs has become one of the fastest expanding consumer sectors in recent years. My own interviews with parents of single children some years ago also suggested an overwhelming interest in their education. This was not only fostered by the state in the interests of raising a 'quality child', but also parents, members of the previous generation 'lost' during the Cultural Revolution, were quite openly making up for their own deprivations. With this new-found interest and with new-found means, the single child has become the focus of expectations of two sets of grandparents and one set of parents. For single-child girls this is something of a new phenomenon and it has led to stresses and strains in family relations, with girls unable to withstand the presssures and in extreme circumstances even running away from home.

One small daughter in grade six primary school wrote a letter to her mother in which she tried to convey to her the negative effects of the high expectations she demanded of her daughter:

> The night is so quiet. I have been bending over the desk for five hours, writing mechanically, the extra homework that you required me to do. Rubbing my sleepy eyes, looking at the endless subjects and those inexplicable problems, I have no way out but write you this letter to tell you what is on my mind![114]

What is on her mind is that her mother has had ambitions for her from the time she was born: 'You often say to me "Clumsy birds have to start flying early – come on, do thirty applied problems" ... Rewards and punishments are set out clearly; your words are an "imperial edict" to which I dare not object.'

If she makes mistakes, her mother cannot control her temper and gives her a heavy slap in the face:

> Mother you may scold me and beat me as you please, for why on earth am I so foolish as not to be able to live up to your expectations! ... Mother, how wonderful it would be if you use the energy it takes to beat me, to help me with my lessons and homework!

Mother, have you ever considered what would happen when you treat me so? Whenever I get bad marks, I dare not show them to you since if you know, I will be beaten and scolded. What is most terrible is that it wounds my self-respect!

I understand that you cherish high aspirations for me and want me to become a college student and a very intelligent girl. I can confidently say that I am a child who is eager to outdo others, and I will study very hard and try every way to make myself an outstanding person even though I might not be a very clever girl.

The night is still quiet and, bending over the desk, I don't feel a bit sleepy, for I really have a lot to say to you. Mother, please trust your daughter so as to help her better![114]

The craving for mothers' affection of several of these young daughters is highly reminiscent of the personal narratives of the early decades of the century quoted in Part I.

A few daughters, feeling pressurized to achieve, have given up on their parents and left home, making 'runaway' or 'vagabond' girls a feature of newspaper reports for the first time since the early decades of the century. Then girls ran away from home in their attempt to further their education; now girls are running away primarily to escape from the pressures to achieve educationally. In 1993, the Women's Studies Forum drew attention to the phenomenon of vagrant girls as a problem 'not to be overlooked'.[115] At about the same time, *Zhongguo Qingnian* (China Youth) also reported on the experience of six girls who had all run away from their families.[116] In a manner reminiscent of the first decades of the century, the newspaper published letters from the daughters explaining their reasons for running away and the replies of their parents. In all the cases featured in the newspapers, including the national daily newspaper, *People's Daily*, the daughters had been only children who could no longer tolerate the pressure to achieve and to live up to parental expectations. In turn, the parents admitted that in retrospect the pressures they had placed on their daughters may have been unnecessarily high. The city parents of one 15-year-old girl runaway were both geologists who had spent the best years of their youth in the countryside during the Cultural Revolution. They later admitted that they had transferred their dreams to their daughter, whom they had named 'making wonders'. According to their daughter's letter published in one of the papers, their expectations had had a detrimental effect: 'I used to swear to study hard and bring honour ... But your autocratic education and indiscriminate physical punishment made me really lose confidence in myself.'[117]

She began to fail her exams and continually fall short of her parents'

requirements, resorting to altering her report cards and returning home
later and later. In the face of increasing criticism and warnings and
fearing her deceptions would be found out, she decided to run away:
'It's better for me to leave home and try to hew out my path in life in
the outside world than stay at home offending my parents.'
In reply, her parents admitted that:

> Aching regret has been gnawing at our hearts for the whole year
> since our only child went away. But it all comes too late. We had
> the child when we were both 30. We ambitiously designed what
> we felt to be a bright future for our daughter: key high school,
> renowned university ... We wanted her to achieve much more
> than we did ... We kept adding pressure on her. Whenever she
> was fond of playing and showed reluctance in study, we would
> scold her or beat her.

What is also interesting about so many of these cases is the role that
peers or friends of the daughters' play as confidantes and advisors to
the girls and as mediators between daughters and parents. It is friends
who keep contact with the girls by posting letters and mediating between
parent and girl by explaining to parents the predicaments of their
daughters. When Beijing children were asked in a recent survey in
whom they would confide, most said they would go to their friends.
Their fathers ranked only fourth and their mothers fifth, with teachers
not even in the top ten.[118] In the new defiance of age-old inter-
generational bonds, it is peer groups who provide more suppport and
it is such surveys, together with these newspapers stories of runaway
girls, that have caused many to fear for future relations between older
and younger generations: 'This disturbing trend may signal that the
traditional relationships that have for centuries bound Chinese youth
with their parents and rest of society may be loosening.'[119]
    It is not just the traditional bonds between the generations that are
observed to be loosening as old juxtaposes with the new, as Chinese
juxtaposes with the West and the traditional juxtaposes with the modern; within the same generation tension between expectations and
female choices make for ambiguity in lifestyle, attitudes and emotions.

Ambiguous women

Young women, especially, feel themselves to be hovering within a
plurality of expectations originating from a variety of sources including
state, family and male, so that the identification of 'proper' or 'appropriate' female behaviour and priorities seems difficult in the absence
of a single rhetoric defining proper female needs and interests appropriate to a modern woman. Indeed, confusion is the prevalent theme

in present-day representations of women and in the written and spoken words of women themselves. Tension and confusion is openly expressed again and again in the numerous short stories published in the past ten years in China. So far there have been three volumes on contemporary Chinese women writers translated and published in English and the stories in each depict very clearly trends in the changing representations of modern woman in China over the past ten years. The first volume, published in 1982, illuminated some of the hitherto hidden areas of women's lives, which were represented as more complex than in previous revolutionary decades, both in their presentation of their selves and of others.[120] In these stories the reader was newly treated to more than just a description of a sequence of events, which was usually secondary to the importance of the stream of consciousness or interior dialogue of the women characters as they think and verbally rationalize their choices or lack of options in working out the priorities of their young or middle-aged lives and in particular the conflicting demands of love, marriage or children with career. Most of these of stories, of which Shen Rong's *At Middle Age* is an example, belong to the genre of wound literature or scar literature in that they focus on expressing social problems of political movements that caused great suffering.

In the second volume the influence of important events and characteristics of society fades into the background and it is the conflict and tension within female minds that are narrated.[121] The stories are of fragmented disorderly lives, with the emphasis on the inconsequential as a device to question the meaning and worth of female lives lived in all their ambiguity and ambivalence. In one very popular short story, *Blue Sky and Green Sea*, the author Liu Suola portrays female characters who display outward confidence but are hiding hearts full of paradoxes, juxtaposing contradictory outward and inward feelings or thoughts robbing them of vital energy. To emphasize this point, the young woman author also writes in an unusually ambiguous tangled style of writing with constant repetititon and confusion said 'to mirror the characters' own depressed and confused mind'.

It is the complexity of life's choices, dilemmas and problems in the everyday of late-reform China that feature in the third volume of short stories published in 1993.[122] They feature one woman's moving tale of stifled aspirations in the countryside; another's exhausting day as a factory worker; another's frustrations at bringing up a child in the consumer age and the anxieties of a successful Shanghai business-woman. The majority of the heroines are shown moving beyond the quest for male protection to develop a sense of their own worth as women. In one short story, entitled *Black Forest*, a young woman who recognizes her own abilities and the large gap between her and her husband, resolutely breaks out from her ailing marriage to start a new life. Labelled 'the new realism', the stories lay stress not only on woman's own search for self-worth within the everyday but also on her own desire to exert some control over her own destiny.

Tension and confusion are also expressed by women directly in their own letters published in the media. In a similar period of rapid social change several decades earlier, when there were also few patterns and cues guiding new behaviour in education, employment, courtship and marriage, daughters especially looked to the new media for help in establishing models for becoming new and modern women. As did the younger generations in the early decades of this century, young women in recent years have also turned to magazines and newspapers for some form of guidance in resolving tensions and reducing confusion. Since 1980 the number of popular magazines and newspapers has mushroomed, with most giving women the opportunity to seek advice on a wide range of social and individual problems generating confusion. In one of my recent interviews, one woman editor of the 'Family and Society' section of *Zhongguo Funu Bao* (Chinese Women's News) outlined the main issues raised in the letters of her correspondents. She thought that a majority of the letters were to do with legal issues or the protection of women's rights and interests, particularly pertaining to family disputes in which they as daughters, daughters-in-law, wives or widows felt discriminated against. Many of the letters had to do with affairs of the heart, particularly with relationships outside of marriage and the problems of divorce including the division of property.

In rural magazines, the editor of *Rural Women* thought that more than half of the problems had to do with requesting information in order to generate income and reduce poverty, with the remaining number divided equally between issues to do with the law and the exercise of their rights in family and marriage. Common problems in the latter category included the opposition of parents to the man of a woman's choice and the refusal of a man to marry a woman after having had sexual relations with her. A subject of both letter and discussion were the problems, including harassment from managers and other men, that young rural women might face as migrants to the cities and special economic zones. Many young village women perceived a dilemma: they wanted to leave the boredom of the villages for the bright lights but they did not want to travel to the confusion of the unknown urban world far from the protection of family and friends.

One novel medium for providing advice and guidance, and one which has received much publicity, has been the establishment of telephone hotlines, which have become fashionable in the cities as sources of advice for women and young persons 'troubled by the confusion of choice in China's changing society'.[123]

A women's hotline in Beijing was set up in September 1991 by a retired newspaper editor who, in the process of studying women's issues, realized that women needed more direct help in alleviating the 'life-confusions and worries' that the changes of the reform era had brought. She thought this was largely because this generation of women 'shoulders the burdens of society and family while strongly desiring emotional compensation'. The hotline promised to do its best for callers who 'pour out their secret sorrows'and it has been so successful that it is said to 'link a society full of problems and grievances'. During the first seven months of its operation, it was reported that more than 80 per cent of the calls were from women with two thirds from callers less than 30 years old.

The main problems were to do with marriage and love (44.6 per cent), maternal and child-care (18.8 per cent), sex problems (6.4 per cent) and human relationships (8.5 per cent). In marriage and love the main questions focused on problems to do with communication within the marriage relationship, affairs, divorce and the sharing of domestic labour. Maternal and child-care problems included contraception, birth, nutrition and correcting child misbehaviour. A report on the hotline has noted that it is quite clear from the questions to do with sex that while some women are now making their 'own claims for sexual life', others are still worrying about and wanting to know the physical signs of 'lost chastity'. Overall, according to the report, most of the requests for advice confirmed that, 'although great changes have taken place in Reform China, the influence of traditional values is still very powerful.' The interviews with the counsellors also suggested that they primarily saw themselves as providing support for women 'caught between tradition and opportunity' and enabling them 'to make independent decisions' for which many women 'still need special help to realise their own strengths and destinies'.

In interviews conducted in the summer of 1994, city women of all but the youngest age cohorts felt themselves ambiguously drawn in several directions at once and confessed to some confusion in these times of rapid change and without clear directions or models to follow. Older women felt they had lived through so many changes in their own lifetimes or twisted and turned in so many different directions. The oldest woman I interviewed had been educated in a Catholic convent school and university before 1949; she had studied and worked at the Academy of Social Sciences since the early 1950s, observing and participating in political movements for socialist education including the anti-Rightist campaign, the Great Leap Forward and the Cultural Revolution; she had since studied in England and North America and returned to Beijing to retire and translate and write on feminist themes in English and Chinese literature; she had married twice, divorced once, lived separately now and her two children, educated in Chinese schools, now studied abroad. No wonder, on her recent return to China after an absence of several years, she said she felt like Rip van Winkle!

Several younger women in their early to mid forties too had lived several lives including Red Guard, *Xiaxiang* or sent-down-to-the-countryside-youth, university student in Beijing and student abroad. One woman whom I have known for several years went from riding horseback on the Mongolian steppes to Harvard University, Massachusetts within the space of a few years. She had been fortunate in that one of her classmates sharing her Mongolian tent had studied English and taught her all she knew, which was enough to gain her entrance to university in Beijing when competitive entrance exams were reinstated. She went on to work for a foreign agency and study international relations at Harvard. For her too, in her own words, 'life and marriage had been cooked up somewhere in this process,' leaving her now newly divorced as a new mother struggling to bring up her school-age daughter previously cared for by her mother-in-law. When I asked her if she would talk about how the modern woman might feel in China today, she replied without a pause – 'Very confused! How can you not be confused?'

Women in their twenties and thirties also admitted to some confusion as to where their priorities lay in the new China – itself ambivalent about its own developing priorities. Should they place the demands of work before or after those of their families or more precisely how could they best juggle the demands of both in these times of piece-work, inflation and uncertainty to the benefit of themselves and their families? There is some ambivalence surrounding the status of the strong independent successful career woman, with the single woman deemed less than successful. In this respect, the women of Taiwan, seeming to combine an alluring femininity and family care with careers, were much more admired than the career women of Hong Kong with their shoulder pads! Again young students in higher education feared that they would neither obtain a good job nor make a good marriage: if they put off one they might lose it all together. Most women felt that only as school students bent on their studies had they escaped the dilemmas of their times. These stories are of privileged women; other young women in other places would have talked of the new choices and the conflict, tension or at least ambivalence involved in making life-choices – perhaps choosing city over village, work rather than school, self- or service- rather than state- or factory-employment or long-term careers over short-term contracting of their labour or even the more lucrative contracting of their bodies given that one of the most observable of changes in the 1990s over the 1980s has been the growing number of bar girls and prostitutes in cities in pursuit of the consumer dream. The visibility of such young women walking the streets and the escalators in smart hotels and in bars was my single most important new observation during a recent trip to Beijing in the summer of 1994. In 1994, each age cohort had very different expectations, and expressed very different ideas, reservations and fears about themselves, their own generation and younger or older cohorts, but in common they seemed to be searching for cues, guidance and models in making sense of the new opportunities for women's social and self-expression in cosmopolitan China of the 1990s.

Cosmopolitan daughters

Perhaps it is the search for opportunity, independent strength or worth and control of their destiny in becoming a modern Chinese woman that are common to the plethora of images and dinstinctions in living. In the search for images and qualities that are female as opposed to male, modern as opposed to traditional and Chinese as opposed to Western, much of the contemporary attempt to reflect on and newly chart the uncharted territory of Reform also recalls similar female attempts during Republican and Revolutionary eras. Just as for the daughters discussed in Parts I and II who searched for and took advantage of new opportunities for education and occupation, so women in reform have found and taken advantage of the new opportunities for education and occupation not only in greater numbers but also with greater variation. If there is one trend that subsumes the major changes for women during the reform era, it is the appropriation of the new opportunities to become educated for and employed in a variety of occupations, making for a new independence in living. The trickle of new opportunities in the Republican era and the river of new opportunities in the Revolution has become the sea during Reform years. A popular saying, *xia hai* or going out or down to the sea, currently in vogue to refer to taking up new business opportunities or 'leaping into the tide of private business' might be expanded to embrace more than just business opportunities:

> Some say that the sea symbolises an immense realm, and going to the sea is an action that incites bold people. Some say that there are more chances of harvest in the sea than on the land. People watch the sea from the shore with some desire, some fear and some mystery. The waves are turbulent, so there may not be plain sailing ahead. Yet many women are among these sea-goers.[124]

Just as some of the early modern women in Republican times became successful in the professions and business and others ended up as 'fallen leaves in an autumn wind', so with new opportunities have come new risks for today's younger generation of women. The number of opportunities has surely risen but the new opportunities of reform rhetoric have not been lived by all: 'These times have made Chinese women's lives sweet and sour. For some their jobs are less secure sometimes and their opportunities fewer, but for others, their futures are more promising and are of their own choosing.'[125] To continue the seaside analogy, some venture into the water boldly and some more timidly, some may swim, some may flounder, but even if the experience of sailing is not smooth the important point is that the sea of opportunity is present.

Although it is difficult during the Reform era to identify a single rhetorical definition of the modern Chinese woman, the many exhortations and expectations of women advocate a strength, independence and adornment that are uniquely female. Model women want not to be five golden warriors but five golden flowers, albeit determined and independent. In Republican times, modern women also searched for sources of strength via education and employment to flower and be independent of their families. Rather than be uniquely female, however, they saw themselves as becoming more like male others or at least taking on masculine characteristics of strength and independence. During the revolution, the modern Chinese woman was exhorted to be physically strong and economically active like her male peers primarily by entering the androgynous category of work. Now, in a shift to concern with the personal, individual and gender qualities, women are exhorted to be strong, independent of spirit and uniquely female, not depending on or reflecting the light of male others. Yet despite this new rhetoric, women are still by their admission influenced by male desires and preferences, especially in love and marriage choices, and daughters who are not married feel incomplete and far from strong and independent in their single status.

While overlapping gender categories are rejected, definitions of female still very much take the qualities of the male other as the yardstick in identifying different and uniquely female characteristics. If men are assumed to be strong and independent then in becoming separate and different, women have been tempted to adopt opposite or female qualities traditionally associated with femaleness and femininity. Both among men, but also among women on their own admission, 'traditional beliefs also run deep.' From the turn of the century during Republican and Revolution and now Reform, even the most strong and independent of women be they pioneers, models or entrepreneurs find themselves succumbing to customary thoughts and practices in public, in the domestic and within themselves as they shape their identities to please very mixed societal, familial and specifically male expectations.

Central to becoming a modern woman throughout the twentieth century and symbolic of so much more has been the adoption of 'modern' dress. In the early decades of the century it might be Western dress or at least mixed Chinese-Western dress and in a few cases male attire; during the Revolution it was the unisex blue trouser suit that was *de rigueur*; and during the Reform era the Western fashion garment various in style, colour and fabric took Chinese women by storm, so speedy, general and changeable has been its adoption by the younger women throughout so much of China.

More generally, if the association of the modern with Western, albeit often both indirect and limited in influence, characterized the Republican era and the explicit and planned dissociation or closing of China to Western influence characterized the years of Revolution, then the overlapping of the 'modern' of socialism with both global consumption and mainly Western influence has distinguished recent years of Reform. As in the early decades of the twentieth century, in the interests of becoming global but retaining what distinguishes Chinese, there has been a continuing official attempt to separate the import of Western culture from Western goods so as to be both modern and Chinese. Thus in China today in the pursuit of both internationalism and cultural specificity, it is politically correct to speak of 'socialism with Chinese characteristics'. So it might be argued that there is a serious attempt to evolve a feminism with Chinese characteristics, femininity with Chinese characteristics or even fashion with Chinese characteristics. Now within women's studies in China, it is common to emphasize the specifically Chinese socio-political context of contemporary Chinese feminism and demarcate its differences from Western feminism.

There is an attempt to define a culturally-specific Chinese womanhood with references to her Chinese, often traditional, qualities that differentiate her from her Western sisters, and contemporary fashionshows predominantly combine both Chinese and Western stylistic features in a single garment.[126] However, for each successive generation anew, the pursuit of the 'modern' has been less nuanced or culturally specific in intent. A survey of new role models among children in Beijing revealed that the people they now respect are from film and popular music shows mostly derived from outside of China.[127] When young schoolgirls in one of my recent research exercises were asked to draw their families now and themselves in twenty years time, the majority illustrated their families in the company of the centrally-placed television sets and portrayed their grown selves as Western-clad singers and dancers with short skirts and microphones and rich in the company of consumer durables ranging from a car to television sets. What exercises such as these, undertaken in both urban or rural locations, suggest is that more than any other factor it is is the global mass media, much of it originating outside of China, that is important in defining female models for becoming a modern woman. Official rhetoric might continue to have a hand in shaping a hybrid or ambiguous Chinese-Western image for today's modern Chinese women, women of most ages might experience tension and confusion in meeting a pluralism of mixed Chinese and Western expectations, but more than ever before China's youngest daughters expect to assume a cosmopolitan culture.

Appendix 1

Regulations governing labour protection for female staff and workers, 1988

Article 1. These regulations are formulated to protect legitimate rights of female staff and workers, reduce and resolve special difficulties encountered in labour and work (subsequently referred to as labour) by female staff and workers due to their physiological characteristics, protect their health, and contribute to the building of socialist modernisation.

Article 2. These regulations will be applicable to female staff and workers of all state organisations, mass organisations, enterprises and institutions (subsequently referred to as units) within the boundary of the PRC.

Article 3. All those units which can be served by women must not reject the employment of female staff and workers.

Article 4. It is not permitted to reduce the basic wage of female staff and workers or cancel their labour contracts during their period of pregnancy, delivery and breast-feeding.

Article 5. It is not permitted to assign female staff and workers to engage in underground mining work or other work with a labour intensity of fourth grade, as stipulated by the state, or certain labour which female staff and workers are forbidden to do.

Article 6. During the menstrual period of female staff and workers, units to which they belong must not assign them to work at high altitude, in places with low temperature, in cold water, or on jobs with a labour intensity of third grade, as stipulated by the state.

Article 7. During the pregnancy of female staff and workers, units to which they belong must not assign them to work on jobs with a labour intensity of third grade, as stipulated by the state, or other labour which should not be done during pregnancy. Their working time must not be extended beyond their normal working hours. Those who are unable to perform their original labour should be allowed to reduce their workload or be assigned to other work in accordance with the certificate issued by a medical department.

Various units generally must not assign female staff and workers who have been pregnant for seven or more months to work night shift and should make arrangements for rest during their work.

Pregnant female staff and workers may take an ante-natal examination during working hours and the time should be considered as their working hours.

Article 8. The period of maternity leave for female staff and workers shall be 90 days, of which 15 days are leave prior to delivery. Those who have difficult labour should be given 15 additional days of leave. Those who give birth to twins, triplets or more shall be given 15 additional days of leave for each additional baby.

Female staff and workers who have a miscarriage shall be given a certain period of leave according to the certificate issued by a medical department.

Article 9. Female staff and workers with a baby of less than one year old shall be allowed by the units to which they belong to breast-feed their babies (or feed their babies with milk or formula) twice, 30 minutes each time, during their working shift. Those who have twins or more babies shall be given 30 additional minutes for each additional baby each time. The two feeding times may be combined by female staff and workers during their working shift. The feeding time and travelling time within their respective units shall be considered as working time.

Article 10. During their breast-feeding period, various units must not assign female staff and workers to work on jobs with a labour intensity of third grade, as stipulated by the state, or other labour which should not be done during the breast-feeding period. During this period the working hours of those female staff and workers shall not be extended and generally they should not be assigned to work night shift.

Article 11. Those units having a relatively large number of female staff and workers should, according to related regulations of the state, gradually establish health clinics, rest-rooms for pregnant women, breast-feeding rooms, child care centres and kindergartens run by themselves or jointly. They should pay attention to properly resolving difficulties of female staff and workers in physiological hygiene, breast-feeding and caring for babies.

Article 12. If their legitimate labour protection benefits are infringed, female staff and workers should have the right to appeal to the responsible department of their respective units or to the local labour department. The department which handles the appeal should make a decision within 30 days of receipt of a letter of appeal. If female staff and workers are not satisfied with the decision made by the department concerned, they may appeal to the people's court within 15 days of receiving a notice on the decision.

Article 13. Responsible persons of departments violating these regulations and infringing upon labour protection rights of female staff and workers and those who are directly responsible for such infringements shall be given administrative punishment by the higher unit in charge of those departments according to the situation. The departments concerned shall be ordered to give reasonable economic compensations to staff and workers whose rights were infringed. The judicial organisations shall investigate and affix responsibility for incidents which constitute crimes.

Article 14. Labour departments at various levels are responsible for inspecting the implementation of these regulations.
   Public health departments, trade unions and women's federations at various levels should have the right to supervise the implementation of these regulations.

Article 15. Labour protection for female staff and workers who violate state regulations on family planning will follow state regulations governing family planning, and these regulations will not be applicable to those who violate state regulations on family planning.

Article 16. The scope of labour, which should not be performed by female staff and workers due to their physiological characteristics, shall be determined by the Ministry of Labour.

Article 17. People's governments of various provinces, autonomous regions and municipalities directly under the jurisdiction of the State Council may formulate specific methods for implementation according to these regulations.

Article 18. The Ministry of Labour shall be responsible for the explanation of these regulations.

Article 19. These regulations will come into force on 1st September 1988. The stipulations governing special treatment in childbirth for female workers and staff according to the "Regulations governing labour insurance of the PRC", revised and promulgated by the government administrative council of the central people's government of the PRC on 2nd January 1953, and the "Circular of the State Council on female workers' maternity leave", dated 26th April 1955, are both hereby rescinded.

Appendix 2

Law of the People's Republic of China on Protection of Rights and Interests of Women

Adopted at the 5th session of the 7th National People's Congress on April 3, 1992

Chapter 1 – General Provisions

Article 1. In accordance with the Constitution and the actual conditions of the country, this Law is formulated to protect women's lawful rights and interests, promote the equality between men and women and allow full play to women's role in socialist modernization.

Article 2. Women shall enjoy equal rights with men in all aspects of political, economic, cultural, social and family life.

The state shall protect the special rights and interests enjoyed by women according to law, and gradually perfect its social security system with respect to women.

Discrimination against, maltreatment of, or cruel treatment in any manner causing injury or even death of women shall be prohibited.

Article 3. The protection of women's lawful rights and interests is a common responsibility of the whole society. State organs, public organizations, enterprises and institutions as well as urban and rural mass organizations of self-government at the grass-roots level shall, in accordance with the provisions of this Law and other relevant laws, protect women's rights and interests.

The state shall take effective measures to provide necessary conditions for women to exercise their rights according to law.

Article 4. The State Council and the people's governments of provinces, autonomous regions and municipalities directly under the Central Government shall, by taking organizational measures, coordinate with relevant departments in ensuring the protection of women's rights and interests. The specific organs shall be designated by the State Council and the people's governments of provinces, autonomous regions and municipalities directly under the Central Government.

Article 5. The All-China Women's Federation and women's federations at various levels shall represent and uphold the rights of women of all nationalities and all walks of life, and strive for the protection of women's rights and interests.

The trade unions and the Communist Youth League organizations shall also, within the scope of their respective work, strive for the protection of women's rights and interests.

Article 6. The state shall encourage women to cultivate a sense of self-respect, self-confidence, self-reliance and self-strengthening, and to safeguard their own lawful rights and interests by utilizing law.

Women shall abide by the laws of the state, respect social morality and perform their obligations prescribed by law.

Article 7. People's governments at various levels and relevant departments shall commend and award the organizations and individuals that have made notable achievements in the protection of women's lawful rights and interests.

Chapter 2 – Political Rights

Article 8. The state shall guarantee that women enjoy equal political rights with men.

Article 9. Women have the right to conduct state affairs, manage economic and cultural undertakings and administer social affairs through various channels and in various ways.

Article 10. Women shall enjoy equal rights with men to vote and to stand for election.

Among deputies to the National People's Congress and local people's congresses at various levels, there shall be an appropriate number of women deputies, and the proportion thereof shall be raised gradually.

Article 11. The state shall actively train and select female cadres.

State organs, public organizations, enterprises and institutions must, in appointing cadres, adhere to the principle of equality between men and women, and attach importance to the training and selection of female cadres for leading posts.

The state shall pay attention to the training and selection of female cadres of minority nationalities.

Article 12. Women's federations at various levels and their member organizations may recommend female cadres to state organs, public organizations, enterprises or institutions.

Article 13. The departments concerned shall listen to and accept criticisms or rational suggestions regarding the protection of women's rights and interests; with respect to complaints or charges against, or exposures of infringement upon women's rights and interests, the departments concerned must ascertain the facts, and be responsible for the disposition thereof; no organization or individual may suppress such complaints, charges or exposures or resort to retaliation.

Chapter 3 – Rights and Interests Relating to Culture and Education

Article 14. The state shall guarantee that women enjoy equal rights with men with respect to culture and education.

Article 15. Schools and departments concerned shall, by implementing the relevant regulations of the state, guarantee that women shall enjoy equal rights with men in such aspects as starting school, entering a higher school, job assignment upon graduation, conferments of academic degrees and dispatch for study abroad.

Article 16. Schools shall, in line with the characteristics of female adolescents, take measures in respect of education, management and facilities so as to ensure their sound development in body and in mind.

Article 17. Parents or other guardians must perform their duty of ensuring that female school-age children or adolescents receive the compulsory education.

Where parents or other guardians fail to send female school-age children or adolescents to school, the local people's governments shall admonish and criticize them and, by adopting effective measures, order them to send their female school-age children or adolescents to school, with the exception of those who, on account of illness or other special circumstances, are allowed by the local people's governments not to go to school.

The governments, society and schools shall, in the light of actual difficulties of female school-age children or adolescents in schooling, take effective measures to ensure that female school-age children or adolescents receive compulsory education for the number of years locally prescribed.

Article 18. People's governments at various levels shall, in accordance with relevant provisions, incorporate the work of the elimination of illiteracy or semi-literacy among women into plans for illiteracy elimination and post-elimination education, adopt organizational forms and working methods suitable to women's characteristics, and organize and supervise the relevant departments in the implementation of such plans.

Article 19. People's governments at various levels and departments concerned shall take measures to organize women in receiving vocational education and technological training.

Article 20. State organs, public organizations, enterprises and institutions shall, by implementing relevant regulations of the state, ensure that women enjoy equal rights with men in their participation in scientific, technological, literary, artistic and other cultural activities.

Chapter 4 – Rights and Interests Relating to Work

Article 21. The state shall guarantee that women enjoy the equal right, with men, to work.

Article 22. With the exception of the special types of work or post unsuitable to women, no unit may, in employing staff and workers, refuse to employ women by reason of sex or raise the employment standards for women.

Recruitment of female workers under the age of sixteen shall be prohibited.

Article 23. Equal pay for equal work shall be applied to men and women alike.

Women shall be equal with men in the allotment of housing and enjoyment of welfare benefits.

Article 24. In such aspects as promotion in post or in rank, evaluation and determination of professional and technological titles, the principle of equality between men and women shall be upheld and discrimination against women shall not be allowed.

Article 25. All units shall, in line with women's characteristics and according to law, protect women's safety and health during their work or physical labour, and shall not assign them any work or physical labour not suitable to women.

Women shall be under special protection during menstrual period, pregnancy, obstetrical period and nursing period.

Article 26. No unit may dismiss women staff and workers or unilaterally terminate labour contracts with them by reason of marriage, pregnancy, maternity leave or baby-nursing.

Article 27. The state shall develop social insurance, social relief and medical and health services to create conditions allowing old, ill or disabled women to obtain material assistance.

Chapter 5 – Rights and Interests Relating to Property

Article 28. The state shall guarantee that women enjoy the equal right, with men, to property.

Article 29. In joint property relationship derived from marriage or family, the rights and interests enjoyed by women according to law may not be infringed upon.

Article 30. Women shall enjoy equal rights with men in the allotment of responsibility for farmland, or grain ration farmland and in the approval of housing sites in rural areas, and women's lawful rights thereto shall not be infringed upon.

After marriage or divorce, women's responsibility for farmland, grain ration farmland and housing sites shall be secured.

Article 31. Women's equal right, with men, of succession to property shall be protected by law. Among the statutory successors in the same order, women shall not be discriminated against.

Widowed women have the right to dispose of the property inherited by them, and no one may interfere with the disposition thereof.

Article 32. Widowed women who have made the predominant contributions in maintaining their parents-in-law shall be regarded as the statutory successors first in order, and their rights of succession thereto shall not be affected by inheritance in subrogation.

Chapter 6 – Rights Relating to the Person

Article 33. The state shall guarantee that women enjoy equal rights with men relating to their persons.

Article 34. Women's freedom of the person shall be inviolable. Unlawful detention or deprivation or restriction of women's freedom of the person by other illegal means shall be prohibited; and unlawful body search of women shall be prohibited.

Article 35. Women's right of life and health shall be inviolable. Drowning, abandoning or cruel infanticide in any manner of female babies shall be prohibited; discrimination against or maltreatment of women who gave birth to female babies or women who are sterile shall be prohibited; cruel treatment causing injury or even death of women by superstition or violence shall be prohibited; maltreatment or abandonment of aged women shall be prohibited.

Article 36. Abduction of and trafficking, or kidnapping of women shall be prohibited; buying of women who are abducted and trafficked in, or kidnapped shall be prohibited.

People's governments and relevant departments must take timely measures to rescue women who are abducted and trafficked, or kidnapped. If such women have returned to their former places of residence, nobody may discriminate against them, and the local people's governments and relevant departments shall well settle the problems arising thereafter.

Article 37. Prostitution or whoring shall be prohibited.

It is prohibited for anyone to organize, force, seduce, shelter or introduce a woman to engage in prostitution or employ or shelter a woman engaged in obscene activities with others.

Article 38. Women's right of portrait shall be protected by law. The use of a woman's portrait for profit-making purposes in advertisements, trademarks, window display, books, magazines, etc., without the consent of the interested woman shall be prohibited.

Article 39. Women's right of reputation and personal dignity shall be protected by law. Damage to women's reputation or personal dignity by such means as insult, libel and giving publicity to private affairs shall be prohibited.

Chapter 7 – Rights and Interests Relating to Marriage and Family

Article 40. The state shall guarantee that women enjoy equal rights with men in marriage and family.

Article 41. The state shall protect women's right of self-determination in marriage. Interference with women's freedom of marriage or divorce shall be prohibited.

Article 42. When a wife terminates gestation as required by the family planning programme, her husband may not apply for a divorce within six months after the operation; this restriction shall not apply in cases where the wife applies for a divorce, or when the people's court deems it necessary to accept the divorce application made by the husband.

Article 43. A woman shall enjoy equal rights with her spouse in possessing, utilizing, profiting from and disposing of the property jointly possessed by the husband and wife according to law, which shall not be affected by the status of income of either party.

Article 44. The state shall protect divorced women's ownership of their houses.

At the time of divorce, the husband and wife shall seek agreement regarding the disposition of their jointly possessed houses; if they fail to reach an agreement, the people's court shall make a judgement in accordance with the actual circumstances of both parties and be taking into consideration the rights and interests of the wife and their child (children), except as otherwise agreed upon by the two parties.

In a case where the husband and wife jointly rent a house or a room, the wife's housing shall, at the time of divorce, be solved according to the principle of taking into consideration the rights and interests of the wife and their child (children).

In a case where the husband and wife live in a house allocated by the unit to which the husband belongs, if the wife has no housing to live in at the time of divorce, the husband shall help her in this regard whenever he can afford to.

Article 45. Both parents shall enjoy the equal right to guardianship of their minor child (children).

In a case where the father is deceased, incapacitated or under any other circumstances that make him unable to act as the guardian of a minor child (children), nobody may interfere with the mother's right of guardianship.

Article 46. At the time of divorce, if the wife becomes sterile because of the sterilization operation or any other reasons, the problem to bring up the child (children) shall be so handled that, while to the advantage of the rights and interests of the child (children), due consideration shall be given to the wife's reasonable demands.

Article 47. Women have the right to child-bearing in accordance with relevant regulations of the state as well as the freedom not to bear any child.

Where a couple of child-bearing age practise family planning according to the relevant regulations of the state, the departments concerned shall provide safe and effective contraceptives and techniques, and ensure the health and safety of the woman receiving any birth-control operation.

Chapter 8 – Legal Responsibility

Article 48. When a woman's lawful rights and interests are infringed upon, she has the right to request the competent department concerned for a disposition or bring a lawsuit in a people's court according to law.

When a woman's lawful rights and interests are infringed upon, she may file a complaint with a women's organisation, which shall request the relevant department or unit to investigate and deal with the case so as to protect the lawful rights and interests of the complainant.

Article 49. Where punishments are prescribed by other laws or regulations for the infringement upon the lawful rights and interests of women in violation of the provisions of this Law, punishments prescribed in such laws or regulations shall apply.

Article 50. Anyone who commits any of the following infringements upon the lawful rights and interests of a woman shall be ordered to make corrections by his or her unit or by an organ at a higher level, and the person who is held directly responsible may, in light of the specific circumstances, be subjected to administrative sanctions:

(1) evading, delaying or suppressing the investigation and disposition of a complaint, a charge or an exposure regarding an infringement upon the rights and interests of a woman;

(2) refusing to employ women or raising the employment standards for women where women shall be employed in accordance with the provisions of relevant laws or regulations;

(3) infringing upon women's rights and interests by violating the principle of equality between men and women in such aspects as allotment of housing, promotion in post or in rank, evaluation and determination of professional and technological titles;

(4) dismissing female staff and workers by reason of their marriage, pregnancy, maternity leave, or baby-nursing;

(5) infringing upon women's rights and interests by violating the principle of equality between men and women in the allotment of responsibility farmland or grain ration farmland or the approval of housing sites; or

(6) infringing upon women's rights and interests by violating the principle of equality between men and women in such aspects as starting

school, entering a higher school, job assignment upon graduation, conferment of academic degrees or dispatch for study abroad.

Anyone who retaliates against a person making a complaint, a charge or an exposure regarding an infringement upon a woman's rights and interests shall be ordered to make corrections or be subjected to administrative sanctions by his or her unit or an organ at a higher level. If a state functionary commits retaliation, which constitutes a crime, the offender shall be investigated for criminal responsibility in accordance with the provisions in Article 146 of the Criminal Law.

Article 51. Anyone who employs or shelters any women to engage in obscene activities with others shall be punished by applying *mutatis mutandis the provisions in Article 19 of the Regulations on Administrative Penalties for Public Security; if the circumstances are so serious as to constitute a crime, the offender shall be investigated for criminal responsibility by applying mutatis mutandis* the provisions in Article 160 of the Criminal Law.

Article 52. Where an infringement upon a woman's lawful rights and interests causes loss of property or other damage, the infringer shall make due compensation or bear other civil liabilities according to law.

Chapter 9 – Supplementary Provisions

Article 53. Relevant departments under the State Council may, on the basis of this Law, formulate relevant regulations, which shall be submitted to the State Council for approval and then be implemented.

The standing committees of the people's congresses of provinces, autonomous regions and municipalities directly under the Central Government may formulate measures for implementation on the basis of this Law.

The people's congresses of national autonomous areas may formulate regulations with appropriate adaptations or supplements in accordance with the principles laid down in this Law and in light of the specific conditions of the national women in respective areas. Regulations formulated by autonomous regions shall be submitted to the Standing Committee of the National People's Congress for the record; regulations formulated by autonomous prefectures or autonomous counties shall be submitted to the standing committees of the people's congresses of the relevant provinces or autonomous regions for approval before entering into effect, and shall also be submitted to the Standing Committee of the National People's Congress for the record.

Article 54. This Law shall enter into force as of October 1, 1992.

Notes

Introduction

1. Andors, P., *The Unfinished Liberation of Chinese Women 1969–1980*, Indiana University Press, 1983; Barlow, T. (ed.), *Gender Politics in Modern China: Writing and Feminism*, Duke University Press, 1993; Broyelle, C., *Women's Liberation in China*, Harvester Press, Sussex, England, 1977; Croll, E., *The Women's Movement in China*, Anglo-Chinese Educational Institute, London, 1974; Croll, E., *Feminism and Socialism in China*, Routledge, London, 1979; Croll, E., *Chinese Women Since Mao*, Zed Press, London, 1983; Croll, E., *Women and Rural Development in China*, ILO, Geneva, 1981 and 1985; Davin, D., *Women's Work: Women and the Party in Revolutionary China*, Clarendon Press, Oxford, 1976; Gilmartin, C., Hershatter, G., Rofel, L., and White, T., *Engendering China: Women, Culture and the State*, Harvard University Press, 1994; Guisso, R.W. and Johannessen S., *Women in China: Current Directions in Historical Scholarship*, Philo Press, New York, 1981; Honig, E. and Hershatter, G., *Personal Voices: Chinese Women in the 1980s*, Stanford University Press, 1988; Johnson, K.A., *Women, the Family and Peasant Revolution in China*, University of Chicago Press, 1983; Judd, E.R., *Gender and Power in Rural North China*, Cambridge University Press, 1994; Kazuko, O., *Chinese Women in a Century of Revolution, 1850–1950*, Heibonsha, Tokyo, 1978; Stanford University Press, 1989; Kristeva, J., *About Chinese Women*, Marion Boyars, London, 1977; Sheridan, M. and Salaff, J., *Lives: Chinese Working Women*, Indiana University Press, 1984; Sidal, R., *Women and Child Care in China*, Penguin, London, 1972; Siu, B., *Women of China: Imperialism and Women's Resistance 1900–1949*, Zed Press, London, 1982; Wolf, M. and Witke, R. (eds.), *Women in Chinese Society*, Stanford University Press, 1975; Wolf, M., *Revolution Postponed: Women in Contemporary China*, Stanford University Press, 1985.

2. Chen Chiyun, *Newsweek*, 16 July 1990.

3. Bloch, M. (ed.), *Political Language and Oratory in Traditional Society*, Academic Press, London, 1982; Parkin, D., *Semantic Anthropology*, Academic Press, London, 1982.

4. Chodorow N., *Psychoanalysis and the Sociology of Gender*, University of California Press, 1978; Friedman, S.S., 'Women's Autobiographical Selves: Theory and Practice', in Benstock, S., *The Private Self: Theory and Practice of Women's Autobiographical Writings*, Routledge, London, 1988.

5. The Personal Narratives Group, *Interpreting Women's Lives: Feminist Theory and Personal Narratives*, Indiana University Press, 1989.

6. Warnock, M., *Memory*, Faber & Faber, London, 1987; Benstock, S., 1988.

7. Clifford, J. and Marcus, G., *Writing Culture*, University of California Press,

1986; Okeley, J. and Callaway, H., *Anthropology and Autobiography*, Routledge, London, 1992.

8. Wu Pei-yi, *The Confucian's Progress: Autobiographical Writings in China*, Princeton University Press, 1990.

9. Moore, H., *Feminism and Anthropology*, Polity Press, Cambridge, 1988, p. 7; Delmar, R., 'What is Feminism' in Mitchell, J. and Oakley, A., *What is Feminism?* A. Blackwell, Oxford, 1987, p. 28.

10. De Beauvoir, S., *The Second Sex*, New English Library Edition, London, 1969, p. 9.

11. Kristeva, J., 'Women's Time', *Signs* 7(1), Autumn 1981, pp. 13–35.

12. Forman, F.J. (ed.), *Taking our Time: Feminist Perspectives on Temporality*, Pergamon Press, Oxford, 1989; Munn, N., 'The Cultural Anthropology of Time: A Critical Essay', *Annual Review of Anthropology*, 1992, Vol. 21, pp. 93–123.

Part I   Not the Sun

1. Tyau, M.T.Z., *China Awakened*, New York, 1922, pp. 59–60.

2. Wong Su-ling, *Daughter of Confucius: A Personal History*, London, 1953.

3. Chow Chung-cheng, *The Lotus Pool of Memory*, London, 1961, p. 13.

4. Chao Buwei Yang, *Autobiography of a Chinese Woman*, Westport, Connecticut, 1970, pp. 3–4.

5. Chow Chung-cheng, p. 9.

6. Guisso and Johannesen, p. 48.

7. *Book of Changes*, section XXXVII, trans. Legge, J. and quoted in Lewis, I.B., *The Education of Girls in China*, New York, 1919, p. 8.

8. *Book of Rites*, IX:24, quoted in *Xin Qingnian* (New Youth), Vol. 2, No. 4. December 1916.

9. *Nu Jie*, Chap. III, trans. Headland, I.T., in Lewis, op. cit., p. 8.

10. *Nu er Jing*, Sections IV and V, see Headland, I.T., *Home Life in China Today*, London, 1914, pp. 69–80.

11. Ayscough F., *Chinese Woman Yesterday and Today*, London, 1938, p. 267.

12. Lewis, op. cit., p. 15.

13. Kulp, H., *Country Life in South China*, Vol. 1. New York, 1925, pp. 278–81.

14. Tsai Chin, *Daughter of Shanghai*, Chatto & Windus, 1988, pp. 35–6.

15. Wei Tao-ming, *My Revolutionary Years*, New York, 1943, pp. 1–5.

16. Chow Ching-li, *Journey into Tears: Memory of a Girlhood in China*, New York, 1978, p. 26.

17. Wei, K. and Quin, T., *Second Daughter: Growing Up in China, 1930–1949*, Boston, 1984, pp. 45–6.

18. Chow Chung-cheng, pp. 12–13.

19. Wong Su-ling, pp. 46–9.

20. Kingston, M.H., *The Woman Warrior: Memoirs of a Girlhood among Ghosts*, Pan Books, London, 1981, pp. 25–6.

21. Ibid.

22. Hsieh Ping-ying, *Autobiography of a Chinese Girl*, London, 1986, p. 37.

23. Pruitt, I., *Daughter of Han: The Autobiography of a Chinese Working Woman* (as told to her by Ning Lao T'ai-t'ai', Stanford University Press, 1967, p. 20.

24. Wai Tao-ming, pp. 3, 8.

25. Ibid., p. 8.
26. Hsieh Ping-ying, p. 37.
27. Ibid., p. 42.
28. Wong Su-ling, p. 174.
29. Chow Chung-cheng, pp. 116–7.
30. Liang Yen, *The House of Golden Dragons*, London, 1961, pp. 27–9.
31. Wong Su-ling, p. 90.
32. Pruitt, p. 23.
33. Hsieh Ping-ying, pp. 42–4.
34. Pruitt, p. 22.
35. Wei Tao-ming, pp. 9–11.
36. Wong Su-ling, pp. 91–2.
37. Chao Buwei, p. 33.
38. *Nu er Jing*, Section VII, translated Headland, op. cit., p. 77.
39. Levy, H.S., *Chinese Footbinding: The History of a Chinese Erotic Custom*, New York, 1966, pp. 26–7.
40. Ibid., p. 30.
41. Wong Su-ling, pp. 10–37, 90.
42. Ibid., pp. 56–8.
43. Smith, A.H., *Village Life in China*, London, 1900, p. 262.
44. Pruitt, p. 29.
45. Ibid.
46. Liang Yen, p. 10.
47. Wei Tao-ming, pp. 79–80.
48. Chow Chung-cheng, p. 115.
49. Hsieh Ping-ying, p. 44.
50. Waley, A., *Translations from the Chinese*, New York, 1941, p. 72.
51. Chow Chung-cheng, p. 105.
52. Wong Su-ling, pp. 86–7.
53. Ibid., p. 119.
54. Chow Chung-cheng, pp. 51, 94.
55. Tsai Chin, p. 49.
56. Waley, op. cit., p. 72.
57. *Book of Poetry*, quoted in *North China Herald*, Shanghai, 10 February 1931.
58. Wong Su-ling, p. 166.
59. Chow Ching-li, pp. 11–13, 39–40.
60. Hsieh Ping-ying, p. 27.
61. Chow Chung-cheng, pp. 14–15.
62. Ibid., pp. 40, 134.
63. Wei, K., pp. 17–19.
64. Ibid., pp. 21–3.
65. Kingston, M.H., p. 48.
66. Wei, K., p. 104.
67. Chow Chung-cheng, p. 133.
68. Wong Su-ling, p. 90.
69. Chow Ching-li, p. 114.
70. Ibid., p. 65.
71. Ibid., p. 114.

72. Lin, A.P., *Grandmother Had No Name*, San Francisco, 1988, pp. 15, 34.
73. Chao Buwei, p. 32
74. Chow Ching-li, p. 28.
75. Wei Tao-ming, p. 16.
76. Chow Chung-cheng, p. 26.
77. Chao Buwei, p. 32.
78. Wong Su-ling, p. 16.
79. Ibid., p. 27.
80. Wei, K., p. 34.
81. Chow Chung-cheng, pp. 59–62.
82. Hsieh Ping-ying, pp. 155–62.
83. Pa Chin, *The Family*, Beijing, 1931, pp. 130–31.
84. Wong Su-ling, p. 192.
85. Wong Su-ling, p. 169.
86. Hsieh Ping-ying, p. 47.
87. Chao Buwei, p. 28.
88. Liang Yen, pp. 16, 53.
89. Chow Chung-li, p. 60.
90. Hseih Ping-ying, pp. 45, 52.
91. Ibid., p. 54.
92. Chow Chung-cheng, p. 147.
93. Hsieh Ping-ying, p. 33.
94. Wei Tao-ming, p. 30.
95. Ibid., p. 13.
96. Hsieh Ping-ying, p. 56.
97. Wei, K., p. 152.
98. Chow Chung-cheng, p. 221.
99. Liang Yen, p. 47.
100. Wong Su-ling, pp. 206–9.
101. Ross, E.A., *The Changing Chinese*, London, 1911, p. 206.
102. Wong Su-ling, pp. 131–2.
103. Chao Buwei, pp. 62–3, 77, 81.
104. Wei, K., pp. 229–30.
105. Wei Tao-ming, pp 23, 25, 27.
106. Chow Ching-li, pp. 81, 87, 91, 106, 245.
107. Hsieh Ping-ying, pp. 138–44.
108. Chow Chung-cheng, pp. 151, 158, 173, 254.
109. Liang Yen, pp. 58–9, 112.
110. Hsieh Ping-ying, p. 199.
111. Wong Su-ling, pp. 268–9.
112. Wei Tao-ming, p. 4.
113. Tang Sheng, *The Long Way Home*, Hutchison, London, 1949, pp. 14, 16.
114. Ibid.
115. Chow Chung-cheng, pp. 24–5, 81.
116. Hsieh Ping-ying, pp. 31–2.
117. Wong Su-ling, p. 167.
118. Tang Sheng, p. 9.
119. Chow Chung-cheng, p. 151.

120. Liang Yeng, p. 58.
121. Tang Sheng, p. 25.
122. Chin Ai-Li S., 'Some problems of Chinese Youth in Transition', *American Journal of Sociology*, Vol. LIV, No. 1, July 1948, pp. 1–9.
123. Wei Tao-ming, p. 13.
124. Wong Su-ling, pp. 92–3.
125. Wei Tao-ming, pp. 28–9.
126. Hsieh Ping-ying, p. 145.
127. Chao Buwei, pp. 45, 81.
128. Liang Yen, p. 9.
129. Wang Su-ling, p. 58.
130. Wei Tao-ming, p. 154.
131. Chow Chung-cheng, pp. 134–5, 138–9.
132. Tang Sheng, p. 15.
133. Wei Tao-ming, p. 154.
134. Pruitt, I., p. 239.
135. Chow Chung-cheng, pp. 219, 221–2.
136. Wei Tao-ming, p. 79.
137. Chao Buwei, p. 155.
138. Wei Tao-ming, pp. 111–13.
139. Chao Buwei, p. 5.

Part II   The Sun and the Moon

1. Wan Mu-chun, 'How the Problem of Women should be Viewed', *Hongqi* (Red Flag), 28 October 1964.
2. 'China's New Womanhood', *China Reconstructs*, 1 March 1956.
3. *The Upsurge of Socialism in the Countryside*, Peking, 1960, p. 286.
4. Lenin, V.I., 'The Tasks of Working Women's Movement in the Soviet Republic', 23 September 1919, in *Women and Society*, New York, 1938, pp. 15–20.
5. Mao Zedong, *Inscriptions for Women of New China*, 20 July 1949.
6. Nan Ting, 'Tien Kuei-ying Earns a Licence', *People's China*, 1 April 1950.
7. Pu Chun-sheng, *Women in China Today*, ACDWF, Peking, 1951, Part 6.
8. Li Chenyung, *Women in China Today*, ACDWF, Peking, 1951, Part 7.
9. 'A Housewife Deputy to the People's Congress', *People's China*, 16 March 1954.
10. Interview with author, private mss.
11. Kung Ying-chao, 'Commune Opens New World for Women', *New China News Analysis*, Peking, 18 December 1958.
12. 'What is Revolutionary Women's True Happiness?', *Zhongguo Funu* (Women of China), 1 October 1963.
13. Liao Suhua, 'In What Respects should we be Self-Conscious?', *Zhongguo Funu*, 1 October 1963.
14. Chen Yuan-tsung. *The Dragon's Village: An Autobiographical Novel of Revolutionary China*, Women's Press, London, 1981, p. 212.
15. *New China News Agency*, 31 July 1958; *Renmin Ribao* (People's Daily), 7 October 1959.
16. Cusack, D., *Chinese Women Speak*, Century Hutchinson, London, 1985, p. 6.

17. *Zhongguo Funu,* 10 August 1966.

18. Wolf, 1985, p. 6.

19. Honig and Hershatter, p. 308.

20. Kristeva, 1977, p. 165.

21. Lévi-Strauss, C., 'Social Structure', in Kroeber, A.L. (ed.), *Anthropology Today,* University of Chicago Press, 1953, p. 517.

22. 'Reference Materials for Training Basic-level Women Cadres', *Zhongguo Funu,* 1 February 1962.

23. Liao Suhua, op. cit.

24. Chen Yunjing. 'Why I undertake Women's Work', *Zhongguo Funu,* 1 August 1964.

25. Letters, *Zhongguo Funu,* 1 September 1963; 1 May 1964; 1 August 1964.

26. Xiu Feng, Letter, *Zhongguo Funu,* 1 September 1963.

27. Commentary, *Zhongguo Funu,* 1 September 1963.

28. Kang Hua, Letter, Ibid.

29. Yu Jin, Letter, Ibid.

30. Tai Yin, Letter, Ibid.

31. Kong Guihua, Letter, Ibid., 1 May 1964.

32. Pan Xiao, 'Why does life's road grow increasingly narrow?', *Zhongguo Qingnian,* No. 5, 1980, pp. 3–5, Trans. *Chinese Sociology and Anthropology,* Summer 1985, pp. 36–41.

34. Liu Song, 'Concerning Pan Xiao's two fundamental assertions', *Zhongguo Qingnian,* No. 10, 1980, pp. 16–18, Trans. *Chinese Sociology and Anthropology,* op. cit.

35. Zhao Lin, 'Only the self is absolute', *Zhongguo Qingnian,* No. 8, 1980, pp. 4–6, Trans. *Chinese Sociology and Anthropology,* op. cit.

36. Lord, B.B., *Eighth Moon* (The story of Sansan's Chinese Childhood as told to the author), Sphere, London, 1966, p. 112.

37. Ibid., p. 115.

38. Ibid., p. 55.

39. Jung Chang, *Wild Swans; Three Daughters of China,* HarperCollins, London, 1991, p. 225.

40. Ibid., p. 390.

41. Ibid., p. 265.

42. Ibid., p. 224.

43. Ibid., p. 210.

44. Ibid., p. 433.

45. Yue Daiyun and Wakeman, C., *To the Storm: The Odyssey of a Revolutionary Chinese Woman,* University of California Press, 1985, p. 312.

46. Min Anchee, *Red Azalea: Life and Love in China,* Gollancz, London, 1993, p. 22.

47. Shen Rong, 'At Middle Age', translated in *Seven Contemporary Chinese Women Writers,* Beijing, 1982, pp. 119–210.

48. Ibid., p. 186.

49. Ibid., p. 160.

50. Lord, op. cit., pp. 13–14.

51. Ibid., p. 56.

52. Chang, J., p. 378.

53. Potter, Sulamith H. and Jack, M., *China's Peasants, The Anthropology of a Revolution*, Cambridge University Press, 1990, pp. 188–95.

54. Ibid., p. 194.

55. Shih Liang, 'Attend Seriously to the Thorough Implementation of the Marriage Law', *Renmin Ribao* (People's Daily), 13 October 1951.

56. Ibid.

57. Yang Yu, 'The Women of Wu Village', *Women in China Today*, Vol. III, 1952.

58. *Zhongguo gudai shenhua gushi*, Shanghai, 1957.

59. Ibid.

60. Cusack, op. cit., p. 54.

61. Yang Yu, op. cit., p. 12.

62. Shih Liang, op. cit.

63. *Renmin Ribao* (People's Daily), 29 September 1951.

64. Directive of the Government Administrative Council Concerning the Thorough Implementation of the Marriage Law, 1 February 1953, in *New China New Analysis*, 1 February 1953.

65. Poem extract quoted in Kristeva, 1977, p. 181.

66. Chen Yuan-tsung, op. cit., p. 86.

67. Simmel, G., 'The Stranger', first published 1908, translated in Wolff, K., *The Sociology of Georg Simmel*, Glencoe, Illinois, pp. 402–8.

68. Levine, D.N., 'Simmel at a Distance', and Schak, W.A., 'Introduction' in Schak, W. and Skinner, W.P. (eds.), *Strangers in African Societies*, University of California Press, 1979.

69. Liao Suhua, op. cit.

70. Wolf, M., 1985, op. cit., p. 137.

71. See Watson, R. and Ebrey, P., *Marriage and Inequality in Chinese Society*, University of California Press, 1991.

72. Henderson, J.B., *The Development and Decline of Chinese Cosmology*, Columbia University Press, 1986 [for an elaboration of the complex notions of heaven in Chinese cosmology].

73. Heidegger, M., *Being and Time*, Harper and Row, New York, 1962.

74. Bordieu, P., 'The Disenchantment of the World', in *Algeria 1960*, Cambridge University Press, 1979 (1963), pp. 1–94.

75. Bordieu, P., 'The Attitude of the Algerian Peasant Towards Time', in Pitt-Rivers, J., *Mediterranean Countrymen*, Mouton, The Hague, 1964, pp. 55–72.

76. Needham, J., *Time and Eastern Man*, The Henry Myers Lecture, Royal Anthropological Institute, London, 1964 [for a summary of Chinese concepts of time].

77. Waln, N., *The House of Exile*, Cresset Press, London, pp. 38–9.

78. Forman, op. cit.

79. Lord, p. 13.

80. Chang, J., p. 250.

81. Mahoney, R., *The Early Arrival of Dreams*, Macdonald, London, 1990.

82. Cui Ling, 'The Age of Maturity for Woman', translated in *Women of China*, 1 November 1990.

83. 'The Other Side of the River', translated in *Women of China*, 1 May 1991.

Part III   Not the Moon

1. Tan Shen, *Women's Studies in China: A General Survey*, Centre for East Asian Studies, University of Copenhagen, Discussion Papers No. 19, April 1993; *Women of China*, 1 December 1994.

2. Honig and Hershatter, p. 30.

3. Wang Fuhua, 'Si Wen' (Four Questions), *Renmin ribao manhua zengkan*, 5 March 1983, quoted in Honig and Hershatter, p. 327.

4. Chan Yiyun, op. cit.

5. This the theme of my *'Women's Rights and New Political Campaigns in China Today'*, Working Paper in Women's History and Development, Institute of Social Sciences, The Hague, No. 1, October 1984.

6. Editor's Note, *Gongren Ribao* (Worker's Daily), 4 August 1982.

7. 'Analysis of Reproduction of Rural Population', *Jingji Yanjiu* (Economic Research), 20 June 1982.

8. Croll, E., 'The Single-child Family in Beijing: A First-hand Report', in Croll, E., Davies, D., and Kane, P. (eds.), *The Single Child Family in China*, Macmillan Press, London, 1985, pp. 190–232.

9. 'Report from Three Counties in Zhejiang Province', *Renkou Yanjiu* (Population Research), No. 3, 1981, pp. 32–7.

10. Yang Fan, 'Save our Baby Girls', *Zhongguo Qingnian* (China Youth), November 1982.

11. *Renmin Ribao* (People's Daily), 7 April 1983.

12. *Xinhua News Agency*, Beijing, 17 April 1983.

13. Croll, E., 'The Single-child Family in Beijing', op. cit.

14. *It's as good to have a girl as a boy*, Beijing Women's Federation, January 1983.

15. Ibid.

16. 'Female Infanticide: Punishable by Law', *Beijing Review*, 25 April 1983.

17. 'Why Female Infanticide Still Exists in Socialist China', *Women of China*, 1 May 1983.

18. Ge Dewei, 'Traditional Values Keep Women in Outdated Roles', *China Daily*, 24 August 1983.

19. *The Report of the People's Republic of China (PRC) on the Implementation of the Nairobi Forward-Looking strategies for the Advancement of Women*, Beijing, February 1994.

20. *China Statistical Yearbook*, Beijing, 1988, pp. 92–114.

21. *The Report of the PRC on the Implementation of the Nairobi*, op. cit.

22. *China Statistical Yearbook*, 1988, op. cit.

23. *Beijing Review*, 12 October 1987; also *China Daily*, 26 February 1988, 8 March 1988.

24. *Beijing Review*, 12 October 1987; *China Daily*, 24 June 1992.

25. *The Report of the PRC on the Implementation of the Nairobi*, op. cit.

26. *Women of China*, 1 September 1988.

27. *The China Business Review*, July–August 1989.

28. *Jiefang Ribao* (Liberation Daily), 20 November 1989.

29. *Xinhua News*, 10 March 1989.

30. *Jiefang Ribao*, op. cit.

31. *China Daily*, 27 March 1990.

32. *China Daily*, 4 December 1988.
33. *Women of China*, 1 November 1988.
34. *China Daily*, 2 April 1988.
35. Ibid., 10 November 1989.
36. Ibid., 6 July 1994.
37. *Women of China*, 1 August 1958; *Xinhua News*, 30 August 1988.
38. *Women of China*, 1 April 1987; *China Daily*, 3 October 1988.
39. *Renmin Ribao* (People's Daily), 8 October 1981.
40. *Xinhua News Agency*, 31 October 1980.
41. *The Report of the PRC on the Implementation of the Nairobi*, op. cit.
42. Ibid.
43. For a full account see Croll, E., 'Domestic Service in China', *Economic and Political Weekly*, Vol. XXI, No. 6, 8 February 1986.
44. *China Daily*, 16 March 1989.
45. Ibid., 25 September 1989.
46. *The Report of the PRC on the Implementation of the Nairobi*, op. cit.
47. *Xinhua News*, 13 June 1992.
48. *The Report of the PRC on the Implementation of the Nairobi*, op. cit.
49. *Xinhua News*, 13 June 1992.
50. Jiang Yongping, 'Ten Years of Reform and the Employment of Women', *Women of China*, 1 December 1989.
51. *The Report of the PRC on the Implementation of the Nairobi*, op. cit.
52. *Women of China*, 1 July 1988; *The Report of the PRC on the Implementation of the Nairobi*, op. cit.
53. My own interviews, June 1990.
54. Ibid.
55. *Women of China*, 1 March 1988.
56. *The Report of the PRC on the Implementation of the Nairobi*, op. cit.
57. *Women of China*, 1 July 1988; 1 October 1988.
58. *State Statistical Yearbook*, 1988, pp. 83–91.
59. *The Report of the PRC on the Implementation of the Nairobi*, op. cit.
60. 'Preparatory Documents', *Summary of World Broadcasts* (*SWB*), 25 April 1978; 4 May 1978; 'Report on Women's Congress', *SWB*, 12 September 1978; 21 September 1978; *Beijing Review*, 29 September 1978 [for reports on the 1978 Congress].
61. Xi Zhongxun Addresses Women's Federation, *SWB*, 20 May 1982.
62. Ibid., 31 October 1980.
63. Ibid., 21 September 1978.
64. Ibid., 25 April 1978.
65. 'Wang Renzhong on the Position of Women', *SWB*, 25 October 1980.
66. *SWB*, op. cit., 15 September 1983; 23 September 1983 [for reports on 1983 Congress].
67. Ibid.
68. *Xinhua News*, 1 September 1988; 5 September 1988; *SWB*, 8 September 1988; *Women of China*, 1 January 1989 [for reports on 1988 Congress].
69. Ibid.
70. The Committee for Women and Children, *Women of China*, February 1994; *The Report of the PRC on the Implementation of the Nairobi*, op. cit.

71. *SWB*, 20 March 1992; for commentaries on the law see *Women of China*, 1 July 1992; 1 March 1993; 1 April 1993.

72. *Women of China*, 1 July 1992; ibid., 1 August 1992.

73. *China Daily*, 3 September 1988.

74. *Women of China*, 1 January 1984.

75. Ibid., 1 January 1983–1 January 1984.

76. Ibid., 1 January 1984.

77. *China Daily*, 4 January 1993.

78. *Women of China*, 1 September 1993; 1 January 1994 [for accounts of the Seventh National Congress].

79. Wan Shanping, 'The Emergence of Women's Studies in China', *Women's Studies International Forum*, Vol. II, No. 5, pp. 458–9; Tan Shen, op. cit.; *Women of China*, 1 March 1987.

80. Li Xiaojiang, *The Development of Women's Studies in China: A Comparison of Perspectives on the Women's Movement in China and the West*, Centre of East Asian Studies, University of Copenhagen, Discussion Paper No. 21, April 1993.

81. 'Beijing Society of Women's Theory', *Women of China*, 1 May 1994.

82. To be written up in *Women of China*, August 1994.

83. Li Xiaojing, 'Gaige yu Zhongguo nuxing qunti yishi de juexing' ('Economic Reform and the Awakening of Women's Consciousness'), *Shehui kexue zhanxian* (Social Science Battlefront), 4 (1988), pp. 300–10; translated in Gilmartin, C. et al., pp. 360–82.

84. *Women of China*, 1 January 1989.

85. Li Xiaojing, 1988, op. cit.

86. *Women of China*, 1 January 1993.

87. *Zhongguo Funu*, 1 February 1985, translated in Honig and Hershatter, op. cit., pp. 39–40.

88. Li ZeZhou, 'Females are the Natural Masters of the Perceptual World', *Women of China*, 1 January 1993, pp. 36–7.

89. Shu Ting, 'Different People, Different Views', *Women of China*, 1 March 1993, pp. 43, 49.

90. Rice, D., *The Dragon's Blood: Conversations with Young Chinese*, HarperCollins, London, 1992, pp. 219–20.

91. Jia Ping'ao, 'About Women', *Women of China*, 1 March 1993.

92. Guan Shujuan, 'The Cafe with Candles', *Women of China*, 1 September 1993.

93. Ting Lan, 'Nüren bushi yueliang' ('Woman is not the Moon'); 'Nuzi Shijie' ('Woman's World'), June 1985, translated in Honig and Hershatter, op. cit., pp. 328–9.

94. Ziming, 'Why is it Hard for a Woman to Find a Spouse?', *Women of China*, 1 April 1993.

95. Jankowiak, W.R., *Sex, Death and Hierarchy in a Chinese City*, University of Columbia Press, 1993, p. 168.

96. Peng Xiaolian, 'Hopes Worn Away', translated in *Contemporary Chinese Women Writers*, Vol. II, Panda Books, Beijing, 1991, pp. 198, 203.

97. Rice, op. cit., pp. 216–17.

98. Ibid.

99. Li Xia, 'Wanted: A Spouse I Can Love', *China Today*, 1 January 1992, p. 42.

100. Peng Xiaolian, op. cit., p. 194.
101. Jankowiak, W.R., op. cit., p. 204.
102. Liu Qian, 'The Inclined Balance', *Women of China*, 1 February 1993.
103. Ibid.
104. Rice, op. cit., p. 196.
105. Hua Yin, 'Hotline for Women', *Women of China*, 1 January 1993, p. 29.
106. 'Female Self-Confidence Must Be Fostered From Childhood', *Zhongguo Funu*, April 1985, p. 34, translated in Honig and Hershatter, op. cit., pp. 38–9.
107. This discussion is based upon Papers presented at the International Seminar on China's 1990 Population Census, 19–23 October 1992, Beijing. In particular it is based on: Hull and Wen Xingyan, 'Rising Sex Ratios at Birth in China: Evidence from the 1990 Population Census'; Tu Ping, 'The Sex Ratios at Birth in China: Results from the 1990 Census'; and Zeng Yi et al., 'An Analysis of the Causes and Implications of the Recent Increase in the Sex Ratio at Birth in China'.
108. *Guardian*, 4 April 1994.
109. *Nongmin Ribao*, 4 December 1992.
110. Ibid.
111. *China Daily*, 22 March 1993.
112. Nie Fangfang, 'My Being a Girl Caused Mother's Death', *Mommy, Daddy and Me*, New World Press, Beijing, pp. 72–5.
113. Wu Shuang, 'Mom Doesn't Think Men are Superior to Women Anymore', Ibid., pp. 31–3.
114. Chen Bo, 'Mother, I Need Your Help Rather Than a Beating', Ibid., pp. 66–8.
115. 'Vagrant Girls – A Problem Not To Be Overlooked', *Women Studies Forum* (Journal), Vol. II, 1993, pp. 25–9.
116. 'Where Did The Six Young Girls Leave For?', *Zhongguo Qingnian* (China Youth), 8 May 1993.
117. *China Daily*, 9 July 1993.
118. Ibid.
119. Ibid.
120. *Seven Contemporary Chinese Women Writers*, Vol. I, Panda Books, Beijing, 1982.
121. *Contemporary Chinese Women Writers*, Vol. II, Panda Books, Beijing, 1991.
122. *Contemporary Chinese Women Writers*, Vol. III, Panda Books, Beijing 1993.
123. This section is based on *China Daily*, 4 May 1992; Hua Yin, 'Hotline for Women', *Women of China*, 1 January 1993; Ibid., 1 September 1993; and interviews with Ding Hui and Wang Xing Juan by Teresa Poole, *Independent*, London, 14 October 1993.
124. Xiao Ming, 'Going to the Sea', *Women of China*, 1 September 1993.
125. 'Young Chinese Women Taste the Sweet and Sour of Modern Life', *Women of China*, 1 May 1994.
126. 'Fashion and Culture in Contemporary China', *Women in China*, 1 November 1991.
127. *China Daily*, 9 July 1993.

Index